RAND McNALLY

the road atlas '07

Questions or suggestions?
Call (800) 777-MAPS (-6277)
or e-mail consumeraffairs@randmcnally.com

D0905261

CONTENTS

More than **350** detailed city maps inside!

Copyright ©2007 by Rand McNally & Company. All rights reserved.

Library of Congress Catalog Number: 92-C60588

For licensing information and copyright permissions, contact us at licensing@randmcnally.com

If you have a question or suggestion, please call (800) 777-MAPS (-6277), or e-mail us at: consumeraffairs@randmcnally.com

or write to:

Rand McNally Consumer Affairs
P.O. Box 7600
Chicago, Illinois 60680-9915

Published in U.S.A.
Printed in Peru

10 9 8 7 6 5 4 3 2 1

Quick Map References

This list contains only 70 of more than 350 detailed city maps in the Road Atlas. To find more city maps, consult the state/province map list to the left and turn to the pages indicated.

BEST of the

» Desert Adventures *Scottsdale to Sedona, Arizona*

Sedona

See pages 7-9

Though Arizona is desert country, it offers surprisingly lush touches if you know where to look: cacti forests, rosy sunsets, and the turquoise that flashes in the bracelets on a cowgirl's arms. This drive leads travelers on a loop through the north central part of this state, beginning just outside Phoenix, curving up to the Grand Canyon, and ending just south in mysterious Sedona.

Best known: Frank Lloyd Wright's Taliesin West in Scottsdale; dude ranches in Wickenburg; the Grand Canyon; Whiskey Row in Prescott; Montezuma Castle National Monument; the red rocks of Sedona.

» Unexpected Arkansas *Eureka Springs to Little Rock*

Little Rock

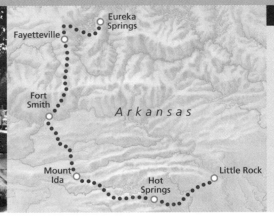

See page 10

There are plenty of reasons Arkansas is called the Natural State. Start with 600,000 acres of lakes. Add 9,700 miles of streams and rivers and 2.4 million acres of national forest. Pack all inside this small state west of the Mississippi River and eureka! You've found an unexpected travel experience.

Best known: "Taking the waters" in Hot Springs; cheering the Razorbacks in Fayetteville; the William J. Clinton Presidential Center and civil rights memorials in Little Rock; the beauty of the Ozarks, and the quartz-filled hills that curve through the state that once was the final frontier of the American West.

» Cruising the Florida Coast *Fort Lauderdale to the Keys*

Fort Lauderdale

See pages 25-27

US 1 epitomizes sunny Florida, basking in the East Coast rays and paralleling the wave-washed beaches from Fort Lauderdale to Key West. There's something for everyone along this drive—family adventures and beachcombing, upscale dining and shopping, turtle watching and kayaking, and sampling key lime pie.

Best known: Mansions along the "Venice of America" seen from Fort Lauderdale water taxis; Miami Beach's fine dining and people watching; Islamorada marina sportfishing; crossing the seven-mile bridge from key to key; Key West's key lime pie.

» Snow on the Eastern Shore *Ocean City to Baltimore, Maryland*

Ocean City

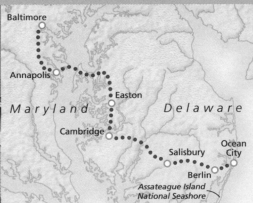

See pages 46-47

Marylanders don't like to call winter off-season. Winter may be a step slower, but the summer amenities are still there and they cost less. At any time of the year wild ponies roam Assateague Island, Harborplace in Baltimore hops, and costumed interpreters give tours at the U.S. Naval Academy in Annapolis. There is one caveat: Since the beaches are closed, you will have to swim in an indoor pool. To see it all, follow the road signs on US 50.

Best known: Crab cakes; antiquing in Berlin; wooden skipjacks; the Chesapeake Bay Maritime Museum; the U.S. Naval Academy.

» Wide Skies of the West *Rapid City to Deadwood, South Dakota*

Prairie land

See page 93

The sky just seems bigger in South Dakota, and this drive through the state's western edge gives travelers plenty of opportunity to admire its spacious, often eerie beauty. This is a land where massive bison appear by the road as if from nowhere, the jagged Badlands loom like monuments to a lost civilization, and locals are on a first-name basis with long-dead gunslingers.

Best known: Badlands National Park; Wall Drug; Crazy Horse Memorial; Mount Rushmore National Monument; casinos and Mount Moriah Cemetery in Deadwood.

ROAD™ 2007

Plan a trip randmcnally.com/BR

Editor's Picks

Lon's at the Hermosa (Scottsdale)
Though it owes its existence to cowboy artist Lon Megargee, Lon's has a sophisticated ambience at odds with its rootin'-tootin' roots. The menu reveals suspiciously city-slicker touches: pats of butter adorned with rosemary sprigs, sour cherry sorbet in a lacy chocolate shell. *5532 N. Palo Cristi Rd., (602) 955-8614*

Kay El Bar Guest Ranch (Wickenburg)
While most guests stay overnight, lodgings at the small, rustic Kay El Bar are overshadowed by the plethora of daytime activities: horseback rides, campfire cookouts, dips in the pool, family-style meals, and romps with the resident Labrador retrievers, Ally and George. Outdoor hammocks beckon to the more inert. *Outside Wickenburg off AZ 89/US 93, (928) 684-7593*

Unravel Yarn and Fiber Arts (Flagstaff)
Unravel lies on old Route 66, hence its motto: "Get Your Knits on Route 66." Co-owner David Coe sometimes sports a t-shirt that reads "Yes, I Knit." The shop carries local and regional yarns, along with esoteric items such as yarn made from recycled silk saris ("I can't seem to keep it in stock," Coe says). *6 Old Route 66, (928) 556-9276*

Starlight Pines Bed and Breakfast (Flagstaff)
Richard Svendsen and Michael Ruiz run this bed-and-breakfast with help from their shih tzu colleagues Moo Shu and Taz. This Victorian-style house offers four guest rooms with many charming touches—chocolates on the pillows, Mason-jar drinking glasses in the bathroom—along with more esoteric objet décor, such as the antique dentist's chair and the vintage cereal brochures. *3380 E. Lockett Rd., (928) 527-1912*

Red Rock Jeep Tours (Sedona)
Sedona's New Age reputation stems from its "vortices," natural areas reputed to emit healing energy. Red Rock Jeep Tours provides a two-and-a-half-hour trek that includes private quiet time at each vortex. "Keep an open mind, an open heart, and see what happens," says one guide. *270 N. AZ 89A, (928) 282-6826*

More great stops

Flagstaff: Hotel Monte Vista, 100 N. San Francisco St., (928) 779-6971, www.hotelmontevista.com
Flagstaff: Riordan Mansion State Historic Park, 409 W. Riordan Rd., (928) 779-4395, www.pr.state.az.us
Scottsdale: Mexican Imports, 3933 N. Brown Ave., (480) 945-6476
Sedona: Body Bliss Factory Direct, 320 N. AZ 89A, Ste. Q, Sedona, (928) 282-1599, www.bodyblissfactorydirect.com
Prescott: Van Gogh's Ear, 156-B S. Montezuma St., (928) 776-1080, www.vgegallery.com

Editor's Picks

Frog Fantasies (Eureka Springs)
This frogs-only gift shop doubles as a museum with displays from three generations of collectors. Collectors can find Fabergé frogs selling between $150 and $250. Frog-themed cookie jars start at $25. Lovable leapers are carved in lapis lazuli and in wood and printed on cookware. *151 Spring St., (479) 253-7227*

Fort Smith Convention and Visitors Center (Fort Smith)
The first stop in Fort Smith should be the visitors center, located in a 19th-century clapboard building. The building was once the

Riverfront Hotel, which doubled as a bordello until 1924. Locals always called the hotel "Miss Laura's," and the name has stuck. *2 North B, (479) 783-8888*

Mt. Ida Café (Mount Ida)
Antlers decorate the pine paneling of this roadside café in the Ouachita National Forest. But it isn't venison that draws customers. It is catfish and burgers. Each Friday the luncheon buffet features catfish with sides of slaw, pinto beans, fried potatoes, and cornbread for $5.49. The charbroiled burger plate arrives with fries and a salad for $5.50. *US 270, (870) 867-2283*

Fordyce Bathhouse (Hot Springs)
This bathhouse has been restored to provide a glimpse of the great American spa experience of the early 20th century. The spring that feeds the hot mineral water to the bathhouse is on view in the basement. The Fordyce doubles as the Hot Springs National Park Visitor Center. *369 Central Ave., (501) 620-6715*

Ottenheimer Market Hall at River Market (Little Rock)
This enclosed marketplace proffers fresh produce and flowers, teas and gourmet coffee, foodstuffs, and gift stalls. Once a month, the River Market Cooking School offers a cooking class. It's only $10 for a hands-on class with a local chef. The market also anchors the Riverfront entertainment area, which jumps with nightspots and restaurants. *400 President Clinton Ave., (501) 375-2552*

More great stops

Eureka Springs: Mount Victoria Bed and Breakfast, 28 Fairmount St., (479) 253-7979, www.mountvictoria.com
Fayetteville: Inn at Carnall Hall, 465 N. Arkansas Ave., (479) 582-0400, www.carnallhall.com
Fort Smith: Fort Smith National Historic Site, Third St. at Rogers Ave., (479) 783-3961, www.nps.gov
Hot Springs: Garvan Woodland Gardens, 550 Arkridge Rd., (501) 262-9300, www.garvangardens.org
Little Rock: William J. Clinton Presidential Center, 1200 President Clinton Ave., (501) 370-5050, www.clintonlibrary.gov

Editor's Picks

Wannado City (Sunrise)
Kids can experience what they want to be when they grow up at this play mini-city in a mall: Play firefighter, arrest a scofflaw, drill a cavity, or model high fashion. Each play job earns play money that can be spent on rock climbing, jewelry making, and other fun stuff. *Sawgrass Mills, 12801 W. Sunrise Blvd., (954) 838-7100; (888) WANNADO*

Versailles Restaurant (Miami)
In the heart of Miami's Little Havana, this venerable restaurant draws locals, dignitaries, and visitors. If restaurant tables are full, grab a seat in the café for a Cuban coffee (thick and very sweet, just 50¢) and a Cuban sandwich. *3555 SW 8th St., (305) 445-7614*

The Fragrance Shop Perfumery (Miami Beach)
This shop blends custom fragrances with pure perfume oils for a fraction of the cost of designer scents. Since there's no alcohol in the blend, the fragrance lasts longer. The shop's 800 essential and perfume oils can be blended into products from aftershave balms (about $11) to massage oils and body lotions (from $19). *612 Lincoln Rd., (305) 535-0037*

Biscayne Nature Center (Key Biscayne)
Families gravitate to Biscayne—which lies within sight of downtown Miami—to explore south Florida habitats, stroll on a self-guided hammock walk, or bask on the beach. Adventure-seekers may want to sign up for a guided kayak tour through the mangroves or a naturalist-led tidal pool hike. *6767 Crandon Blvd., (305) 361-6767*

Big Pine Kayak Adventures (Big Pine Key)
Paddle alongside small sharks, barracuda, and sea turtles on a kayak adventure with Captain Bill Keogh. He literally wrote the book on Keys paddling and knows all the spots for finding marine life. You might even spot tiny Key deer grazing on the island. *1791 Bogie Dr., (305) 872-7474*

Key West Kite Company (Key West)
Buy a nylon version of a clown fish ($20) or racy mermaid ($30), a cool banner for the porch back home, or a spiraling wind deva ($13) that spins in the breeze. Spinners, twisters, basic kites . . . they're all in a shop that's been in business for 25 years. *408 Green St., (305) 296-2535*

More great stops

Fort Lauderdale: Johnny V Restaurant, 625 E. Las Olas Blvd., (954) 761-7920, www.johnnyvlasolas.com
Miami: El Rey de Los Habanos, 1120 SW 8th St., (305) 858-0001
Miami Beach: Fly Boutique, 650 Lincoln Rd., (305) 604-8508
Grassy Key: Dolphin Research Center, 58901 Overseas Highway, (305) 289-0002, www.dolphins.org
Key West: Blond Giraffe, 107 Simonton St., (888) 432-6283, www.blondgiraffe.com

Editor's Picks

Ocean City Life Saving Station Museum (Ocean City)
Via displays and sound effects, visitors witness efforts to rescue a 19th-century ship that has run ashore on the barrier islands. The clapboard museum is filled with exhibits about life on the shore, including a display of boardwalk souvenirs and a collection of china and silver recovered from shipwrecks. *813 S. Boardwalk, (410) 289-4991*

Blackwater National Wildlife Refuge (Cambridge)
Visitors take to this 28,000-acre refuge by water and by land. Nearby outfitters offer

kayaks and canoes, along with bicycles for those who prefer the five-mile paved drive or 20-mile loop. To help spot a bald eagle, the Visitor Center has installed a mounted video camera to maintain live-cam coverage of an eagle perch. *2145 Key Wallace Dr., (410) 228-2677*

The Ward Museum of Wildfowl Art (Salisbury)
Duck into the Ward to witness the evolution of the duck decoy from tool to folk art to status as wildfowl sculpture. The museum features the world's largest public collection of decorative and antique decoys. Take a walk outside along a fully accessible foot trail made of crushed seashells. *909 S. Schumaker Dr., (410) 742-4988*

Chick and Ruth's Delly (Annapolis)
Each morning a voice on a loudspeaker invites all customers to rise, face the flag behind the lunch counter, and recite the Pledge of Allegiance. What a way to start the day! A plate of fresh eggs with homemade corned beef hash and patriotism! The "delly" is located only blocks from the capitol. *165 Main St., (410) 269-6737*

The National Aquarium (Baltimore)
Go ahead and dive right in! 11,000 aquatic creatures make the aquarium on the busy Inner Harbor their home. Newest residents can be found in Animal Planet Australia Wild Extreme, a permanent exhibit located near the entrance, where visitors are greeted by the roar of a 35-foot waterfall. *Pier 3, 501 E. Pratt St., (410) 576-3800*

More great stops

Berlin: Atlantic Hotel, 2 N. Main St., (410) 641-3589, www.atlantichotel.com
Salisbury: Salisbury Zoo and Park, 755 S. Park Dr., (410) 548-3188, www.salisburyzoo.org
Easton: Academy Art Museum, 106 South St., (410) 822-2787, www.art-academy.org
St. Michaels: Chesapeake Bay Maritime Museum, Navy Point, (410) 745-2916, www.cbmm.org
Annapolis: Glazed and Fuzed, 1908 Forest Dr., (410) 268-4529, www.glazedandfuzed.com

Editor's Picks

Prairie Edge Trading Company and Galleries (Rapid City)
No "made in China" tags here—most of the exquisite paintings, traditional apparel, and other works in Prairie Edge, which focuses exclusively on Plain Indians culture, are supplied by local artists. The bead library on the mezzanine holds jar after jar of sparkling bijous. *606 Main St., (605) 342-3086*

Corn Exchange (Rapid City)
Chef M.J. Adams, who's been featured in *Gourmet*, moved here from New York to "save the country from chain restaurants." She's often found chatting to patrons about locally raised menu items such as trout with capers or, for dessert, satiny raspberries with a dollop of whipped cream. *727 Main St., (605) 343-5070*

Black Hills Wild Horse Sanctuary (near Hot Springs)
Ponderosa pines and sinewy brown rabbits dot this vast, hilly 11,000-acre sanctuary. On two-hour bus tours, visitors not only watch mustangs grazing and galloping, but also have the chance to get out of the bus for more close-up encounters. Other stops include a ceremonial site used by local Lakota Sioux. *About 12.5 miles S of Hot Springs, (605) 745-5955*

Prairie Berry Winery (Hill City)
On-site tastings of up to five Prairie Berry products—which include wines made from chokecherries, cranberries, rhubarb, and buffalo berries—are free. Designated drivers, meanwhile, can purchase a bottle or two to take home. Winemaker Sandra Vojta's family has been making wines from South Dakota fruit since 1876. *23837 US 385, (877) 226-9453*

Adams House (Deadwood)
Guided tours of this opulent 1892 house allow visitors to imagine the wealth that its electricity, telephones, and servant call button system represented in the turn-of-the-century West. All but two of the house's contents are original, including the surprisingly well preserved cookies in the cookie jar. *22 Van Buren St., (605) 578-3724*

More great stops

Custer: Sage Creek Grille, 611 Mt. Rushmore Rd., (605) 673-2424
Hill City: Artforms Inc., 347 Main St., (605) 574-4894
Lead: Homestake Gold Mine Visitors' Center, 160 W. Main St., (605) 584-3110, www.homestaketours.com
Philip: Prairie Homestead, 21141 SD 240, (605) 433-5400, www.prairiehomestead.com
Rapid City: Black Hills Reptile Gardens, 5 miles S of Rapid City on US 16, (605) 342-5873, www.reptile-gardens.com

SUNDAY Drives

Ever just want to get in the car and drive? Not every trip has to be a dash between two points. Rand McNally editors have collected **26** choice drives, the kind you might take on a lazy Sunday afternoon. The mileages vary, but most don't take more than four hours— unless you stop at every fruit stand, antique store, and ice cream parlor along the way. These jaunts are meant to be driven, however, and showcase scenery that calls for the camera.

To orient you on a Road Atlas map, a page and grid location for each drive's starting point is provided.

West Virginia's Farm Heritage Road

1 Alaska

This day trip from Anchorage wanders south down the Seward Highway (AK 1) and along the shores of Turnagain Arm (an arm of Cook Inlet) to Portage Lake, where iceberg remnants float. At mile 99, Bird Point offers tidal views; down the road at mile 106, mountain goats and Dall's sheep can be spotted at Windy Point. Also en route: Beluga Point, which offers beluga and orca sightings, and the drive-through Alaska Wildlife Conservation Center, where bison, moose, and other animals roam. To fully appreciate the stops along this drive, plan on at least a half-day's journey.

Find the starting point on p. 6, G-8.

2 Arkansas-Oklahoma

All 54 miles of the Talimena Scenic Drive, which stretches from Mena, Ark., to Talihina, Okla., lie within the Ouachita National Forest. After leaving Mena on AR 1, travelers will pass the Blue Ridge Overlook, where an area of sandstone outcroppings called Earthquake Ridge lies. Other sights to watch out for along the way: the Ouachita River, fire towers, pine and hardwood trees, historic sites, and hang gliders. Keep an eye out, too, for wildlife including golden eagles (in winter and spring), deer, turkey, quail, and even black bear.

Find the starting point on p. 10, F-1.

3 California

San Francisco Bay area residents love to take their guests on a drive to Sonoma County, at least as far as Santa Rosa. Beginning at the CA 1 exit off US 101 north of the city, the drive slices through the coastal hills toward the Pacific for a short jaunt past Point Reyes National Seashore, where sightings of dramatic ocean breaks are a regular occurrence. If you make this drive between January and April, you may be lucky enough to witness the annual gray whale migration. Turn east into the Sonoma Valley on Bodega Bay Road. On this interior stretch verdant vineyards, sprawling olive groves, and truck farms lure visitors from the road.

Find the starting point on p. 12, NM-5.

4 California

Locals call CA 160 south out of Sacramento the River Road because it curves along the banks of the Sacramento River toward and past Isleton. Just outside the city it passes through the Clarksburg appellation, where vineyards line the road, and near Delta Meadows River Park with its numerous sloughs and acres of meadowland. This area of the Sacramento Valley provides a glimpse of what the area was like before levees were introduced. Be alert for wildlife such as black-tailed deer along this stretch. Further along, the river provides nesting areas for heron, egrets, and other waterfowl. Isleton hosts a number of festivals including the Crawdad Festival on Father's Day.

Find the starting point on p. 12, NK-7.

5 Colorado

US 24 west out of Colorado Springs borders Pike National Forest en route to Breckenridge. The road crosses the Platte River before turning north on CO 9 and traversing the Platte twice more, heading ever upwards into the mountains. At Hoosier Pass (11,539 ft.) you may see to the west some of Colorado's famous "Fourteeners"—the peaks that reach more than 14,000 ft.—including Mt. Lincoln (14,286 ft.) and Mt. Elbert, the highest point in Colorado at 14,433 ft. End the drive in Breckenridge, a Victorian-era (1847) town that retains an Old West flavor.

Find the starting point on p. 21, H-14.

6 Delaware

It takes only about an hour to drive the loop of this newly designated National Scenic Byway (Delaware's first) with no stops, but these 12.25 miles are packed with so many mansions, gardens, and historic estates that few travelers can imagine not pulling over for multiple photo ops. From the Pennsylvania state line, take DE 52 south to Wilmington. The route passes by 18th-century Quaker settlement Centerville and the lush gardens of the Winterthur Museum and Country Estate before easing into Wilmington, then back up DE 52 to DE 100. Just three miles north of Wilmington lies Brandywine Creek State Park, where travelers can stretch their legs underneath 190-year-old tulip poplar trees.

Find the starting point on p. 24, B-2.

7 Florida

With one western turn onto FL 9336 from US 1, road trippers can experience the subtropical natural plenitude of Everglades National Park. Along the way to Flamingo on Florida Bay, first-time visitors should stop at the Ernest Coe Visitors Center. At Pa-hay-okee Overlook at Shark Basin, a 12-foot tower provides a grand view of Cypress Tree Island and the vast expanses of sawgrass that thrive in the park. At Mahogany Hammock, you can stretch your legs on a half-mile elevated boardwalk that leads into the country's largest growth of mahogany before continuing the drive through the mangrove swamp to the bay.

Find the starting point on p. 27, R-13.

8 Georgia

South of Savannah, live oaks shade US 17 as it parallels the Intracoastal Waterway. The original north-south route to Florida, the road winds through miles of grasslands. It passes remnants of rice farming and plantations. Evidence of the road's glory days takes the shape of a plethora of gas stations and coffee shops peppering the road. As it wends its way toward the marshes near Brunswick, US 17 leads to the toll bridge over to St. Simons Island, where crab cakes and dock fishing await.

Find the starting point on p. 29, K-13.

Bryce Canyon National Park, Utah

Olympic Mountains, Washington

9 Hawaii

From Kailua Kona, on Hawai'i's west coast, circle the island along the lush coastline. Wander through the famous kona coffee farms off HI 11 near Holualoa. Samples and tours are available at many farms and grinders. At Hōnaunau, turn on Puuhonua Rd. to Pu'uhonua o Hōnaunau National Historic Park—the Place of Refuge—where taboo breakers once sought safety from the wrath of Hawaiian royalty. Back on HI 11, turn south at Waiohiunu on Kamaoa Road to Kalae (South Cape), the southernmost tip of the United States, and the nearby green sand beach. Return to HI 11 north, through Hawai'i Volcanoes National Park to see the lava still flowing, and on to Hilo, the island's biggest town.

Find the starting point on p. 30, M-8.

10 Kansas

Trailing down the eastern edge of the state, the 167-mile Frontier Military Scenic Byway is bounded by Leavenworth in the north and the Oklahoma border on the south. This (mostly) two-lane route traces the military trail that once connected Fort Leavenworth and Fort Scott. From Leavenworth, take KS 5 south to I-435 South, then south on US 69. Along the way, see wildflowers, the Louisburg Cider Mill, the Marais des Cygnes Wildlife Area, and numerous historic sites, such as the Mine Creek Civil War battlefield.

Find the starting point on p. 41, C-18.

Fort Scott National Historic Site, Kansas

11 Maine

When asked for directions to the area's famous lighthouses, Mainers in Portland say "just follow the water." Start this drive on Broadway at "Bug" Light on Casco Bay, in South Portland. Head south on Madison Street, then east on Breakwater Drive, continuing onto Benjamin Pickett Street. After a left on Fort Road, you'll see Spring Point Light at the end of a breakwater, the Portland Harbor museum, and the clipper ship *Snow Squall*. Take Fort Road back south, turning left onto Preble Street, which becomes Shore Road. The roadway straightens and glides past waterfront mansions in Cape Elizabeth. At the sign for Fort Williams Park, turn left and anticipate the first glimpse of Portland Head Light, Maine's celebrated lighthouse.

Find the starting point on p. 45, J-9.

12 Maryland

Don't be fooled by the name; the National Freeway, a.k.a. I-68, offers views to rival those alongside any rural two-lane road. Start out from Hancock on I-70, then veer west immediately onto I-68. The freeway slices through Sideling Hill, then makes its way through the 43,000-acre Green Ridge State Forest before sloping into a valley and traversing a bridge over the city of Cumberland. As it continues westward, the route passes through miles of mountains and crosses the Eastern Continental Divide—west of the divide, water eventually flows into the Mississippi River, while east of it, water eventually flows to the Atlantic Ocean—before hitting Friendsville just east of the state line.

Find the starting point on p. 46, A-6.

13 Massachusetts

When Bostonians want to beat the city blahs, they take a step back in time and drive to Plymouth Bay. The exodus begins on I-93, then veers southeast onto MA 3A, which hugs the seaboard. Along the way you'll pass Wompatuck State Park, popular for its trails and a freshwater spring that provides free water for the taking. MA 3A continues through a rural landscape, where you begin to smell the salt breezes before arriving at the Myles Standish Monument at the northern end of Plymouth Bay. The two-lane road then curves around the bay to Plymouth Rock and Plimoth Plantation before continuing its winding route to Cape Cod.

Find the starting point on p. 49, F-14.

14 Michigan

A ride out "the peninsula" keeps locals and visitors in a kicked-back mood. The Old Mission Peninsula north of Traverse City is only 22 miles long and just a mile wide in spots. What lies along MI 37 and between the East Arm and West Arm of Grand Traverse Bay are miles of orchards, some apple but mostly cherry, as this area is a prime cherry-growing area. The Old Mission Lighthouse (circa 1870) and a park by the same name are located at the tip. On the way back, turn on Swaney Road toward Old Mission village for an ice cream stop.

Find the starting point on p. 50, J-6.

15 Mississippi-Alabama

Started in 1938 and not completed until 2005, the Natchez Trace Parkway stretches more than 400 miles, making it far too long a haul for the weekend traveler. Take it in chunks instead, such as the one that starts in Tupelo, Miss., and ends in the Shoals area of Alabama some 80 miles later. Start at the Natchez Trace Visitor Center in Tupelo, then follow the parkway north and east, passing Confederate grave sites, tree-filled Dogwood Valley, ancient mounds, Freedom Hills Overlook (the parkway's highest point), and (in season) plentiful wildflowers.

Find the starting point on p. 56, C-9.

16 Nebraska

From Henry, Neb. (near the Wyoming border), take US 26 east and south to Lewellen. You'll be tracing—albeit in reverse—part of the historic Oregon and Mormon trails, which followed the cottonwood-lined North Platte River. And you'll see some of the landmarks that guided early pioneers en route: Scotts Bluff, Chimney Rock, Courthouse Rock, and Jail Rock. Near Lewellen, the route passes Ash Hollow State Historical Park; stop to see wagon ruts from pioneer days. From Lewellen itself, take NE 92 east, then US 26 west to make a scenic loop around Lake McConaughy, the state's largest reservoir.

Find the starting point on p. 62, G-1.

17 Nevada

From Las Vegas, head northeast on I-15, passing Nellis AFB and into the desert. Rolling tumbleweeds and gravel fill the landscape to the edge of the Moapa River Indian Reservation, where you turn onto NV 169 towards Valley of Fire State Park. The route runs through the park, where great vistas of the flaming rocks give the park its name. Check out the natural arches; then head east and north through the small Muddy River valley towns of Overton (at the north end of Lake Mead) and Logandale to I-15 and a return to the bright lights of Las Vegas.

Find the starting point on p. 64, M-8.

18 New York

This bucolic jaunt begins just east of where the Long Island Expressway ends. Pick up New York State's Route 25 in Riverhead and head east onto the North Fork. Vineyards, old barns, farm pastures and fences line the two-lane, rural road. Signs for fresh fruit, roasted corn, fresh goat cheese, and wine invite passersby to stop and try tasty wares. Small villages punctuate the drive with pockets of historic buildings and quaint shops. The fork narrows eastward, drawing the water closer to the road. Farmers have turned to the sea and now sell daytrippers fresh seafood. George Washington commissioned the Horton's Point lighthouse perched on the bluffs overlooking Long Island Sound in Southold, a quick detour north on Horton Road. The schooner used in the film *Mutiny on the Bounty* is moored in seaside Greenport. When both Long Island Sound on the left and Gardiner's Bay on the right are in view, you're near the end of both the Fork and the road.

Find the starting point on p. 69, SE-11.

19 Oregon

Wine country awaits on this drive, but you'll get there on the roundabout route. Start on Portland's gateway to the coast, US 26 heading northwest. The city gives way to rolling hills as fir trees press in on either side of the incline. At the summit you begin the drop to the sea. Turn south on US 101 and climb 700 feet above the Pacific, the rugged coastline staying just in view. Tillamook offers a taste of renowned cheese. The road bends inland among the forest, then back to the sea. Turn back Portland-ward on OR 18 near Otis. Vineyards and signs beckoning wine enthusiasts and beginners line the route northeast. Sip responsibly (if at all) before continuing on OR 18, which becomes OR 99W as the drive returns to Portland.

Find the starting point on p. 84, C-5.

20 Pennsylvania

A scenic drive usually focuses on natural features, right? Not so on the Lincoln Highway Heritage Corridor, a 200-mile stretch of road (most of it along US 30) that spans six counties and passes man-made highlights such as murals, vintage gas pumps transformed into works of art, a giant coffee pot, and a 200-year-old tavern. They're all part of the corridor's "roadside museum," which stretches from New Oxford to Ligonier. Other, non-artificial sights to enjoy include apple orchards, cornfields, hills, and mountains. Country stores, diners, and antique shops all along the route provide leg-stretching opportunities.

Find the starting point on p. 89, EQ-4.

21 Texas

This drive west of Austin dips, rises, and bends through Hill Country. Head out of Austin on US 290, passing through Dripping Springs and Henly. US 290 hooks up with US 281 for a few miles; then 281 jogs north until the western turn onto FM 1323 for a gradual climb toward Willow City. Spring brings carpets of wildflowers, most notably the famed Texas bluebonnet. In Eckert, head south on TX 16. The landscape grows more lush on the approach to Fredericksburg. Look for German architecture while driving through this town settled by German immigrants in the 1840s. Turning back toward Austin, US 290 follows the Pedernales River Valley. Rolling hills, tall trees, and occasional vineyards infuse a Tuscan flavor to the Texas terrain.

Find the starting point on p. 100, EJ-6.

22 Utah

Brigham Young's home in St. George could be a starting point for this jaunt through southern Utah. Heading north of town on I-15, turn east on UT 9 toward Hurricane, crossing the Virgin River and heading toward the granite peaks of Zion National Park. Driving into the park is not allowed (shuttle buses take visitors to the canyons and hiking paths), but UT 9 climbs high along the southern edge on its eastward route. It passes ancient volcanic fields before becoming US 89 northbound through little towns like Orderville and Glendale. Turn east again onto UT 12, which slices across the northern lobe of Bryce Canyon National Park, where pointy rock formations called hoodoos jut into the sky. Stop in tiny Tropic for lunch or dinner.

Find the starting point on p. 102, N-4.

Joyce, Washington

23 Washington

Just north of its intersection with US 101, WA 112—the Strait of Juan de Fuca Highway—spans the Elwha River canyon to begin its meandering 61-mile journey. At first the Olympic Mountains form the backdrop to lushly green foothill farms. Stop at the historic Joyce General Store and Depot Museum. After about 20 miles, the strait comes into view. Eagles skim the shoreline to scoop exposed sea creatures at low tide. Lucky passengers may spot gray whales and sea otters. The road forms a crescent as it follows the bay between Clallam Bay and Sekiu, home to Roe-z, the wood-carved female running fish. For the last 10 or so miles, the road curves close to the water and around rock formations with names like Slipper Rock and Sail and Seal Rocks. The drive ends at Neah Bay in the Makah Indian Reservation.

Find the starting point on p. 108, D-4.

24 West Virginia

The Farm Heritage Road staggers across West Virginia's Monroe County, alternately winding north and south. True to its name, the road carries travelers through rural landscapes, made even more authentic by the county's utter lack of fast-food chains. Take WV 3 from Sweet Springs to Union, where you'll see antebellum homes and churches. Then follow US 219 south through the former spa town of Salt Sulphur Springs to WV 122, a westerly course that will take you to Greenville, home of the 19th-century Old Mill. Head south on WV 12 and end with an orchard tour in Ballard, or continue south to Peterstown. Even a round-trip journey will get you home before dinner.

Find the starting point on p. 112, I-7.

25 Wisconsin

Some of Wisconsin's most dramatic rolling hill country and charming settlements are just west of Madison. Taking US 12 west to WI 78 south and then west again on US 18/151, the road passes close by Blue Mound State Park as it climbs and descends through the Driftless Area—the region in southwest Wisconsin beyond the reach of the last glaciers. US 18 heads west while you stay on US 151, veering south on WI 23 to Mineral Point. First settled by Cornish miners in the 1820s, Mineral Point was the first city in Wisconsin to be listed on the National Register of Historic Places. Treat yourself to a walk on High Street and take home some figgyhobbin, the Cornish dessert of pastry, brown sugar, raisins, and caramel. The route back to Madison (WI 39 east to WI 69/92 north to US 18/151 east) runs through New Glarus, a Swiss village with chalet-crowded streets.

Find the starting point on p. 115, N-10.

26 Wyoming

Begin at the arch of elk antlers in downtown Jackson for an awesome scenic drive through Grand Teton National Park. Take US 26/89/191 north past the National Elk Refuge, wintering home to more than 5,000 elk. Head up to Moose, veering left off the main road onto Teton Park Road and into the national park. Pullouts abound for great photos: the log-hewn Chapel of the Transfiguration in Moose; the eight peaks, including Grand Teton (13,770 ft.) and Mt. Moran (12,605 ft.); the top of Signal Mountain for its view of the Snake River and Flathead Valley below. At Jackson Lake Junction, head east on US 89/191/287, then check out wildlife at Oxbow Bend, a turnout on the right. Reconnect with US 26/89/191 at Moran, heading south, for a fast yet scenic return to Jackson.

Find the starting point on p. 116, D-5.

Winterthur Museum, Delaware

NUMBERS to Know

Toll Roads

State	Name	Location (Start point to end point)	Cash Miles	Price
Alabama	Foley Beach Expressway	AL 59 north of Foley to AL 180 in Orange Beach	15.0	$2.00
California	CA 241 Section	CA 91 to Foothill Transportation Corridor	12.2	$2.50
	CA 261 Section	Jamboree Rd. to CA 241	6.0	$1.25
	Eastern Transportation Corridor CA 133 Section	I-5 to Foothill Transportation Corridor	4.3	$1.50
	Foothill Transportation Corridor (CA 241)	Eastern Transportation Corridor to Oso Pkwy.	9.5	$2.75*
	San Joaquin Hills Trans. Corridor (CA 73)	MacArthur Blvd. to I-5	17.7	$4.25*
Colorado	E-470	I-25 N to I-25 S	46.1	$9.75
	I-25 Express Lanes	HOV lanes in I-25 to/from downtown Denver to US 36	7.0	$3.25
	Northwest Parkway	I-25 and US 36	10.0	$2.00
Delaware	DE 1	S. Dover to Biddles Corner	32.9	$2.00
	John F. Kennedy Memorial Highway	Maryland state line to jct DE 141	11.0	$3.00
Florida	Airport Expressway (FL 112)	Miami Int'l. Airport to I-95	4.1	$1.25
	Bee Line Expressway (FL 528)	I-4 to FL 520	31.0	$3.25
	Central Florida Greenway (FL 417)	I-4S to Seminole county line	38.0	$3.75
	Southern Connector	I-4 to the Central Florida Greenway	3.9	$0.75
	Crosstown Expressway	Gandy Blvd (US 92) to I-75	13.9	$2.25
	Dolphin Expressway (FL 836)	Florida's Turnpike's Homestead Extension to I-95	11.8	$1.25
	Don Shula Expressway (FL 874)	Florida's Tpk. Homestead Ext. to the Palmetto Expressway	7.2	$1.25
	East-West Expressway (FL 408)	Colonial Dr. (east) to Florida's Turnpike	22.0	$2.50
	Everglades Parkway (Alligator Alley)	Naples to Andytown	78.0	$2.50
	Florida's Turnpike			
	Mainline Ticket System	South of St. Cloud, FL to jct with FL 804 near Greenacres	143.0	$13.70
	Homestead Extension	Miramar to Florida City	47.0	$4.00
	Northen Coin System	I-75 to Three Lakes Toll Plaza (start of ticket system)	84.0	$2.00
	Southern Coin System	Lantana Toll Plaza to Miami	39.0	$2.00
	Gratigny Parkway (FL 924)	Palmetto Expwy. to NW 32nd Ave.	5.4	$1.25
	Osceola Parkway (FL 522)	Florida's Turnpike to Walt Disney World Drive	12.4	$1.25
	Polk Parkway (FL 570)	I-4 near Clark Rd. to I-4 near Mt. Olive Rd.	25.1	$3.00
	Sanibel Causeway	Connecting Sanibel Island to the mainland	3.0	$6.00
	Sawgrass Expressway (FL 869)	I-75 to I-95	23.0	$2.00
	Seminole Expressway (FL 417)	I-4 near FL 46 to Seminole County line	18.0	$2.00
	Snapper Creek Expressway (FL 878)	US 1 to FL 874 (Don Shula Expressway)	2.7	$1.25
	Suncoast Parkway (FL 589)	Veterans Expwy. to US 98	42.0	$3.00
	Veterans Expressway (FL 589)	Dale Mabry Hwy. to Courtney Campbell Causeway	15.0	$1.75
	Western Expressway (FL 429)	US 192 to US 441 (FL 429)	25.0	$2.00
Georgia	GA 400	Lenox Rd. to I-285	3.6	$0.50
Illinois	Chicago Skyway (I-90)	I-94 to Indiana state line	7.8	$2.50
	North-South Tollway (I-355)	I-290, Addison, to I-55	17.5	$2.00
	Northwest Tollway (I-90)	Des Plaines to South Beloit	76.0	$4.20
	Ronald Reagan Memorial Tollway (I-88)	I-294 to Rock Falls	97.0	$5.40
	Tri-State Tollway			
	northbound (I-294 & I-94)	I-94 / IL 394 to Wisconsin state line	83.0	$4.90
	southbound (I-94 & I-294)	Wisconsin state line to I-94 / IL 394	83.0	$4.70
Indiana	Indiana Toll Road			
	barrier portion (I-90)	Illinois state line to LaPorte ticket plaza	24.0	$0.50
	ticket portion (I-80/90)	LaPorte, IN to Ohio state line	133.0	$4.60
Kansas	Kansas Turnpike (I-70 & I-35 & I-335)	Kansas City to Oklahoma state line	236.0	$8.75
Kentucky	Audubon Parkway	Henderson to Owensboro	23.4	$0.50
	William H. Natcher Parkway	Bowling Green to Owensboro	70.2	$1.50
Maine	Maine Turnpike	York to Augusta	100.0	$4.00
Maryland	John F. Kennedy Memorial Highway	Toll bridge b/t Havre de Grace and Perryville	50.0	$5.00
Massachusetts	Massachusetts Turnpike Westbound	East Boston to New York state line	138.0	$7.60
New Hampshire	Blue Star Turnpike	Portsmouth to Seabrook	15.0	$1.00
	F.E. Everett Turnpike	Nashua to Concord	44.7	$1.50
	Spaulding Turnpike	Portsmouth to Milton, NH	33.2	$1.00
New Jersey	Atlantic City Expressway	Turnersville to Atlantic City	44.0	$2.50
	Garden State Parkway Southbound	Montvale to Cape May	173.0	$3.50
	New Jersey Turnpike	Delaware Memorial Bridge to US 46	148.0	$6.45
New York	New York Thruway			
	eastbound	Pennsylvania state line to New York City	496.0	$22.50
	westbound	New York City to Pennsylvania state line	496.0	$18.50
	Berkshire Section	Selkirk to Massachusetts Turnpike	15.0	$1.50
	New England Section	New York City to Connecticut state line	15.0	$1.25
	Niagara Section	Buffalo to Niagara Falls	21.0	$1.50
Ohio	J.W. Shocknessy Ohio Turnpike	Pennsylvania state line to Indiana state line	241.2	$8.95
Oklahoma	Cherokee Turnpike	East of US 69 to east of US 59	32.8	$2.25
	Chickasaw Turnpike	Ada to Sulphur	27.1	$0.55
	Cimarron Turnpike	I-35 to Tulsa	59.2	$2.50
	Creek Turnpike	Turner Turnpike to Will Rogers Turnpike	33.2	$2.45
	H.E. Bailey Turnpike	Oklahoma City to Texas state line	86.4	$4.00
	Indian Nation Turnpike	Henryetta to Hugo	105.2	$4.75
	Kilpatrick Turnpike	I-40 to I-35/44	25.3	$2.00
	Muskogee Turnpike	Tulsa to Webbers Falls	53.1	$2.50
	Turner Turnpike	Oklahoma City to Tulsa	86.0	$3.50
	Will Rogers Turnpike	Tulsa to Missouri state line	88.5	$3.50
Pennsylvania	Amos K. Hutchinson Bypass (PA 66)	US 119 to US 22	13.2	$1.00
	James E. Ross Hwy Northbound (PA 60)	Beaver Falls to New Castle	16.5	$1.00
	Mon/Fayette Expressway (PA 43)	PA 51 to US 40	24.0	$1.75
	Pennsylvania Turnpike			
	Main Section	New Jersey state line to Ohio state line	359.0	$22.75
	Northeast Section	Norristown to Scranton	110.0	$6.25
Texas	Camino Colombia Toll Road	I-35 to Mexican border	22.0	$2.00
	Dallas North Tollway	I-35 E to TX 121	22.0	$2.25
	Hardy Toll Road	I-45 to I-610	21.6	$2.50
	President George Bush Turnpike	I-35 E to TX 78	29.2	$3.75
	Sam Houston Tollway		61.3	
	East Sam Houston Tollway	I-45 to I-10		$1.25
	North Sam Houston Tollway	US 290 to I-45		$1.25
	South Sam Houston Tollway	US 59 to I-45		$9.50
	West Sam Houston Tollway	US 59 to US 290		$1.25
	Westpark Tollway	I-610 to Wildcrest Road		$1.00
Virginia	Chesapeake Expressway (VA 168)	I-64 to the North Carolina border	16.0	$2.00
	Downtown Expressway	I-195 to I-95	2.5	$0.50
	Dulles Greenway	VA 28 to Leesburg	14.3	$3.20
	Dulles Toll Road	VA 123 to VA 28	14.0	$0.75
	Pocahontas Parkway	I-95 connecting to I-295	7.5	$2.25
	Powhite Parkway Extension	VA 150 to Old Hundred Rd	12.5	$0.75
West Virginia	West Virginia Turnpike	Charleston to Princeton	88.0	$3.75

*During peak hours (M-F 7-9 a.m. NB lanes and M-F 4-7 p.m. SB lanes)

Hotel Toll-free Numbers and Websites

Adam's Mark Hotels & Resorts
(800) 444-2326
www.adamsmark.com

AmericInn
(800) 634-3444
www.americinn.com

Baymont Inns & Suites
(800) 301-0200 or
(866) 999-1111
www.baymontinn.com

America's Best Inns & Suites
(800) 237-8466
www.americasbestinns.com

Best Western
(800) 780-7234
www.bestwestern.com

Budget Host
(800) 283-4678
www.budgethost.com

Clarion Hotels
(877) 424-6423
www.clarioninn.com

Coast Hotels & Resorts
(800) 716-6199
www.coasthotels.com

Comfort Inns
(877) 424-6423
www.comfortinn.com

Comfort Suites
(877) 424-6423
www.comfortsuites.com

Courtyard by Marriott
(800) 321-2211
www.courtyard.com

Crowne Plaza Hotel & Resorts
(877) 227-6963
www.crowneplaza.com

Days Inn
(800) 329-7466
www.daysinn.com

Delta Hotels & Resorts
(888) 778-5050
(877) 814-7706
www.deltahotels.com

Doubletree Hotels & Guest Suites
(800) 222-8733
www.doubletree.com

Drury Hotels
(800) 378-7946
www.druryhotels.com

Econo Lodge
(877) 424-6423
www.econolodge.com

Embassy Suites Hotels
(800) 362-2779
www.embassysuites.com

Exel Inns of America
(800) 367-3935
www.exelinns.com

Extended StayAmerica
(800) 804-3724
www.extstay.com

Fairfield Inn by Marriott
(800) 228-2800
www.fairfieldinn.com

Fairmont Hotels & Resorts
(800) 257-7544
www.fairmont.com

Four Points Hotels by Sheraton
(800) 368-7764
www.fourpoints.com

Four Seasons Hotels & Resorts
(800) 819-5053
www.fourseasons.com

Hampton Inn
(800) 426-7866
www.hamptoninn.com

Hilton Hotels
(800) 445-8667
www.hilton.com

Holiday Inn Hotels & Resorts
(800) 465-4329
www.holiday-inn.com

Homewood Suites
(800) 225-5466
www.homewood-suites.com

Howard Johnson Lodges
(800) 446-4656
www.hojo.com

Hyatt Hotels & Resorts
(888) 591-1234
www.hyatt.com

InterContinental Hotels & Resorts
(888) 424-6835
www.intercontinental.com

Jameson Inns
(800) 526-3766
www.jamesoninns.com

Knights Inn
(800) 843-5644
www.knightsinn.com

La Quinta Inn & Suites
(866) 725-1661
www.lq.com

Le Meridien Hotels
(800) 543-4300
www.lemeridien.com

Loews Hotels
(800) 235-6397
www.loewshotels.com

MainStay Suites
(877) 424-6423
www.mainstaysuites.com

Marriott International
(888) 236-2427
www.marriott.com

Microtel Inns & Suites
(888) 771-7171
www.microtelinn.com

Motel 6
(800) 466-8356
www.motel6.com

Omni Hotels
(888) 444-6664
www.omnihotels.com

Park Inn/Park Plaza
(800) 670-7275
www.parkinns.com

Preferred Hotels & Resorts
(800) 323-7500
www.preferredhotels.com

Quality Inns & Suites
(877) 424-6423
www.qualityinn.com

Radisson Hotels & Resorts
(800) 333-3333
www.radisson.com

Ramada Inn/Ramada Limited/Ramada Plaza Hotels
(800) 272-6232
www.ramada.com

Red Lion Hotels
(800) 733-5466
www.redlion.com

Red Roof Inns
(800) 733-7663
www.redroof.com

Renaissance Hotels & Resorts
(888) 236-2427
www.renaissancehotels.com

Residence Inn by Marriott
(888) 236-2427
www.residenceinn.com

The Ritz-Carlton
(800) 241-3333
www.ritzcarlton.com

Rodeway Inn
(877) 424-6423
www.rodeway.com

Sheraton Hotels & Resorts
(800) 598-1753
www.sheraton.com

Signature Inns
(800) 822-5252
www.signatureinns.com

Sleep Inn
(877) 424-6423
www.sleepinn.com

Super 8 Motel
(800) 800-8000
www.super8.com

Travelodge Hotels
(800) 578-7878
www.travelodge.com

WestCoast Hotels
(800) 325-4000
www.westcoasthotels.com

Westin Hotels & Resorts
(888) 625-5144
www.westin.com

Wyndham Hotels & Resorts
(877) 999-3223
www.wyndham.com

To find a bed-and-breakfast at your destination, log on to www.bedandbreakfast.com®

NOTE: All toll-free reservation numbers are for the U.S. and Canada unless otherwise noted. These numbers were accurate at press time, but are subject to change. Find more listings or book a hotel online at randmcnally.com.

Cell Phone Emergency Numbers

Alaska 911
Arizona 911
Arkansas 911
California 911
Colorado 911
*277, (303) 329-4501
Connecticut 911
Delaware 911
D.C. 911
Florida 911
Georgia 911
Hawaii . . . . None
Idaho *477
Illinois 911
Indiana 911
Iowa 911, *55
Kansas *47
Kentucky . . (800)222-5555
Louisiana 911
Maine 911
Maryland 911
Massachusetts 911
Michigan 911
Minnesota 911
Mississippi 911
Missouri *55
Montana 911
Nebraska 911
Nevada *647
New Hampshire 911
New Jersey 911
New Mexico 911
New York 911
North Carolina 911
North Dakota *2121
Ohio 911
Oklahoma 911
Oregon 911
Pennsylvania 911
Rhode Island 911
South Carolina 911
South Dakota 911
Tennessee 911
Texas 911
Utah 911
Vermont 911
Virginia 911
Washington 911
West Virginia 911
Wisconsin 911
Wyoming 911

TOURISM
Concierge

On the road or before you go, log on to the official tourism website of your destination. These websites offer terrific ideas about organizing a visit and often include calendars of special events and activities. Prefer calling? Most states offer toll-free numbers.

United States

Alabama Bureau of Tourism & Travel
(800) 252-2262
www.800alabama.com

Alaska Travel Industry Association
(907) 929-2200
www.travelalaska.com

Arizona Office of Tourism
(866) 239-9712
www.arizonaguide.com

Arkansas Department of Parks & Tourism
(800) 628-8725
www.arkansas.com

California Travel & Tourism Commission
(800) 862-2543*
(916) 444-4429
www.visitcalifornia.com

Colorado Tourism Office
(800) 265-6723
www.colorado.com

Connecticut Tourism
(800) 282-6863
www.ctbound.org

Delaware Tourism Office
(866) 284-7483
(302) 739-4271
www.visitdelaware.com

Visit Florida
(888) 735-2872
www.visitflorida.com

Georgia Office of Tourism
(800) 847-4842
www.georgiaonmymind.org

Hawaii Visitors & Convention Bureau
(800) 464-2924
www.gohawaii.com

Idaho Tourism
(800) 847-4843
www.visitid.org

Illinois Bureau of Tourism
(800) 226-6632
www.enjoyillinois.com

Indiana Tourism Division
(888) 365-6946
www.enjoyindiana.com

Iowa Tourism Office
(800) 345-4692*
(888) 472-6035
(515) 242-4705
www.traveliowa.com

Kansas Travel & Tourism
(800) 252-6727
www.travelks.com

Kentucky Department of Travel
(800) 225-8747
(502) 564-4930
www.kentuckytourism.com

Louisiana Office of Tourism
(800) 334-8626
www.louisianatravel.com

Maine Office of Tourism
(888) 624-6345
(225) 342-8100
www.visitmaine.com

Maryland Office of Tourism
(800) 634-7386
www.visitmaryland.org

Massachusetts Office of Travel & Tourism
(800) 227-6277
(617) 973-8500
www.massvacation.com

Travel Michigan
(888) 784-7328
www.michigan.org

Minnesota Office of Tourism
(800) 657-3700
(651) 296-5029
www.exploreminnesota.com

Mississippi Division of Tourism
(800) 927-6378
(601) 359-3297
www.visitmississippi.org

Missouri Division of Tourism
(800) 810-5500
(573) 751-4133
www.visitmo.com

Travel Montana
(800) 847-4868
(406) 841-2870
www.visitmt.com

Nebraska Division of Travel & Tourism
(877) 632-7275
(800) 228-4307
(402) 471-3796
www.visitnebraska.org

Nevada Commission on Tourism
(800) 638-2328
www.travelnevada.com

New Hampshire Division of Travel and Tourism Development
(800) 386-4664
(603) 271-2665
www.visitnh.gov

New Jersey Office of Travel & Tourism
(800) 847-4865
(609) 777-0885
www.visitnj.org

New Mexico Department of Tourism
(800) 733-6396
www.newmexico.org

New York State Tourism
(800) 225-5697
(518) 474-4116
www.iloveny.com

North Carolina Division of Tourism
(800) 847-4862
(919) 733-8372
www.visitnc.com

North Dakota Tourism Division
(800) 435-5663
(701) 328-2525
www.ndtourism.com

Ohio Division of Travel & Tourism
(800) 282-5393
www.ohiotourism.com

Oklahoma Tourism & Recreation Department
(800) 652-6552
www.travelok.com

Oregon Tourism Commission
(800) 547-7842
www.traveloregon.com

Pennsylvania Center for Travel & Marketing
(800) 847-4872
www.visitpa.com

Rhode Island Tourism Division
(888) 886-9463
(800) 556-2484
(401) 222-2601
www.visitrhodeisland.com

South Carolina Department of Parks, Recreation & Tourism
(888) 727-6453*
(803) 734-1700
www.discoversouthcarolina.com

South Dakota Department of Tourism
(800) 732-5682
(605) 773-3301
www.travelsd.com

Tennessee Department of Tourist Development
(800) 462-8366*
(615) 741-2159
www.tnvacation.com

Texas Tourism Division
(800) 888-8839*
www.traveltex.com

Utah Travel Council
(800) 200-1160
(801) 538-1030
www.utah.com

Vermont Department of Tourism and Marketing
(800) 837-6668
www.vermontvacation.com

Virginia Tourism Corporation
(800) 321-3244
(800) 847-4882
www.virginia.org

Washington State Tourism
(800) 544-1800
www.experiencewashington.com

Washington, D.C. Convention & Tourism Corporation
(800) 422-8644*
(202) 789-7000
www.washington.org

West Virginia Division of Tourism
(800) 225-5982
www.callwva.com

Wisconsin Department of Tourism
(800) 432-8747
www.travelwisconsin.com

Wyoming Travel & Tourism
(800) 225-5996
www.wyomingtourism.org

Canada

Travel Alberta
(800) 252-3782
www.travelalberta.com

Tourism British Columbia
(800) 435-5622
www.hellobc.com

Travel Manitoba
(800) 665-0040
www.travelmanitoba.com

Tourism New Brunswick
(800) 561-0123
www.tourismnbcanada.com

Newfoundland & Labrador Department of Tourism
(800) 563-6353
(709) 729-2830
www.gov.nf.ca/tourism

Nova Scotia Department of Tourism & Culture
(800) 565-0000
novascotia.com

Ontario Travel
(800) 668-2746
www.ontariotravel.net

Prince Edward Island Tourism
(888) 734-7529
www.peiplay.com

Tourisme Québec
(877) 266-5687
www.bonjourquebec.com

Tourism Saskatchewan
(877) 237-2273
www.sasktourism.com

Mexico

Mexico Tourism Board
(800) 446-3942
www.visitmexico.com

* To request travel materials only

MAP LEGEND

Roads and related symbols

	Free limited-access highway
	Toll limited-access highway
	New road (under construction as of press time)
	Other multilane highway
	Principal highway
	Other through highway
	Other road (conditions vary — local inquiry suggested)
	Unpaved road (conditions vary — local inquiry suggested)
	Ramp; one way route
	Ferry
96 BR 96	Interstate highway; Interstate highway business route
31 BUS 31	U.S. highway; U.S. highway business route
1 15	Trans-Canada highway; Autoroute
1	Mexican highway or Central American highway
18	State or provincial highway
147	Secondary state, secondary provincial, or county highway
NM	County trunk highway
	Construction site or construction zone
	Scenic route; Best of the Road™ route
TOLL	Service area; toll booth or fee booth
	Tunnel; mountain pass

Interchanges and exit numbers (For most states, the mileage between interchanges may be determined by subtracting one number from the other.)

Highway mileages (segments of one mile or less not shown):
Cumulative miles (red): the distance between arrows
Intermediate miles (black): the distance between intersections

Comparative distance
1 mile = 1.609 kilometers   1 kilometer = 0.621 mile

Cities & towns (size of type on map indicates relative population)

⊗ ⊛	National capital; state or provincial capital
◉ ○	County seat or independent city
● ○	City, town, or recognized place; neighborhood
	Urbanized area
	Separate cities within metropolitan area

Parks, recreation areas, & points of interest

	U.S. or Canadian national park
	U.S. or Canadian national monument, other National Park Service facility, state/provincial park or recreation area
▲ ⋔	Park with camping facilities; park without camping facilities
▲ 禾	Campsite; wayside or roadside park
	National forest, national grassland, or city park
	Wilderness area; wildlife refuge
■ ▪	Point of interest, historic site or monument
✈	Airport
	Building
- - - - -	Foot trail
⌐	Golf course or country club
⊞	Hospital or medical center
	Indian reservation
?	Information center or Tourist Information Center (T.I.C.)
✈	Military or governmental installation; military airport
☎	Rest area with toilets; rest area without toilets

Physical features

	Dam
△ ▲	Mountain peak; highest point in state/province
	Lake; intermittent lake; dry lake
	River; intermittent river
	Desert
	Glacier
	Swamp or mangrove swamp

Other symbols

	Area shown in greater detail on inset map
52	Inset map page indicator (if not on same page)
☼	Great River Road
◇	Port of entry
• • • • •	Intracoastal waterway
	Railroad
COOK	County or parish boundary and name
	State or provincial boundary
	National boundary
• • • • •	Continental divide
	Time zone boundary
33°00′ 95°00′	Latitude; longitude

Population figures are from the latest available census or are Census Bureau or Rand McNally estimates.

For a complete list of abbreviations that appear on the maps, go to www.randmcnally.com/ABBR.

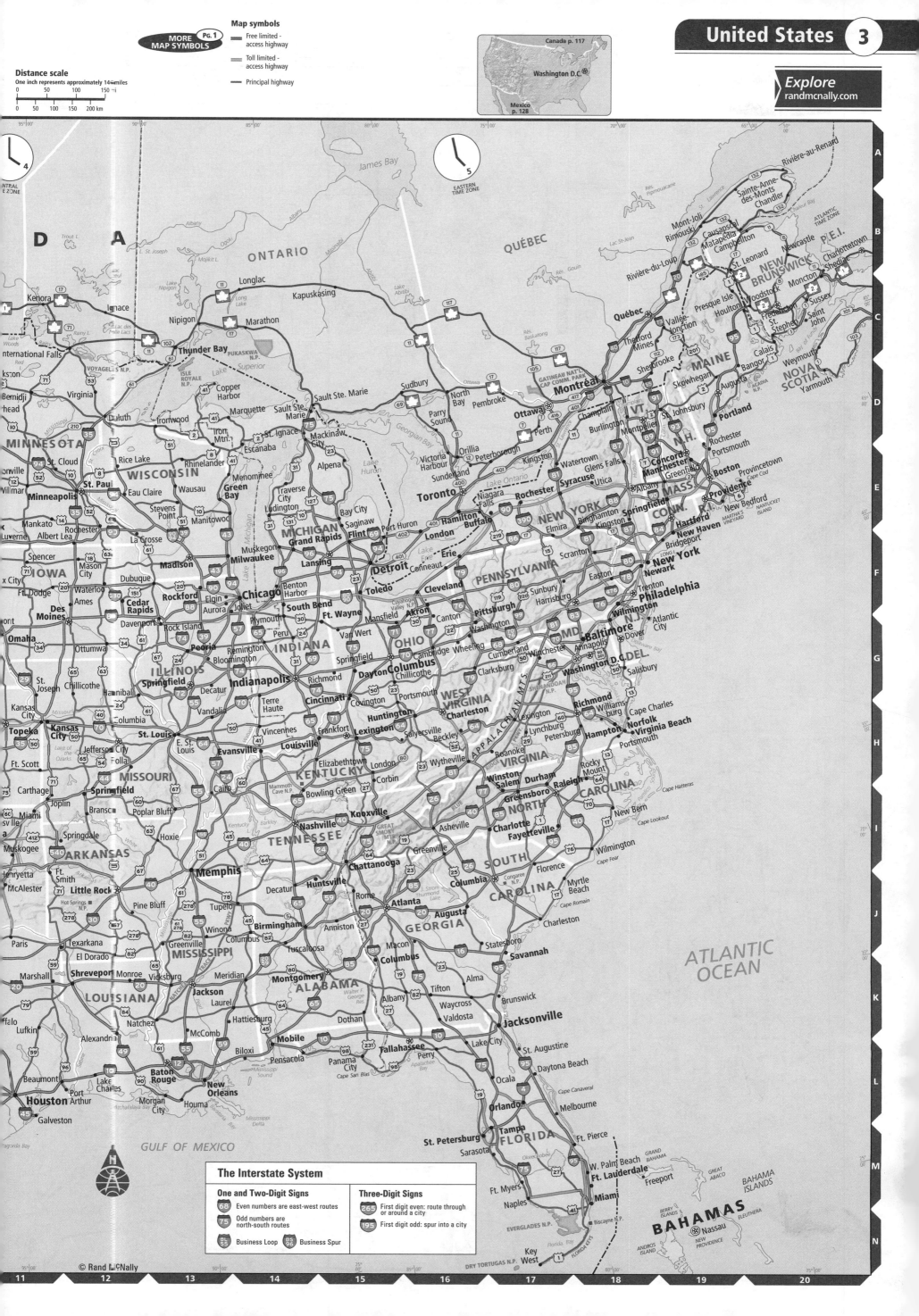

Nickname: The Heart of Dixie
Land area: 50,744 sq. mi. (rank: 28th)
Population: 4,500,752 (rank: 23rd)
Largest city: Birmingham, 236,620

INDEX OF CITIES PG. 129

Mileage between cities	Andalusia	Anniston	Atlanta, GA	Auburn	Birmingham	Chattanooga, TN	Decatur	Dothan	Eufaula	Florence	Gadsden	Huntsville	Meridian, MS	Mobile	Montgomery	Pensacola FL	Phenix City	Selma	Tuscaloosa	Troy
ATLANTA, GA	249	90		106	148	115	227	202	151	275	120	193	188	290	329	160	319	105	210	193	203
BIRMINGHAM	181	66	148	111		143	80	199	182	128	61	98	41	146	261	92	251	141	94	142	59
CHATTANOOGA, TN	319	116	115	218	143		130	314	263	87	86	65	183	289	399	230	389	217	232	280	202
DOTHAN	75	210	202	124	199	314	277		51	325	255	295	238	253	201	107	156	97	151	57	212
HUNTSVILLE	277	103	193	244	98	105	26	295	278	67	73		90	240	357	188	347	176	190	238	153
MOBILE	125	282	329	225	261	399	339	201	255	387	317	357		300	134		169	55	257	173	206
MONTGOMERY	89	113	160	56	92	230	170	107	90	218	148	188	131	152	169		159	88	50	50	105
TUSCALOOSA	194	121	203	161	59	202	135	212	195	122	120	153	56	93	206	105	261	193	75	155	

Total mileage through Alabama
- 10: 66 miles
- 20: 215 miles
- 59: 241 miles
- 65: 367 miles

MORE MILEAGES PG. 138

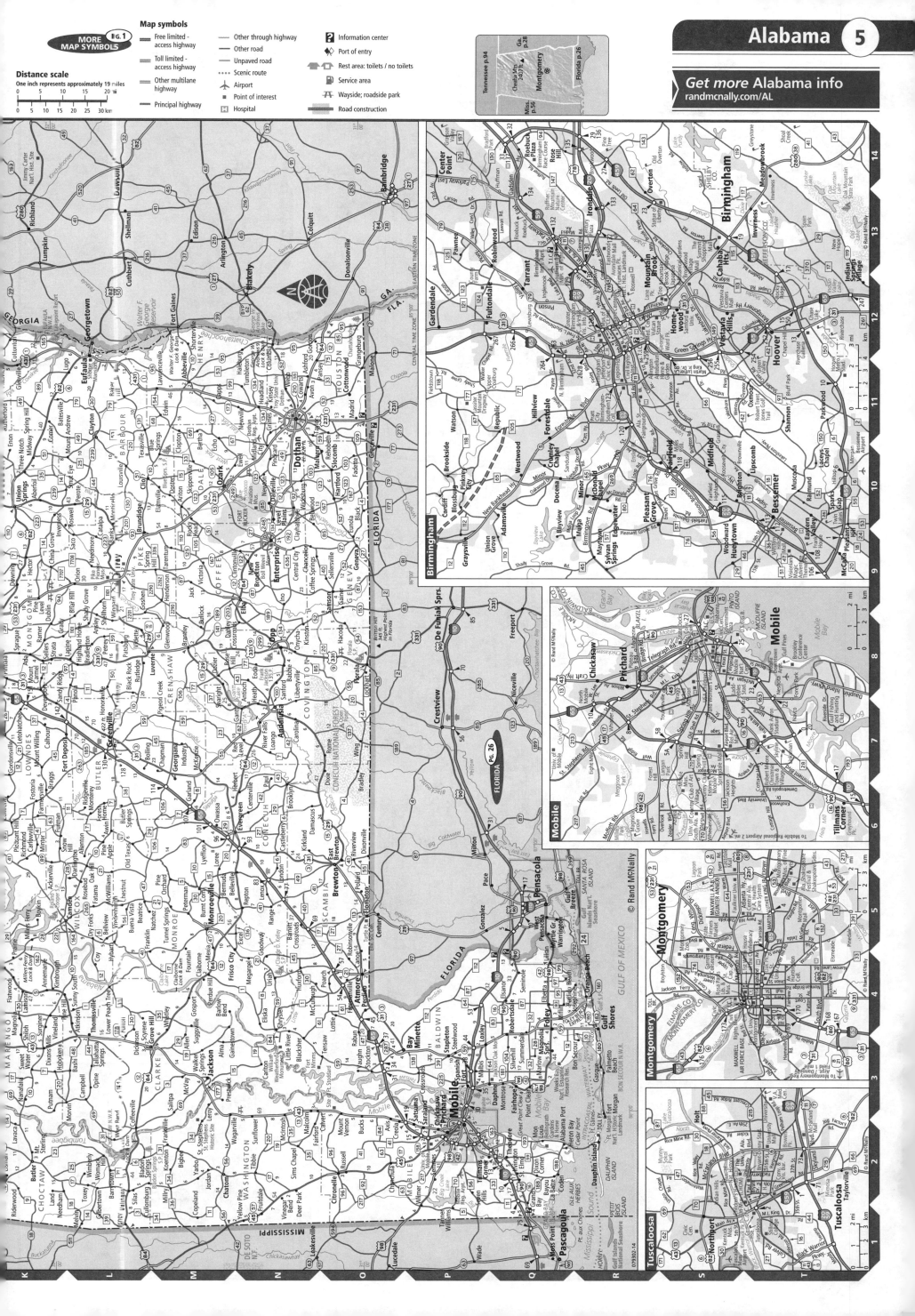

Plan a trip
randmcnally.com/AK

Nickname: The Last Frontier
Land area: 571,951 sq. mi. (rank: 1st)
Population: 648,818 (rank: 47th)
Largest city: Anchorage, 270,951

INDEX OF CITIES PG. 129

Distance scale
One inch represents approximately 134 miles

Mileage between cities	Anchorage	Fairbanks	Glennallen	Haines	Homer	Kenai	Seward	Tok	Valdez
ANCHORAGE		360	187	782	225	158	127	325	304
FAIRBANKS	360		253	665	585	518	487	208	366
HAINES	782	665		595	1007	940	909	457	708
HOMER	225	585	412	1007		89	174	550	529
KENAI	158	518	345	940	89		107	483	462
SEWARD	127	487	314	909	174	107		452	431
TOK	325	208	138	457	550	483	452		251
VALDEZ	304	366	117	708	529	462	431	251	

Total mileage through Alaska
① 408 miles ③ 325 miles
② 202 miles

MORE MILEAGES PG. 138

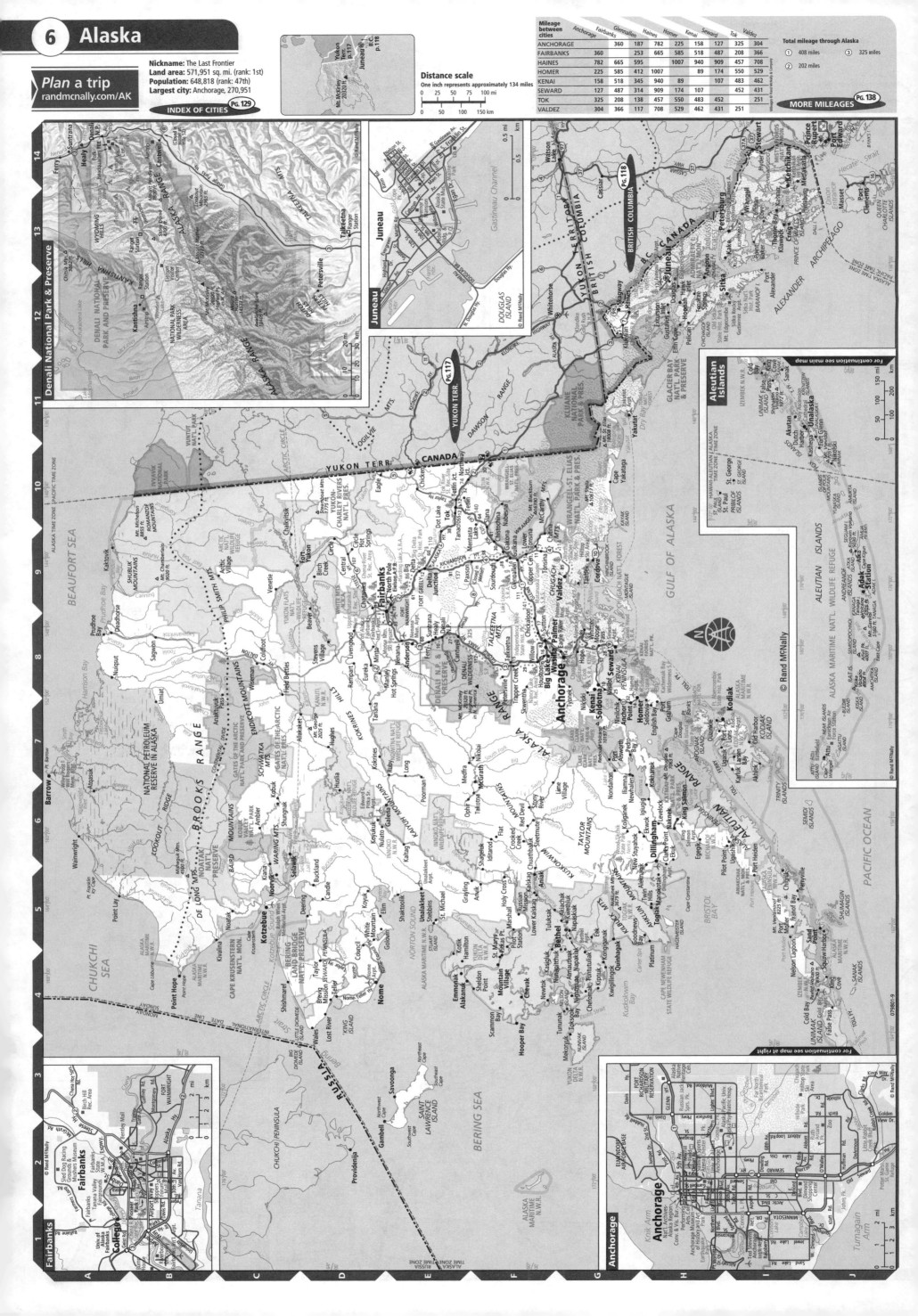

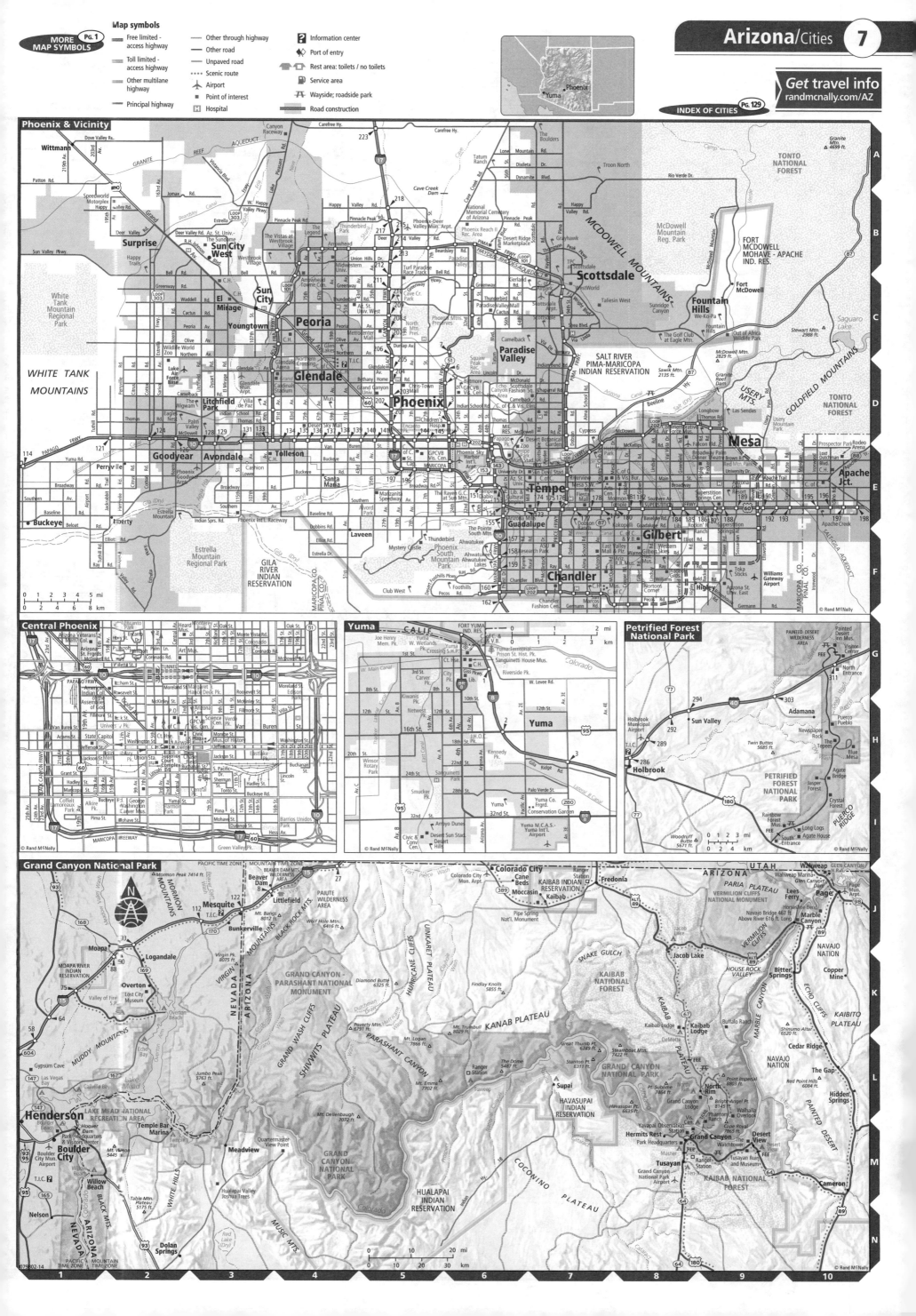

Nickname: The Grand Canyon State
Land area: 113,635 sq. mi. (rank: 6th)
Population: 5,580,811 (rank: 18th)
Largest city: Phoenix, 1,388,416

INDEX OF CITIES Pg. 129

Mileage between cities	Blythe, CA	Casa Grande	Eagar	Flagstaff	Gallup, NM	Grand Canyon	Holbrook	Lake Havasu City	Las Vegas, NV	Lordsburg, NM	Nogales	Page	Phoenix	Shiprock, NM	Tucson	Yuma
CASA GRANDE	197		221	187	318	268	221	236	249	341	224	131	324	51	145	411	67	172
FLAGSTAFF	282	187	179		188	81	92	144	204	249	410	317	137	136	93	281	253	318
HOLBROOK	374	221	87	92	97	169		236	296	341	265	305	217	228	185	190	241	410
KINGMAN	157	236	323	144	332	167	236		60	105	459	366	279	185	146	425	302	215
PHOENIX	146	51	225	136	324	217	228	185	296	310	181	274	181		94	417	117	182
PRESCOTT	155	145	272	93	281	123	185	146	206	251	368	275	230	94		374	211	214
TUCSON	263	67	241	253	334	334	241	302	315	407	157	64	390	117	211	431		237
YUMA	103	172	397	318	506	317	410	215	155	596	394	301	182	214	599	237	

Total mileage through Arizona

8	178 miles	17	146 miles
10	392 miles	40	355 miles

MORE MILEAGES Pg. 138

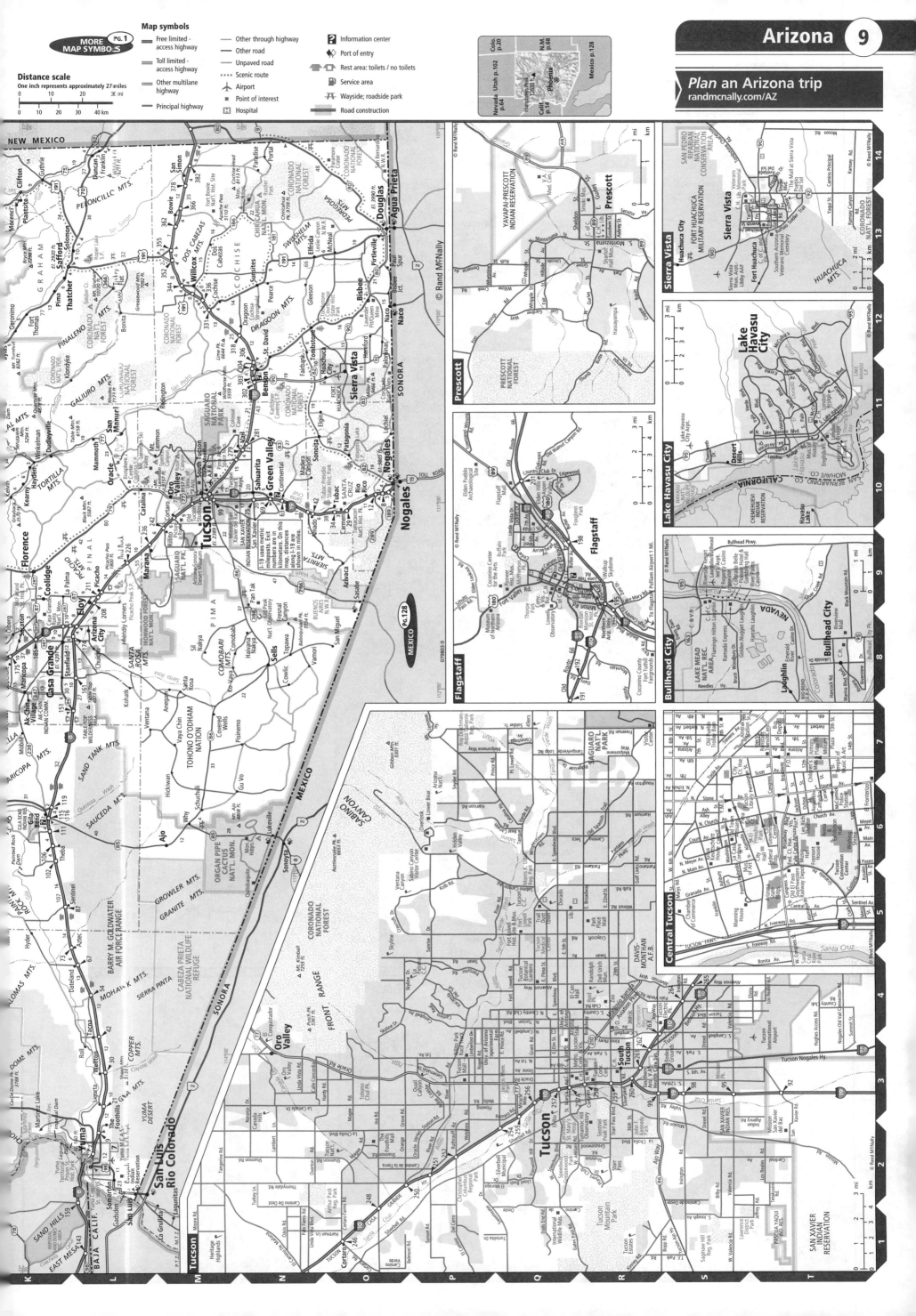

Plan an Arizona trip
randmcnally.com/AZ

Get travel info
randmcnally.com/AR

Nickname: The Natural State
Land area: 52,068 sq. mi. (rank: 27th)
Population: 2,725,714 (rank: 32nd)
Largest city: Little Rock, 184,053

INDEX OF CITIES PG. 129

Distance scale
One inch represents approximately 29 miles

0 10 20 30 40 km

Mileage between cities	El Dorado	Fayetteville	Fort Smith	Harrison	Jonesboro	Little Rock	Pine Bluff	Texarkana	West Memphis
EL DORADO		310	275	255	248	117	91	90	244
FAYETTEVILLE	310		61	88	294	195	235	239	316
FORT SMITH	275	61		150	259	160	200	180	281
HARRISON	255	88	150		170	140	180	272	261
JONESBORO	248	294	259	170		133	173	273	63
LITTLE ROCK	117	195	160	140	133		42	140	129
TEXARKANA	90	239	180	272	273	140	151		269
WEST MEMPHIS	244	316	281	261	63	129	135	269	

Total mileage through Arkansas		
30	143 miles	55	72 miles
40	284 miles	US 65	309 miles

MORE MILEAGES PG. 138

© Rand McNally

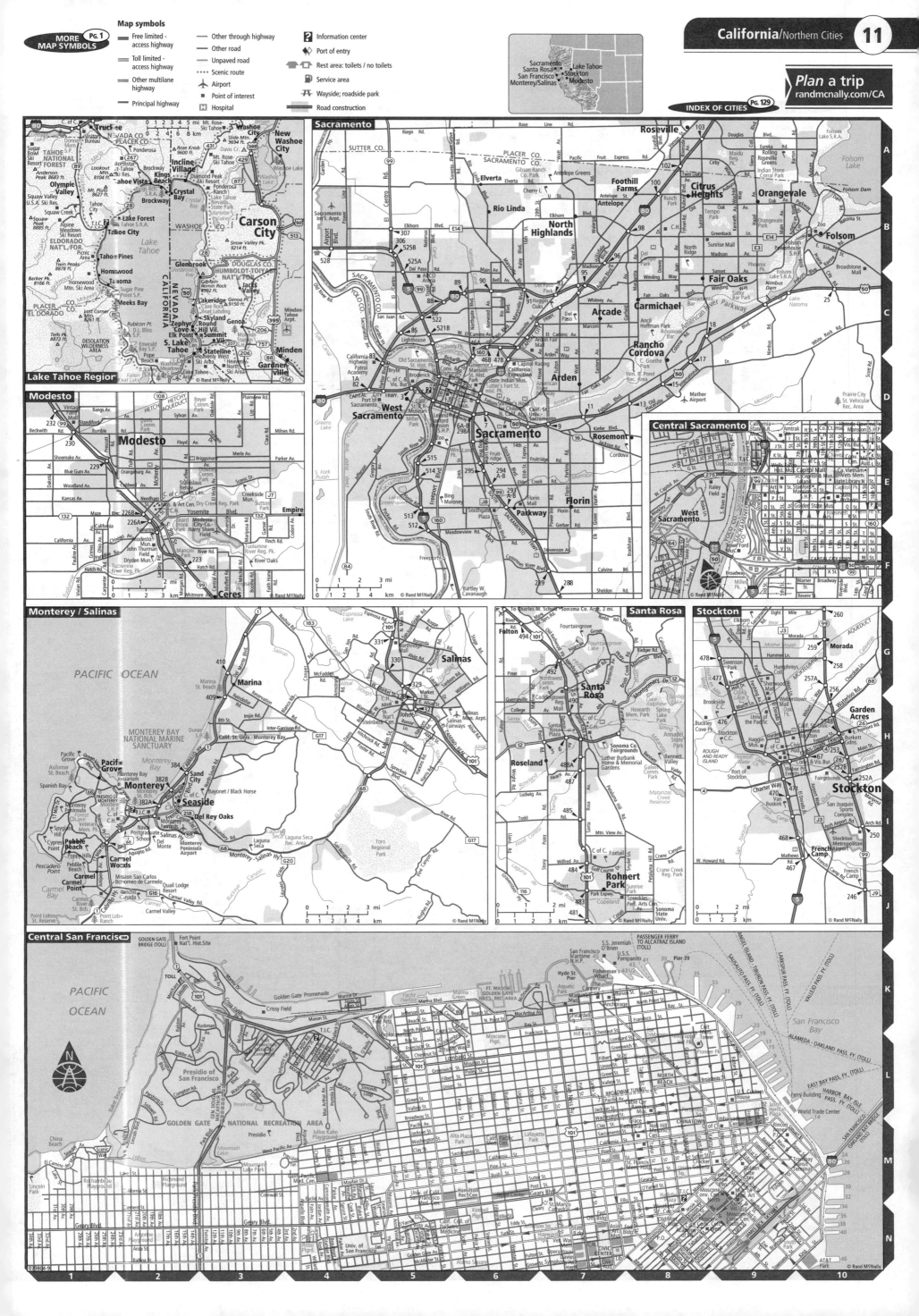

Nickname: The Golden State
Land area: 155,959 sq. mi. (rank: 3rd)
Population: 35,484,453 (rank: 1st)
Largest city: Los Angeles, 3,819,951

INDEX OF CITIES Pg. 129
MORE MILEAGES Pg. 138

Mileage between cities	Alturas	Bishop	Crescent City	Eureka	Oakland	Oroville	Redding	Sacramento	San Francisco	San Jose	South Lake Tahoe	Stockton	Susanville	Ukiah	Vallejo	Yosemite NP	Yreka
BISHOP	385		623	556	289	333	402	273	297	286	347	180	237	288	421	298	139	458
EUREKA	300	556	82		281	223	154	296	281	324	223	398	342	268	162	264	463	214
REDDING	146	402	217	154	209	98		165	217	246	226	267	211	114	189	336	97
SACRAMENTO	307	273	378	296	83	72	165		91	116	100	102	47	197	148	63	171	260
SAN FRANCISCO	359	297	363	281	8	149	217	91		44	58	193	80	269	119	32	190	312
SAN JOSE	388	286	406	324	43	178	246	116	44		101	218	69	298	162	63	179	341
S. LAKE TAHOE	239	180	477	398	185	155	267	102	193	218		52	149	142	250	165	187	312
VALLEJO	331	298	346	264	24	121	189	63	32	63	52	165	68	241		102	191	284

Total mileage through California

5 — 797 miles
101 — 791 miles
80 — 199 miles

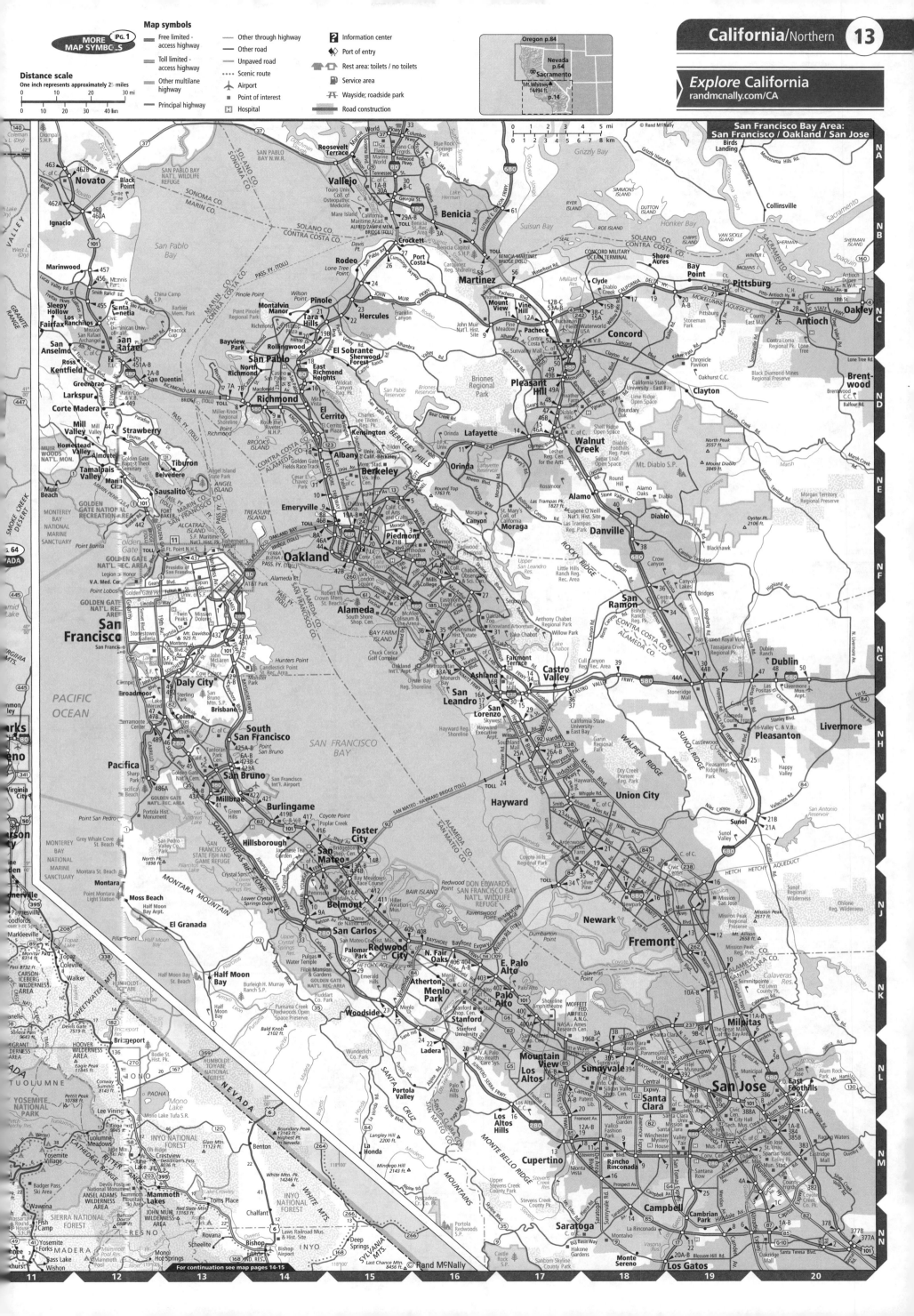

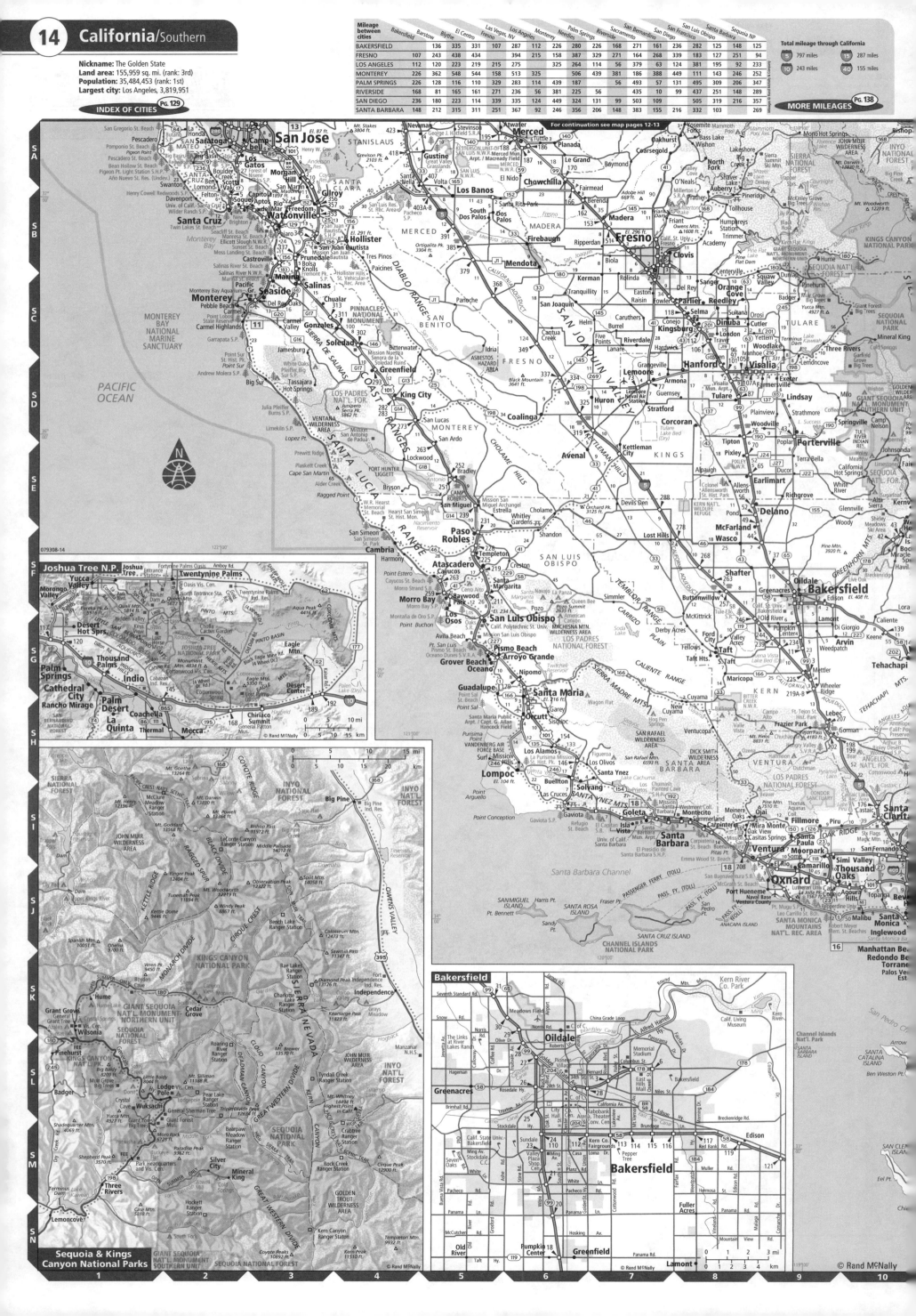

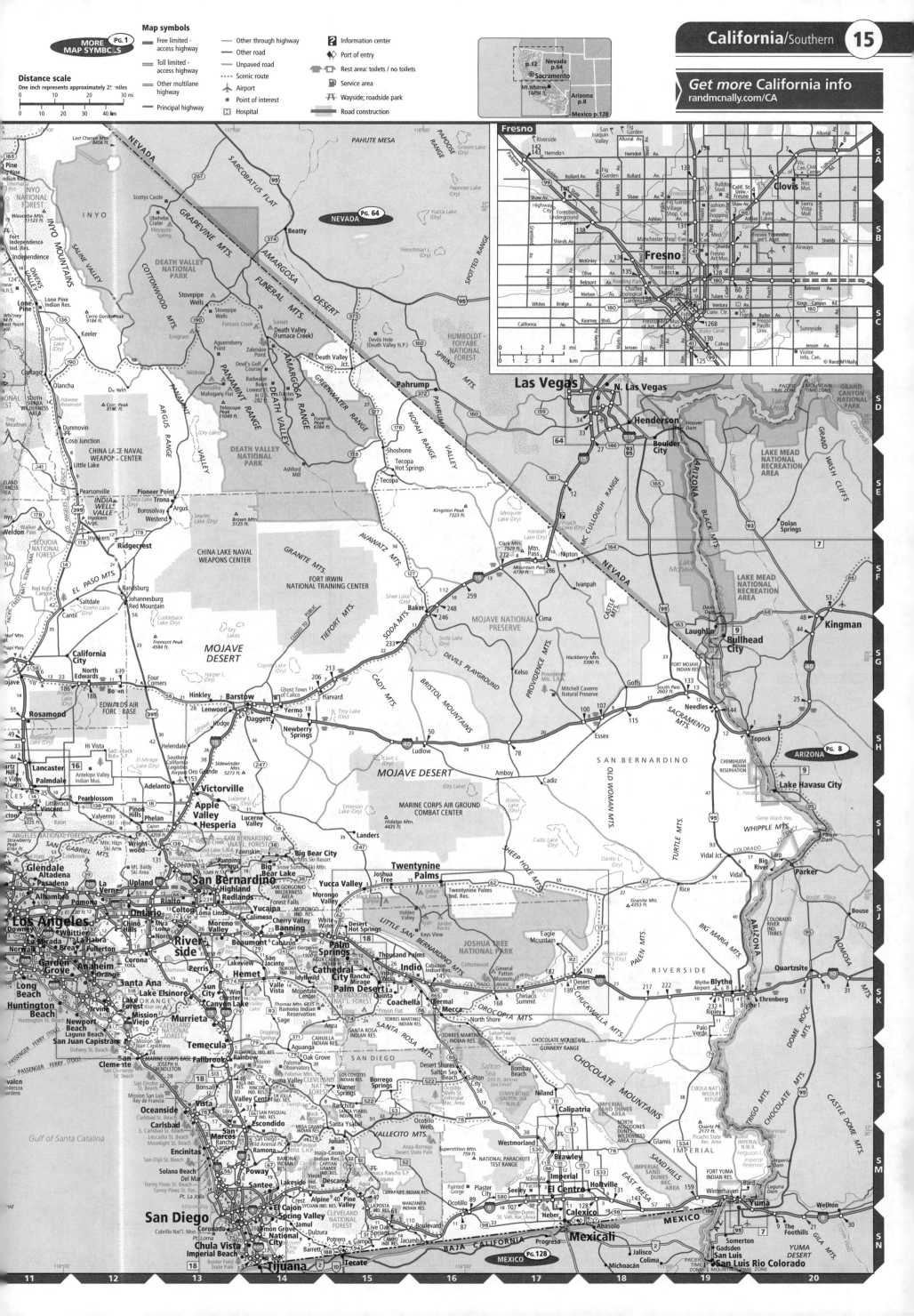

Get more California info
randmcnally.com/CA

Map symbols

Free limited-access highway
Toll limited-access highway
Other multilane highway
Principal highway
Other through highway
Other road
Unpaved road
Scenic route
Airport
Point of interest
Hospital

? Information center
Port of entry
Rest area: toilets / no toilets
Service area
Wayside; roadside park
Road construction

MORE MAP SYMBOLS PG. 1

Distance scale
One inch represents approximately 25 miles
0 10 20 30 mi
0 10 20 30 40 km

Fresno

NEVADA PG. 64

ARIZONA PG. 8

MEXICO PG.128

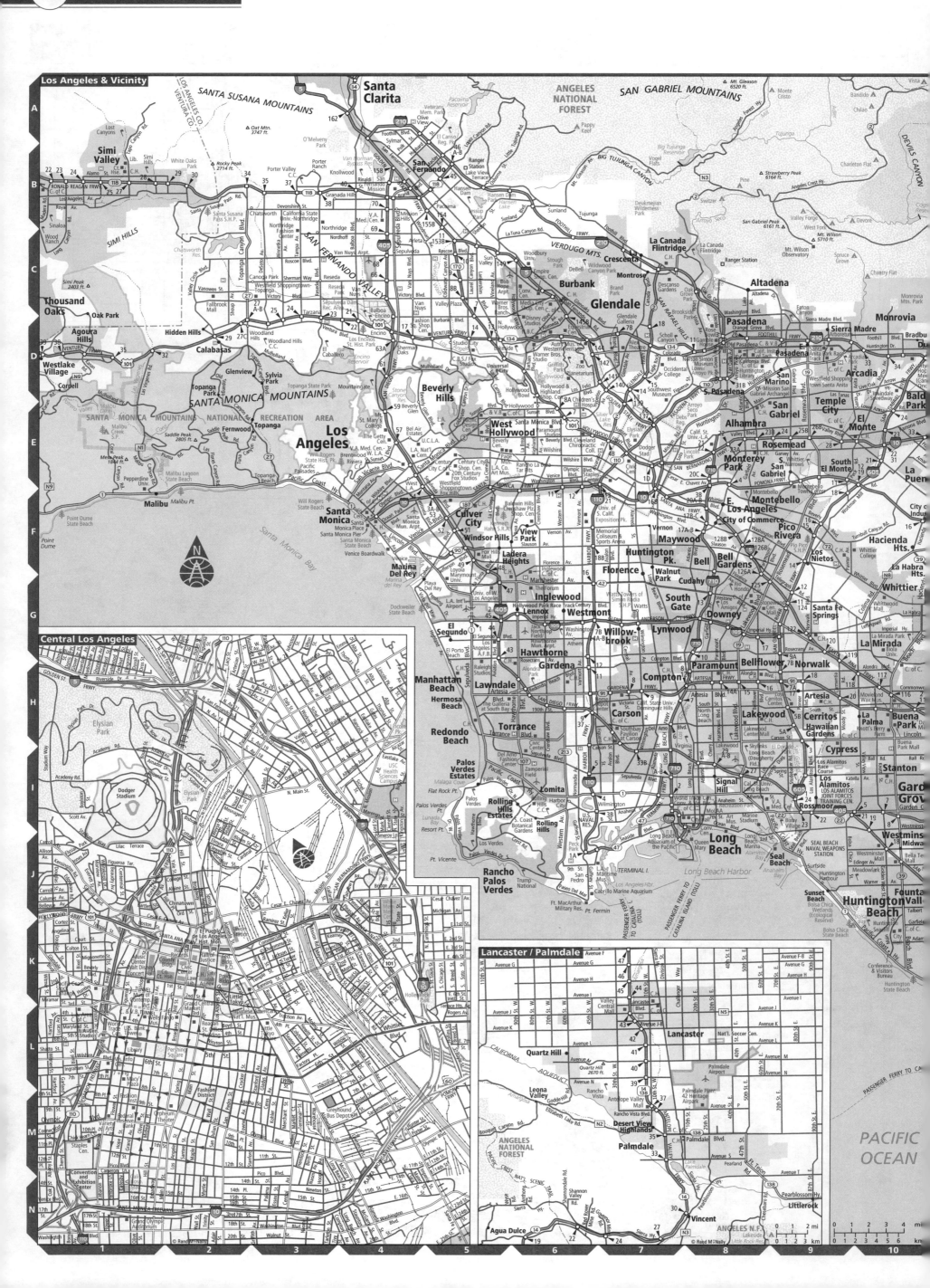

Map symbols

MORE MAP SYMBOLS PG. 1

- Free limited-access highway
- Toll limited-access highway
- Other multilane highway
- Principal highway
- Other through highway
- Other road
- Unpaved road
- Scenic route
- Airport
- Point of interest
- Hospital
- Information center
- Port of entry
- Rest area: toilets / no toilets
- Service area
- Wayside; roadside park
- Road construction

Los Angeles   Lancaster/Palmdale

Plan a California trip
randmcnally.com/CA

SAN GABRIEL MOUNTAINS

ANGELES NATIONAL FOREST

SAN BERNARDINO NATIONAL FOREST

Hesperia

Cajon Junction

San Bernardino

Riverside

Moreno Valley

Glendora · Claremont · Upland · Rancho Cucamonga · Fontana · Rialto · Colton · Redlands

Covina · West Covina · Pomona · Ontario · Chino · Montclair

Diamond Bar · Rowland Heights · Chino Hills

Corona · Norco · Home Gardens · El Cerrito

Anaheim · Orange · Santa Ana · Tustin · Irvine

Lake Forest · Mission Viejo · Laguna Hills · Aliso Viejo · Laguna Niguel

San Juan Capistrano · Dana Point · San Clemente

CLEVELAND NATIONAL FOREST

SANTA ANA MTS.

Lake Elsinore · Wildomar · Murrieta · Temecula

Perris · Sun City · Menifee

Newport Beach

CAMP PENDLETON MARINE CORPS BASE

PECHANGA INDIAN RESERVATION

© Rand McNally

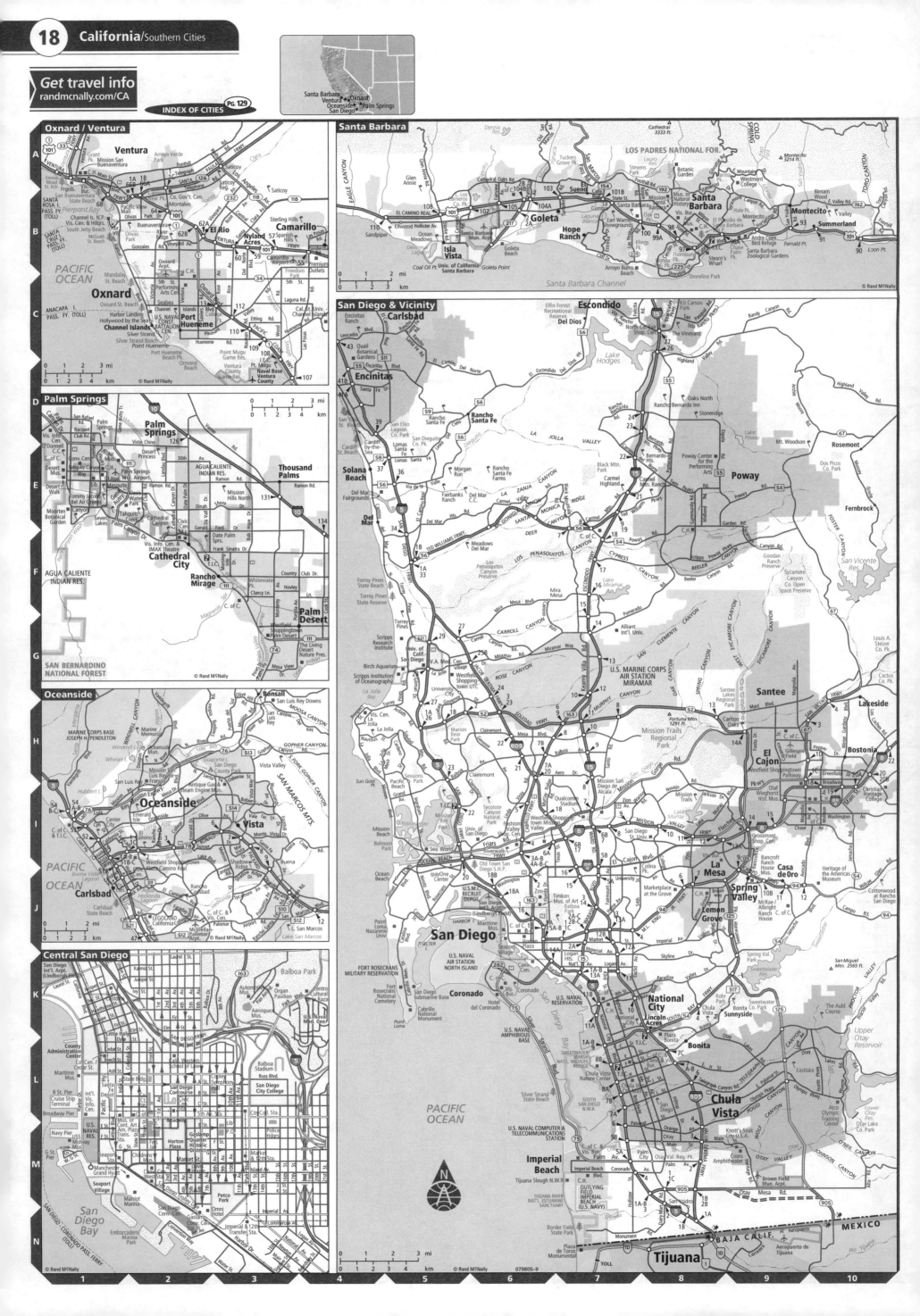

Map symbols

Free limited-access highway
Toll limited-access highway
Other multilane highway
Principal highway
Other through highway
Other road
Unpaved road
Scenic route
Point of interest
Hospital

? Information center
Port of entry
Rest area: toilets / no toilets
Service area
Airport
Wayside; roadside park
Road construction

MORE MAP SYMBOLS PG. 1

INDEX OF CITIES PG. 129

Plan a trip
randmcnally.com/CO

Boulder

Fort Collins

Rocky Mountain National Park

Estes Park
Grand Lake
ROCKY MOUNTAIN NATIONAL PARK
ARAPAHO NATIONAL FOREST
ROOSEVELT NAT'L. FOR.
MUMMY RANGE

Colorado Springs

PIKE NATIONAL FOREST
U.S. AIR FORCE ACADEMY
Manitou Springs
Security-Widefield
FORT CARSON MILITARY RESERVATION

Central Denver

Denver & Vicinity

Lafayette
Louisville
Superior
Broomfield
Westminster
Northglenn
Thornton
Federal Hts.
Sherrelwood
Western Hills
Arvada
Wheat Ridge
Mountain View
Edgewater
Golden
Lakewood
Denver
Sheridan
Englewood
Cherry Hills Village
Greenwood Village
Morrison
Columbine Valley
Littleton
Centennial
Highlands Ranch
Lone Tree
Parker
Roxborough Park
Sedalia
Commerce City
Dupont
Irondale
Henderson
Brighton
Barr
Lochbuie
Glendale
Aurora
Foxfield
Waterton
Louviers

DENVER INTERNATIONAL AIRPORT
ROCKY MOUNTAIN ARSENAL NAT'L. WILDLIFE REFUGE
BUCKLEY AIR FORCE BASE

© Rand McNally

Nickname: The Centennial State
Land area: 103,718 sq. mi. (rank: 8th)
Population: 4,550,688 (rank: 22nd)
Largest city: Denver, 557,478

INDEX OF CITIES PG. 129

Mileage between cities	Alamosa	Aspen	Boulder	Burlington	Colorado Springs	Craig	Denver	Durango	Estes Park	Fort Collins	Glenwood Springs	Grand Junction	Gunnison	Lamar	Leadville	Pueblo	Sterling	Trinidad
BURLINGTON	304	308	181		151	361	163	455	218	217	319	408	311	109	265	185	142	243
COLORADO SPRINGS	161	157	93	151		264	67	312	130	129	222	311	166	162	128	42	194	126
DENVER	228	162	26	163	67	199		379	63	62	157	246	233	208	103	109	127	193
DURANGO	151	250	405	455	312	317	379		442	441	253	170	174	353	256	270	506	260
FORT COLLINS	290	221	56	217	129	201	62	441	42		216	305	295	262	162	171	102	255
GRAND JCT.	248	131	256	408	311	153	246	170	285	305	89		126	453	175	285	370	345
LEADVILLE	138	59	113	265	128	161	103	256	149	162	86	175	119	275		122	227	215
PUEBLO	119	184	135	265	42	306	109	270	172	171	264	285	159	122	155		235	84

Total mileage through Colorado
25 300 miles 76 185 miles
70 451 miles 50 467 miles

MORE MILEAGES PG. 138

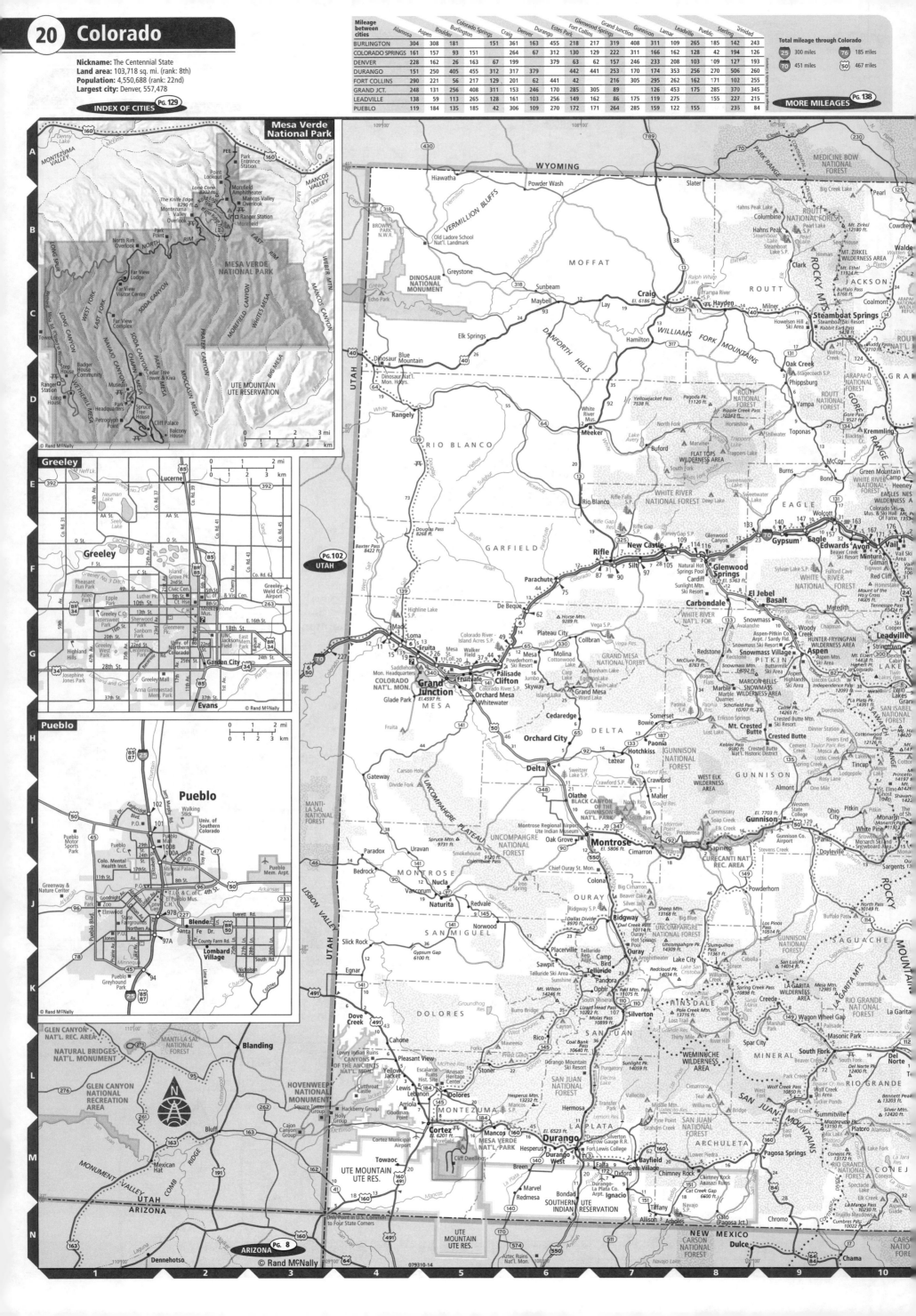

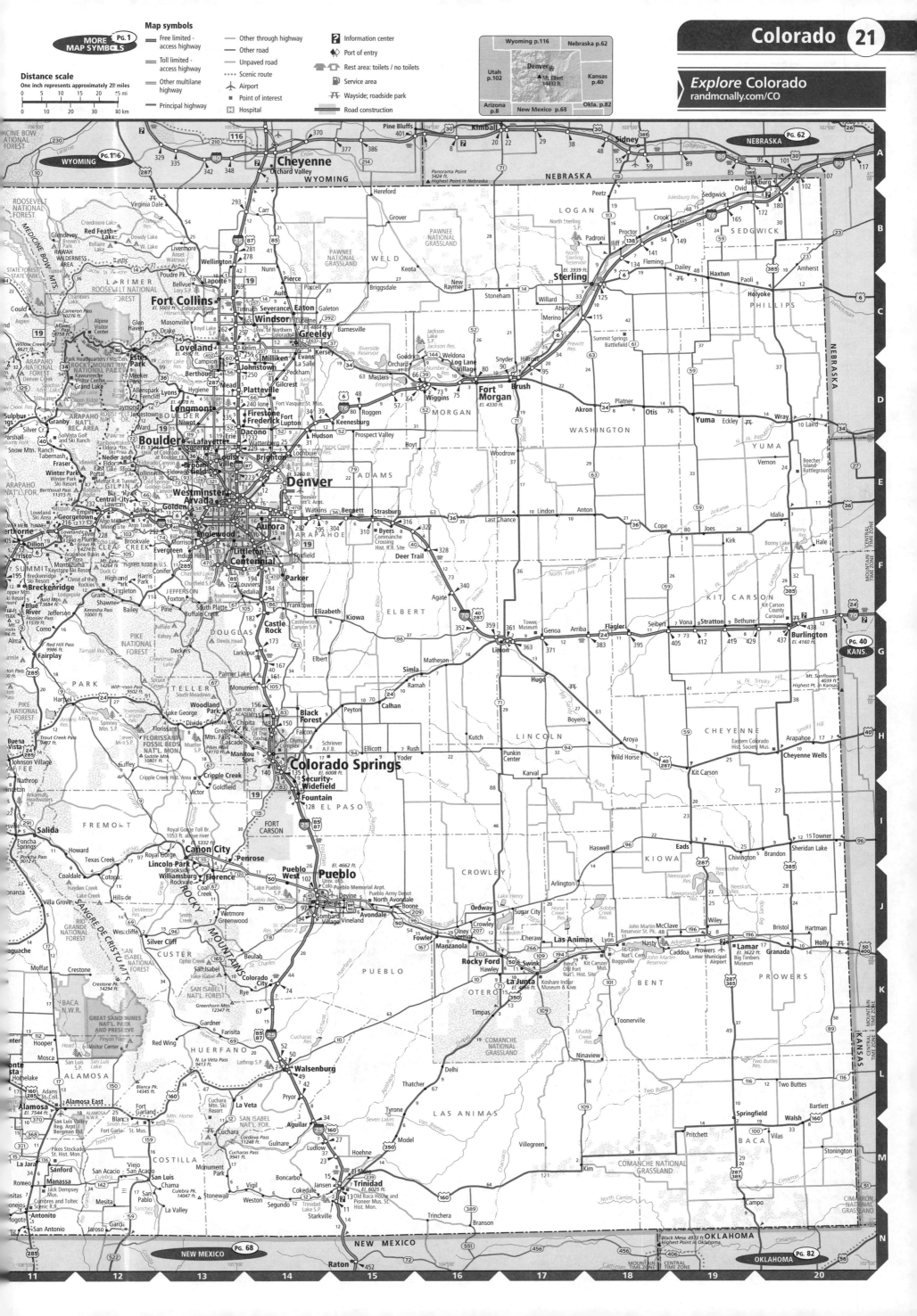

Nickname: The Constitution State
Land area: 4,845 sq. mi. (rank: 48th)
Population: 3,483,372 (rank: 29th)
Largest city: Bridgeport, 139,664

INDEX OF CITIES PG. 129

MORE MILEAGES PG. 138

Mileage between cities	Bridgeport	Canaan	Clinton	Danbury	Hartford	Meriden	Middletown	New Haven	New London	New York, NY	Norwich	Providence, RI	Putnam	Springfield, MA	Stamford	Torrington	Waterbury	Willimantic
BRIDGEPORT		75	41	29	57	42	45	19	69	54	76	123	112	83	22	51	31	83
DANBURY	29	53	57		61	44	54	35	85	61	100	146	107	87	31	49	29	91
HARTFORD	57	43	40	61		24	17	40	46	111	41	87	46	26	79	36	32	30
NEW HAVEN	19	69	22	35	40		25	28	50	73	57	106	93	66	41	45	25	66
NEW LONDON	69	89	30	85	46	56	44	50		123	13	56	49	72	91	89	69	28
PUTNAM	112	122	73	107	46	68	70	93	49	166	39	33		63	134	82	78	31
TORRINGTON	51	26	67	49	36	35	45	45	89	105	77	123	82	51	73		20	66
WATERBURY	31	44	47	29	32	15	25	25	69	85	71	117	78	58	53	20		62

Total mileage through Connecticut

84 98 miles	**95** 112 miles
91 58 miles	**395** 55 miles

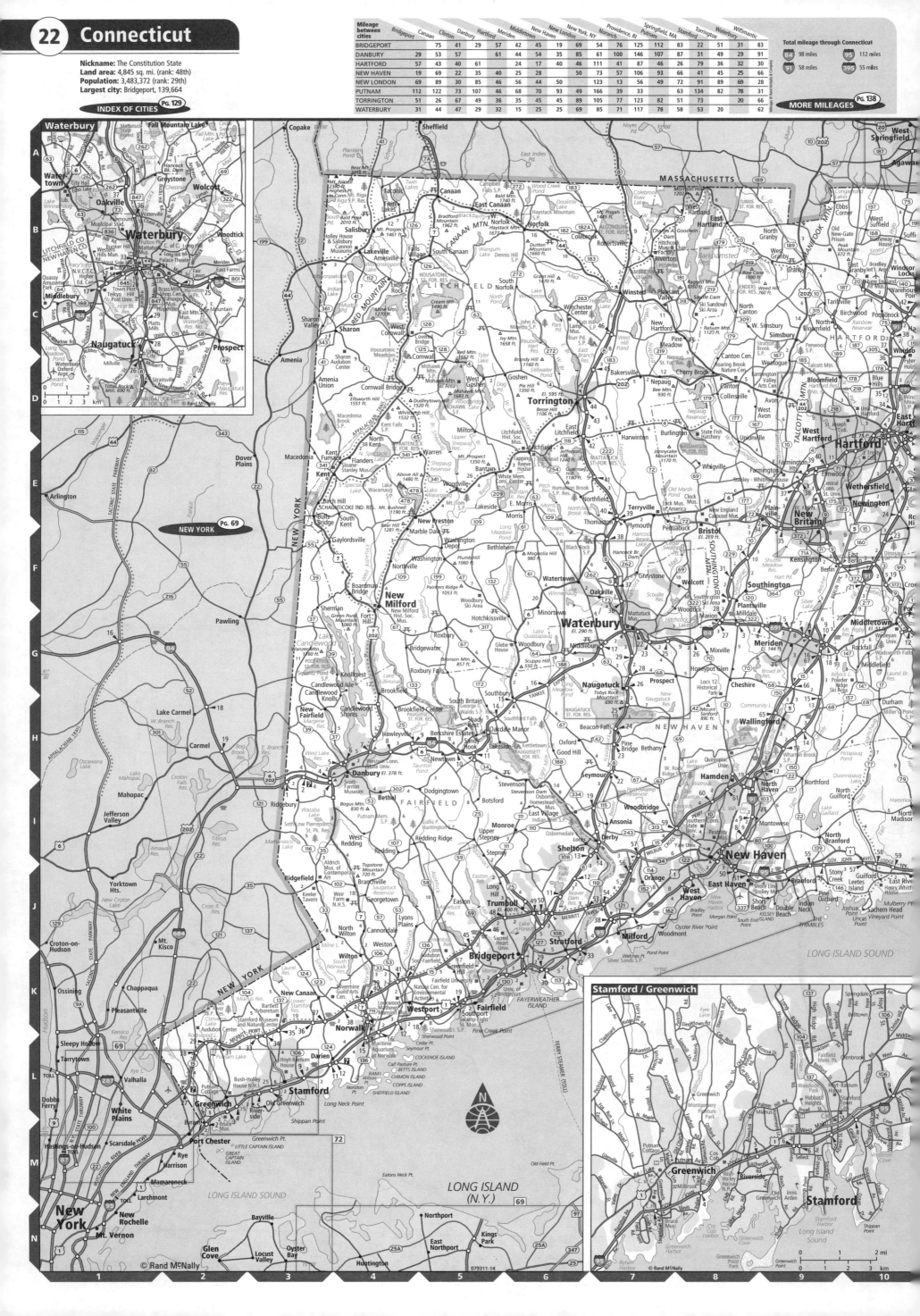

© Rand McNally

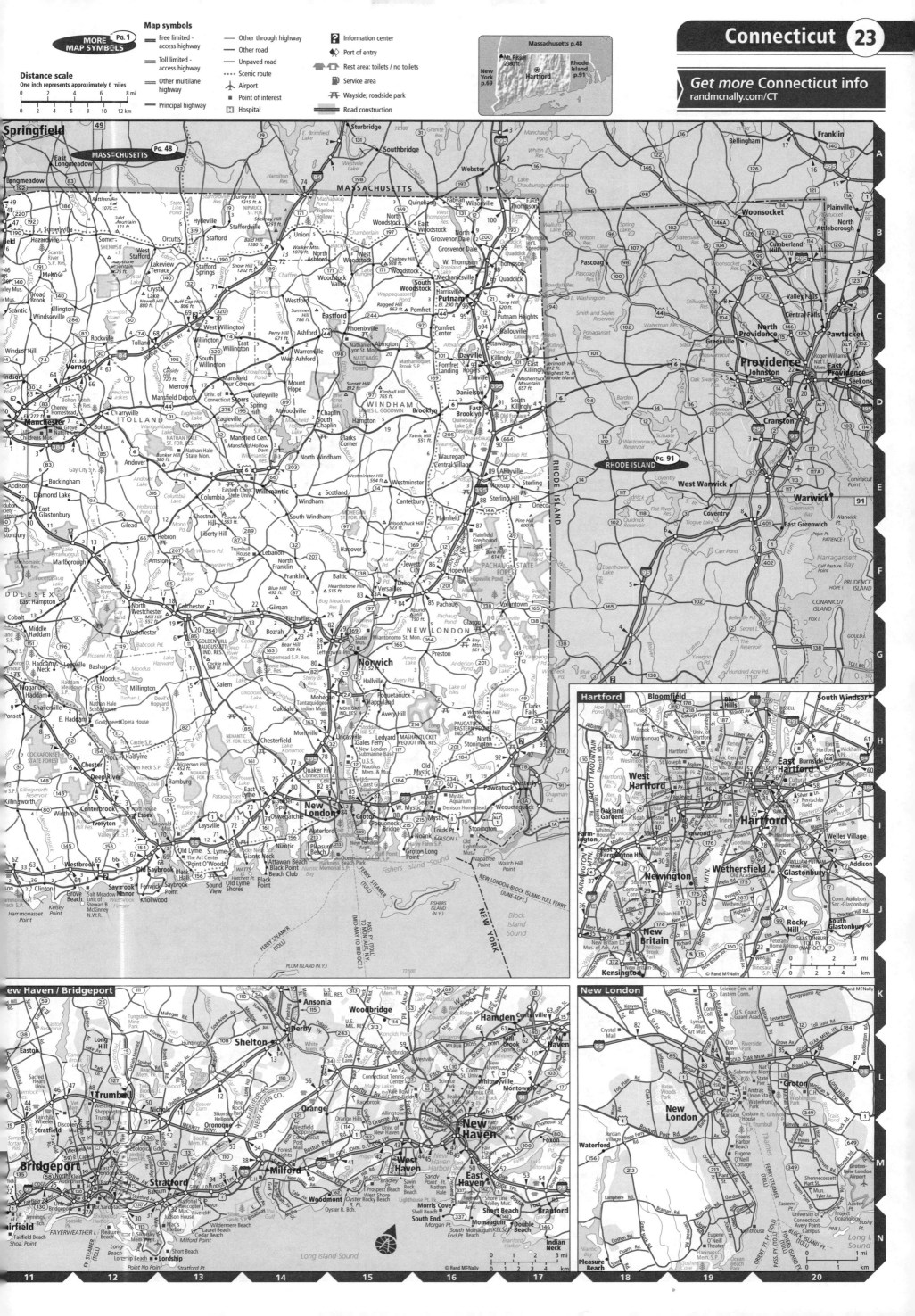

Get more Connecticut info
randmcnally.com/CT

Plan a trip
randmcnally.com/DE

Nickname: The First State
Land area: 1,954 sq. mi. (rank: 49th)
Population: 817,491 (rank: 45th)
Largest city: Wilmington, 72,051

INDEX OF CITIES PG. 129

Pennsylvania p.88
New Castle County
448 ft.
N.J. p.66
Maryland p.46
Dover
Virginia p.106

Distance scale
One inch represents approximately 9 mi
0 5 mi
0 5 km

Mileage between cities	Dover	Georgetown	Lewes	Milford	Newark	Salisbury, MD	Selbyville	Wilmington
DOVER		35	38	19	46	56	55	47
GEORGETOWN	35		14	16	83	27	21	84
LEWES	38	14		20	86	41	33	87
MILFORD	19	16	20		67	42	36	68
NEWARK	46	83	86	67		104	133	13
SALISBURY, MD	56	27	41	42	104		24	105
SELBYVILLE	55	21	33	36	103	24		104
WILMINGTON	47	84	87	68	13	105	104	

Total mileage through Delaware
23 miles ① 104 miles
108 miles

MORE MILEAGES PG. 138

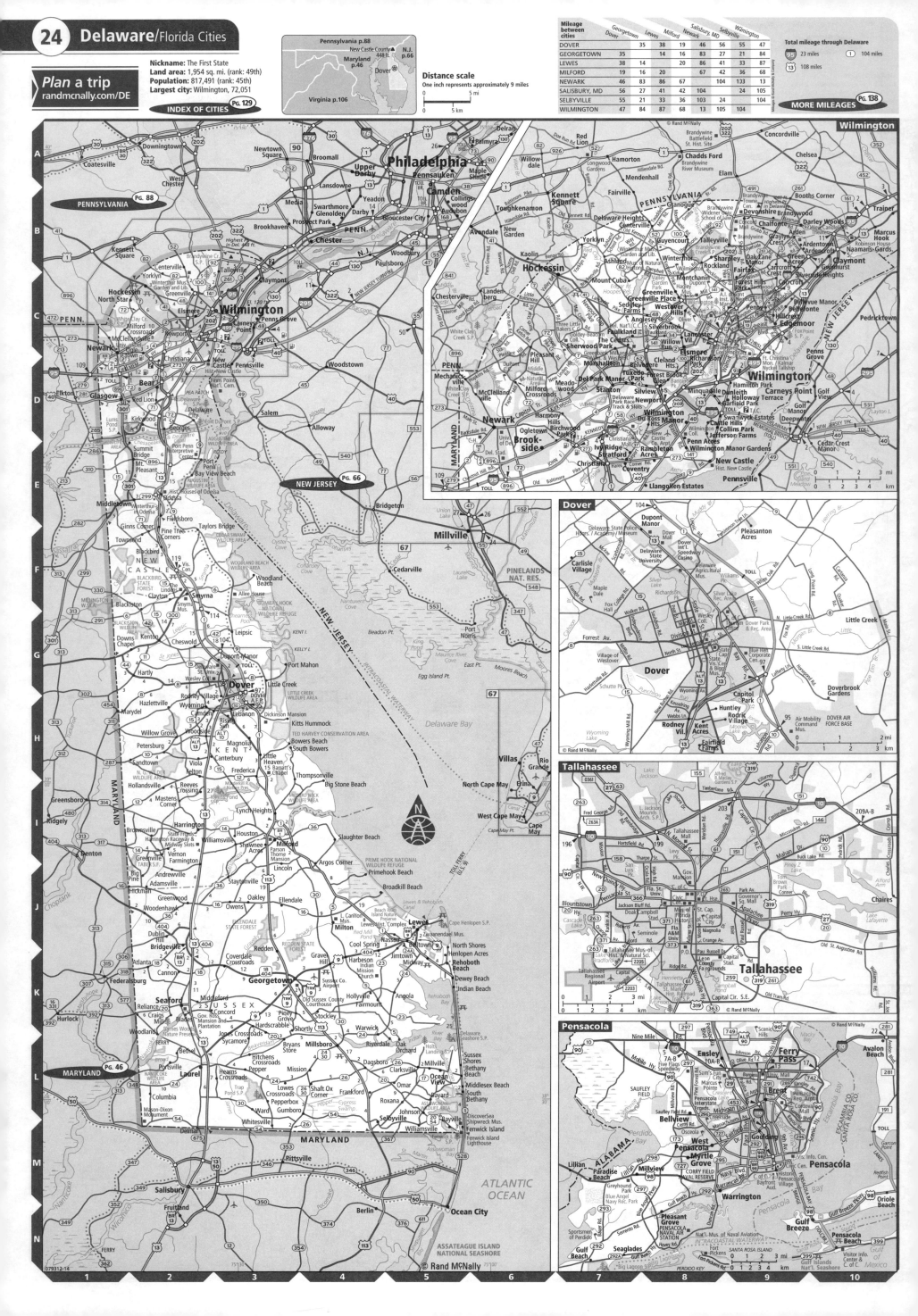

Wilmington

Dover

Tallahassee

Pensacola

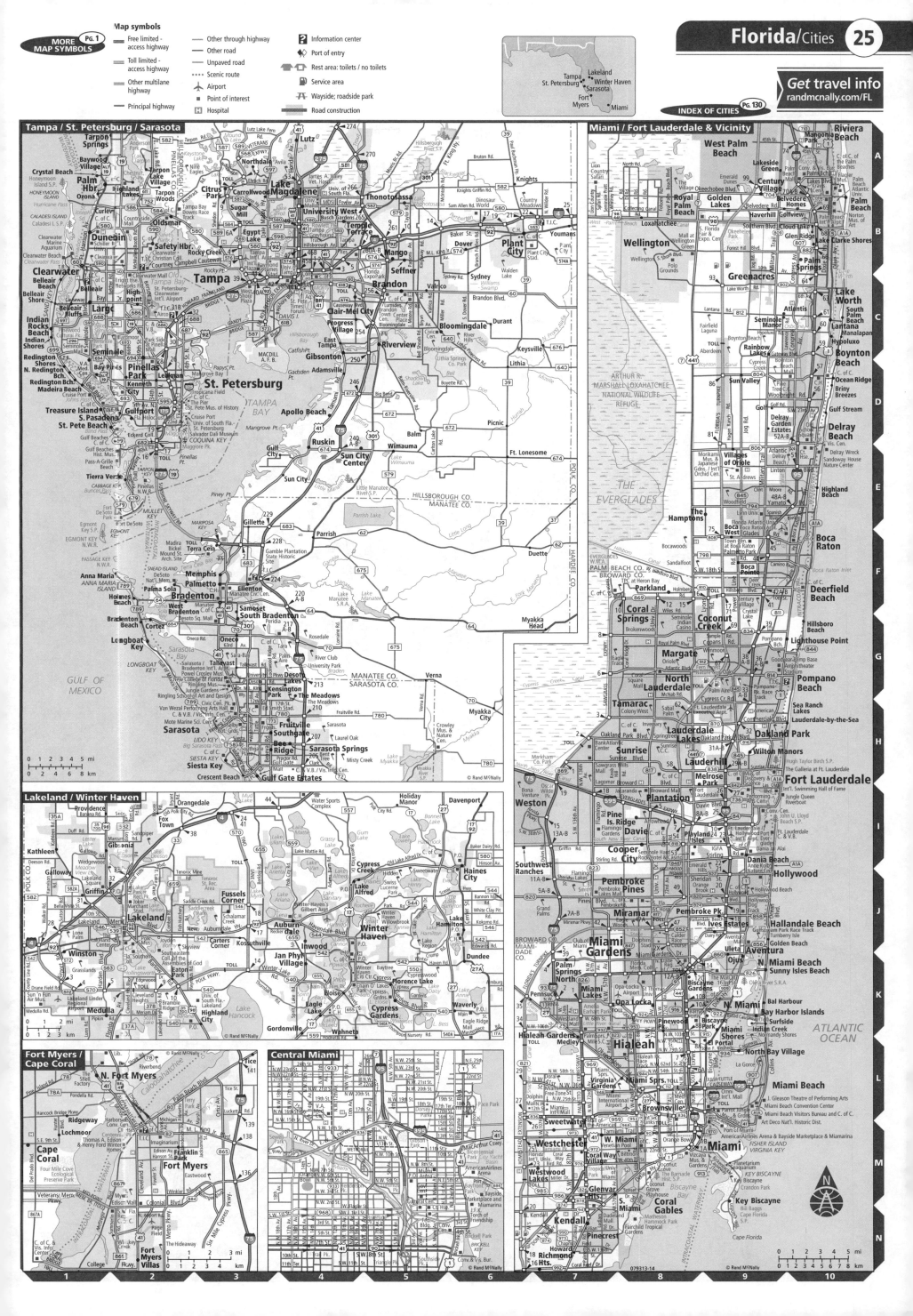

Nickname: The Sunshine State
Land area: 53,927 sq. mi. (rank: 26th)
Population: 17,019,068 (rank: 4th)
Largest city: Jacksonville, 773,781

INDEX OF CITIES PG. 130

Mileage between cities	Atlanta, GA	Daytona Beach	Fort Lauderdale	Fort Myers	Fort Pierce	Gainesville	Jacksonville	Key West	Lakeland	Melbourne	Miami	Orlando	Panama City	Pensacola	St. Petersburg	Sarasota	Tallahassee	Tampa	West Palm Beach Titusville
FORT MYERS	581	212	141		128	253	298	289	111	172	152	156	517	593	261	116	78	398	129	195	129
JACKSONVILLE	346	90	318	298	223	73		503	196	176	341	142	282	358	41	226	252	163	202	133	278
MIAMI	661	253	27	152	126	333	341	164	223	170		229	597	673	304	260	222	478	273	212	66
ORLANDO	440	56	206	156	119	112	142	391	54	72	229		376	452	108	128	257	84	39	166
PENSACOLA	319	446	650	593	566	344	358	835	467	519	673	452	103		397	494	520	196	470	489	610
TALLAHASSEE	270	251	455	371	371	149	163	640	272	324	478	257	98	196	302	299		325	275	294	415
TAMPA	458	140	262	129	151	130	202	410	33	130	273	84	394	470	189	24	56	275		123	202
WEST PALM BEACH	598	190	43	129	57	270	278	173	107	66	166	534	610	241	226	197	415	202	149

Total mileage through Florida

4	132 miles	75 471 miles
10	362 miles	95 382 miles

MORE MILEAGES PG. 138

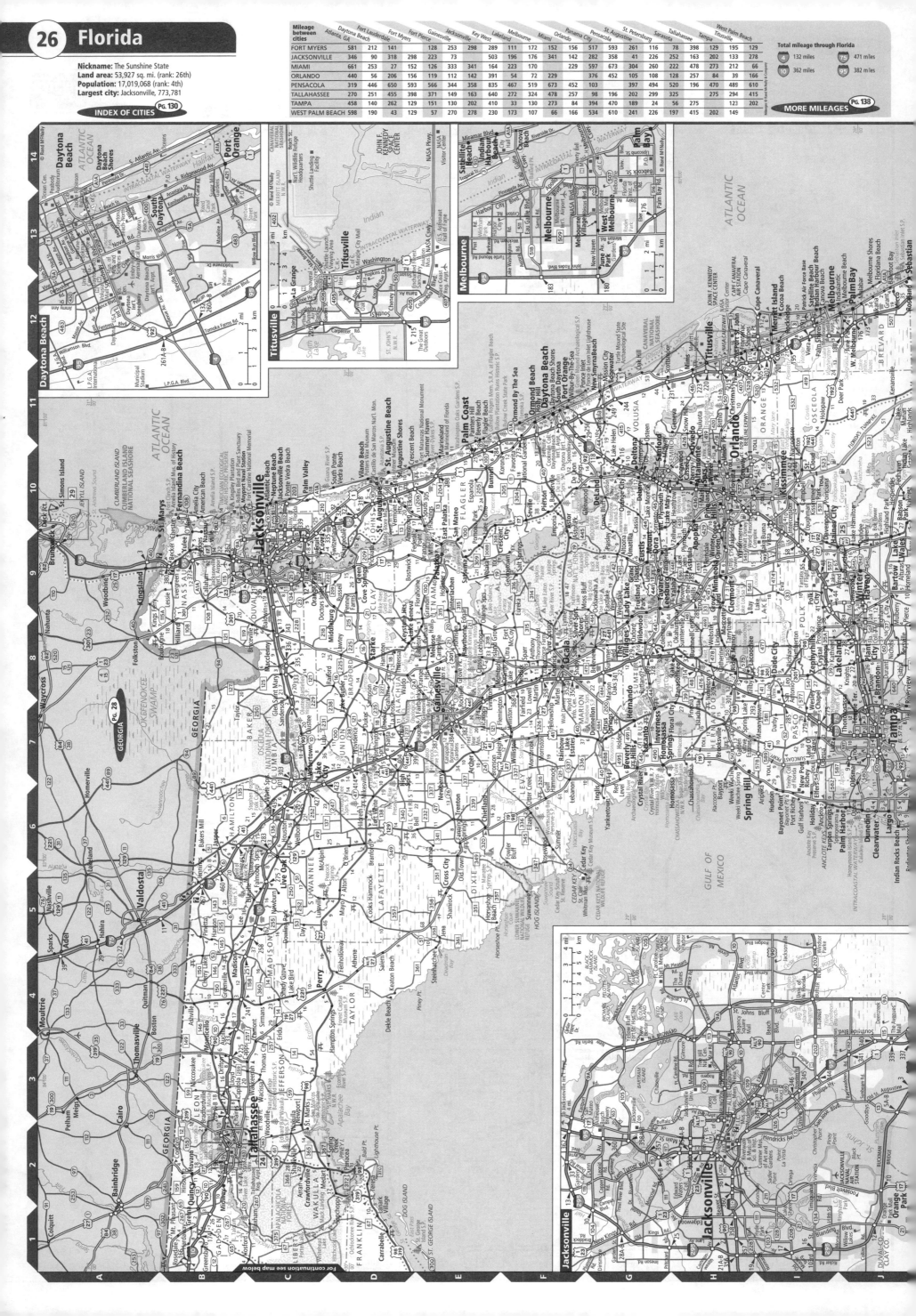

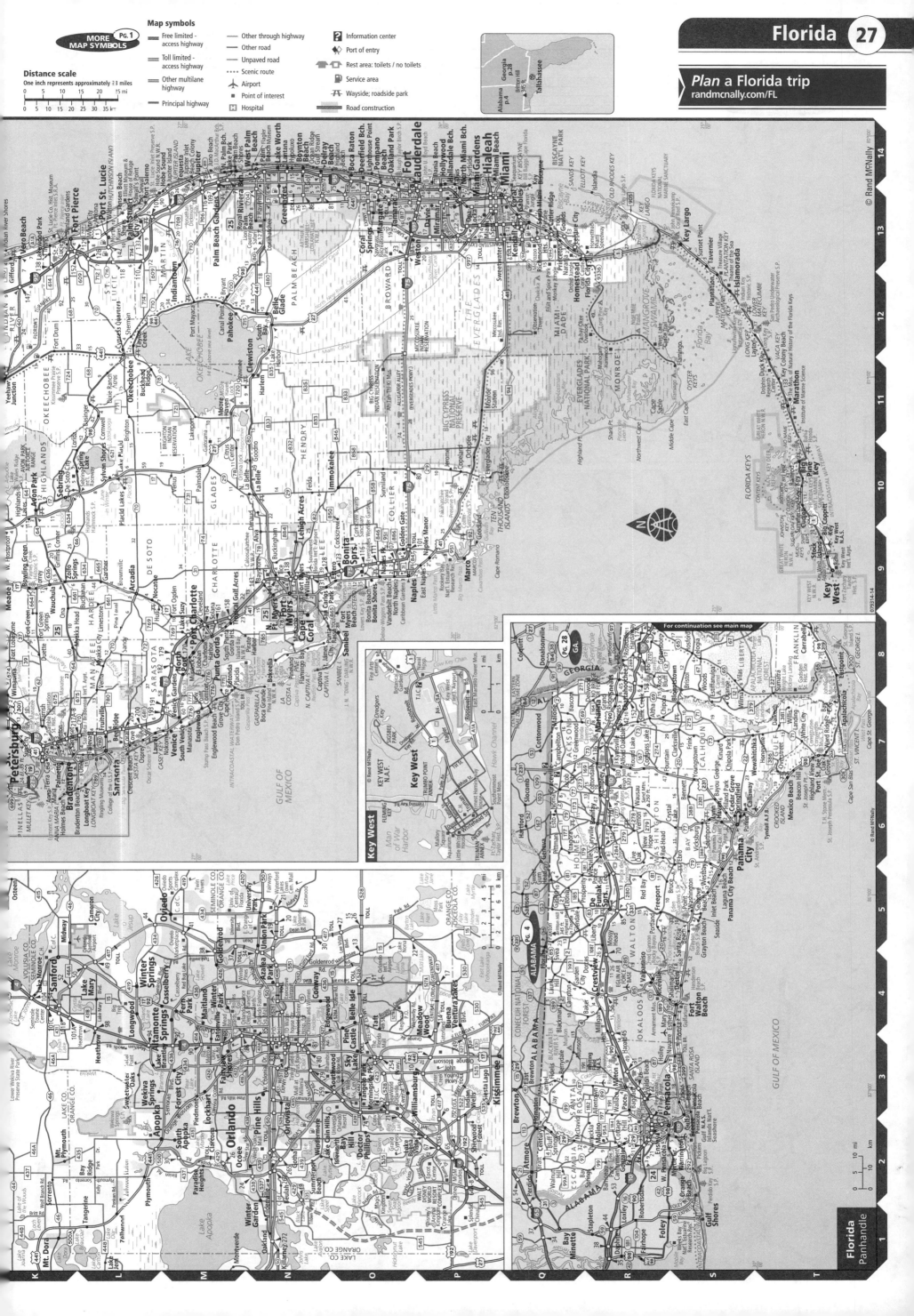

Plan a Florida trip
randmcnally.com/FL

Nickname: The Peach State
Land area: 57,906 sq. mi. (rank: 21st)
Population: 8,684,715 (rank: 9th)
Largest city: Atlanta, 423,019

INDEX OF CITIES PG. 130

MORE MILEAGES PG. 138

Mileage between cities	Albany	Americus	Athens	Atlanta	Augusta	Bainbridge	Brunswick	Chattanooga, TN	Columbus	Gainesville	Greenville SC	Jacksonville, FL	La Grange	Macon	Rome	Savannah	Toccoa	Valdosta	Vidalia	Warner Robins	Waycross
ATLANTA	182	129	67		150	240	310	115	104	51	132	346	65	81	66	252	90	229	177	98	254
AUGUSTA	229	197	97	150		287	198	265	249	138	115	260	210	124	216	140	130	223	97	141	188
CHATTANOOGA, TN	297	244	168	115	265	355	425		216	128	243	461	177	196	66	367	191	344	292	213	369
COLUMBUS	89	62	171	104	249	129	262	216		155	246	295	45	97	148	268	194	178	193	90	204
JACKSONVILLE, FL	207	238	342	346	260	203	71	461	295	393	390		340	269	414	140	432	120	164	260	79
MACON	105	73	90	81	124	163	229	196	97	128	269	112		147	171	167	152	96	17		162
SAVANNAH	231	210	222	252	140	250	78	367	268	299	256	140	283	171	318		264	168	95	166	106
VALDOSTA	90	121	242	229	223	82	120	344	178	276	367	120	223	152	295	168	315		112	143	62

Total mileage through Georgia
20 = 203 miles
75 = 355 miles
85 = 180 miles
95 = 112 miles

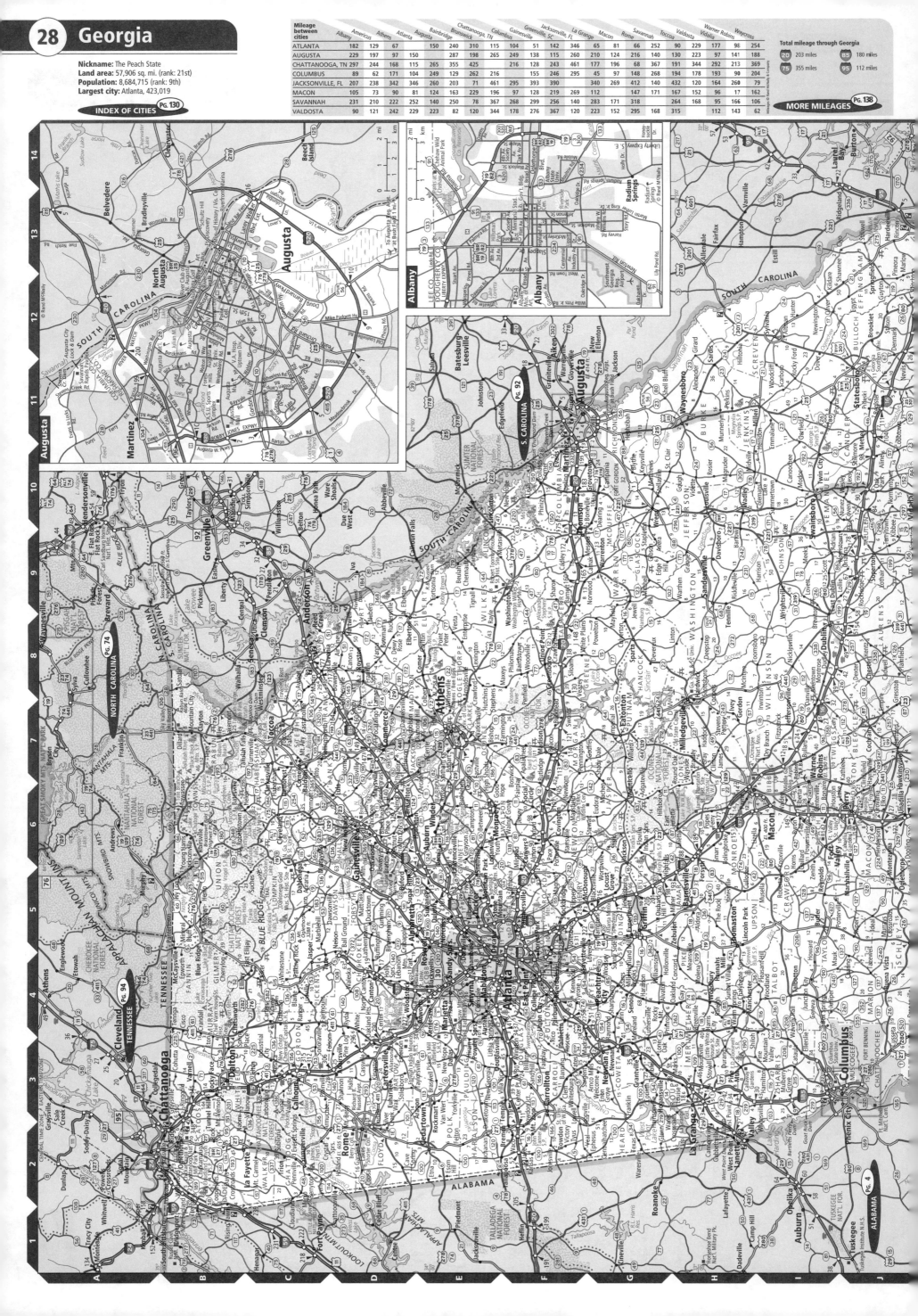

MORE MAP SYMBOLS PG. 1

Map symbols

Free limited - access highway
Toll limited - access highway
Other multilane highway
Principal highway
Other through highway
Other road
Unpaved road
Scenic route
Airport
Point of interest
Hospital

? Information center
◆ Port of entry
🚻 Rest area: toilets / no toilets
🍴 Service area
🏝 Wayside; roadside park
▦ Road construction

Distance scale
One inch represents approximately 22 miles

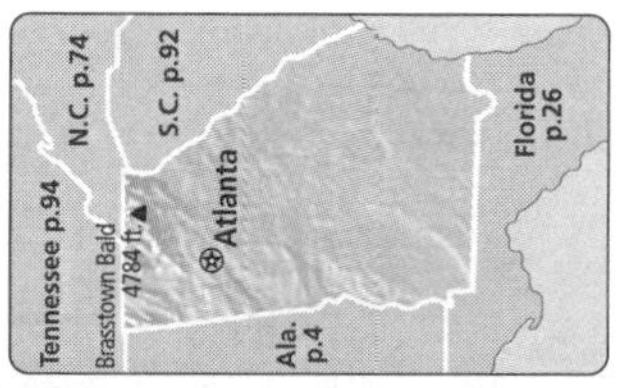

0 5 10 15 20 25 mi
0 5 10 15 20 25 30 35 40 km

Explore Georgia
randmcnally.com/GA

© Rand McNally

ATLANTIC OCEAN

Savannah

Brunswick

Macon

Columbus

Plan a trip
rand mcnally.com/HI

Nickname: The Aloha State
Land area: 6,423 sq. mi. (rank: 47th)
Population: 1,257,608 (rank: 42nd)
Largest city: Honolulu, 380,149

INDEX OF CITIES   PG. 130

Distance scale
One inch represents approximately 39 miles
0 10 20 30 40 km
0 10 20 30 mi

MORE MILEAGES   PG. 138

Mileage between cities	Honolulu Hilo	Kahului	Kailua Kona	Kapaa	Lahaina	Maunaloa	*Via Air
HILO	221*	123*	234*	87	320*	146*	179*	237*
HONOLULU	221*		105*	12	196*	115*	128*	66*	20
KAHULUI	123*	105*		118*	118*	213*	23	58*	121*
KAILUA	234*	12	118*		209*	128*	141*	79*	31
KAILUA KONA	87	196*	118*	209*		305*	141*	174*	212*
KAPAA	320*	115*	213*	128*	305*		236*	175*	131*
LAHAINA	146*	128*	23	141*	141*	236*		81*	144*
WAHIAWĀ	237*	20	121*	31	212*	131*	144*	82*	

Total mileage through Hawaii
H1 27 miles   H3 15 miles
H2 8 miles

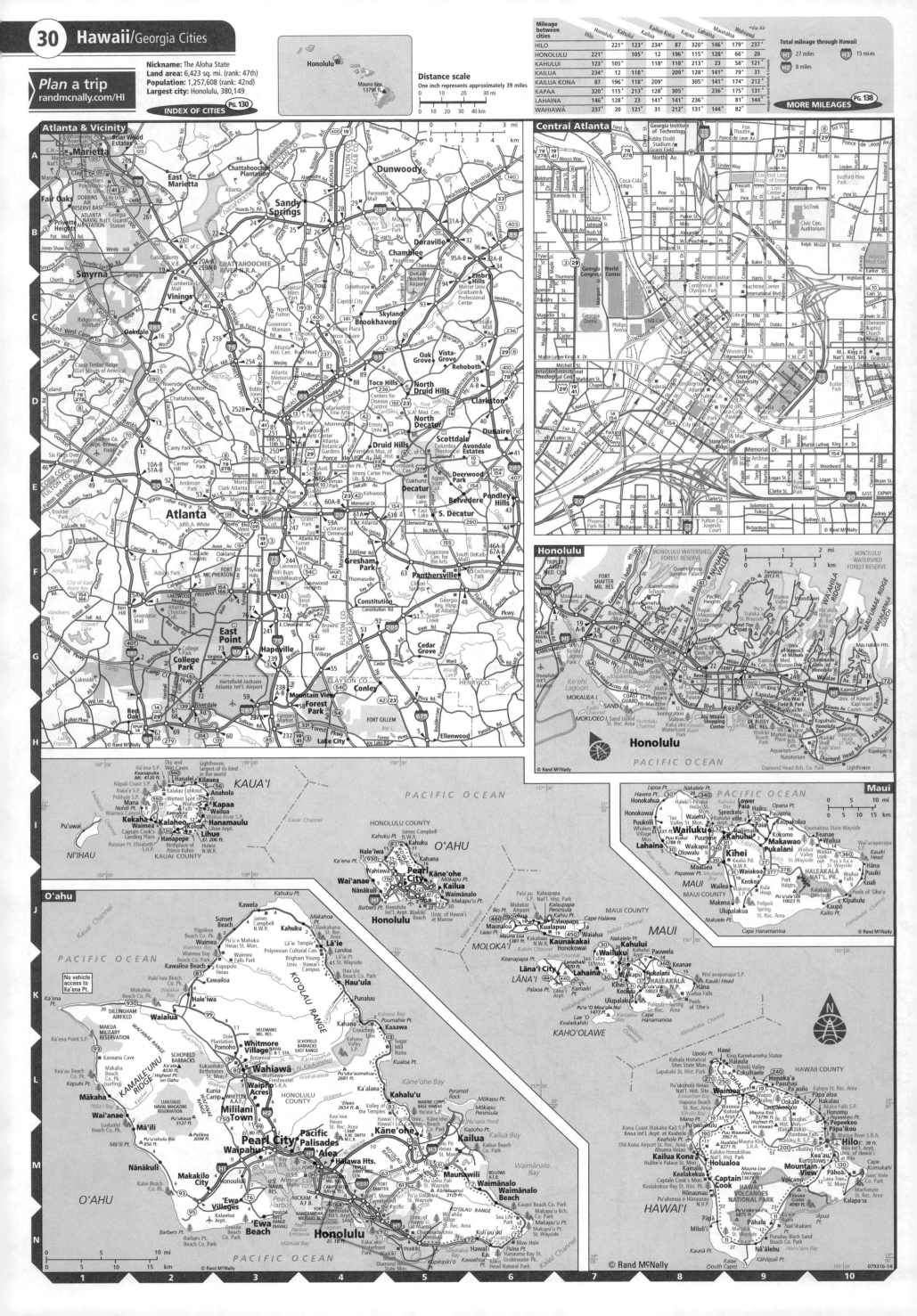

Atlanta & Vicinity

Central Atlanta

Honolulu

KAUA'I

Maui

O'ahu

MOLOKA'I

LĀNA'I

KAHO'OLAWE

MAUI

HAWAI'I

© Rand McNally

079316-14

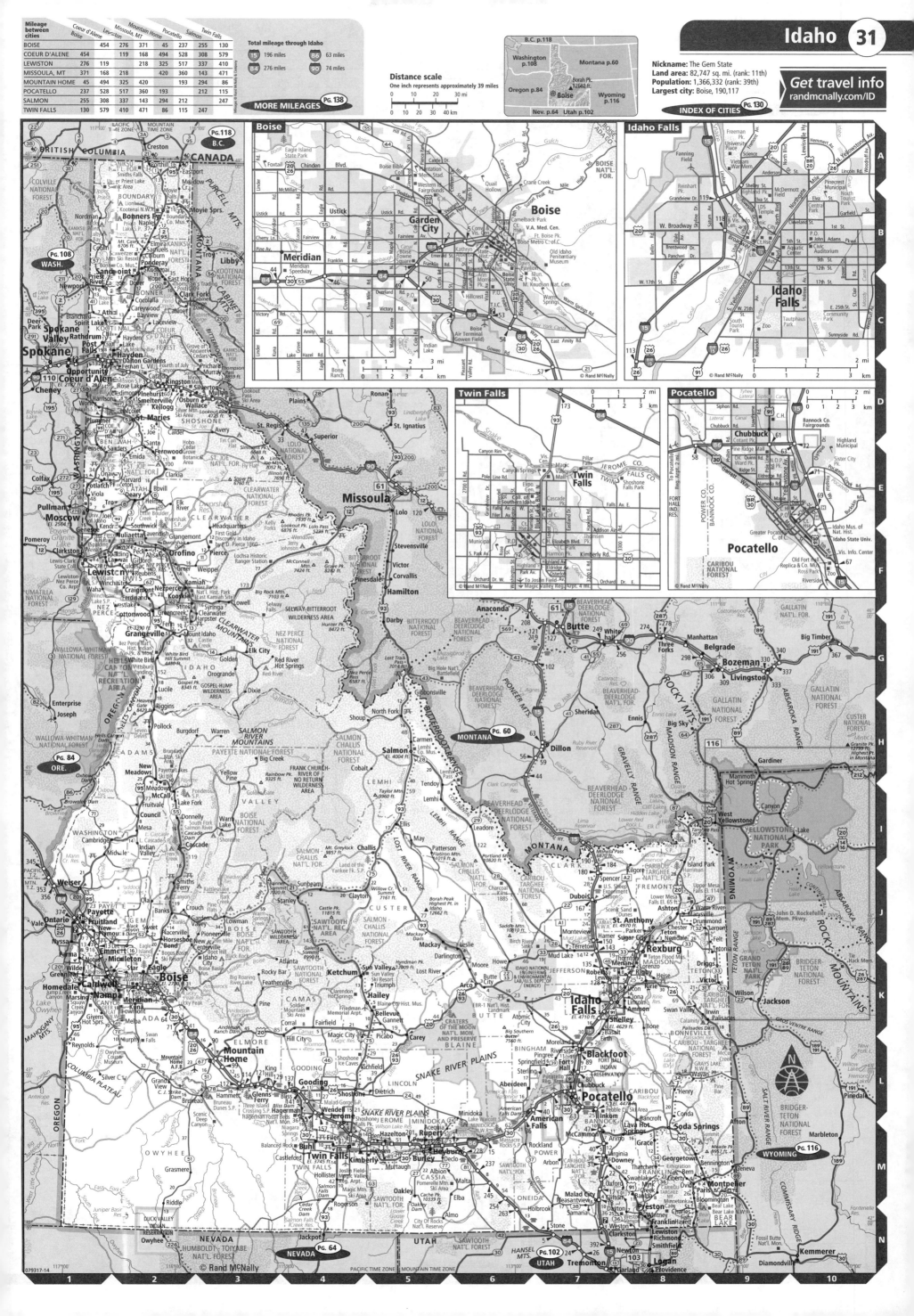

Nickname: Land of Lincoln
Land area: 55,584 sq. mi. (rank: 24th)
Population: 12,653,544 (rank: 5th)
Largest city: Chicago, 2,869,121

INDEX OF CITIES — PG. 130

Mileage between cities	Bloomington	Cairo	Carbondale	Champaign	Chicago	Decatur	De Kalb	Dubuque, IA	Effingham	Elgin	Galesburg	Kankakee	Lawrenceville	Moline	Mt. Vernon	Peoria	Quincy	Rockford	St. Louis, MO	Springfield	Waukegan
CARBONDALE	249	59		244	202	333	185	370	415	124	369	297	274	149	340	58	248	231	384	108	178	377
CHAMPAIGN	51	244	202		135	47	172	257	78	171	139	76	127	182	148	90	195	186	182	85	179
CHICAGO	136	375	333	135		178	66	175	209	38	198	56	250	165	279	170	310	84	300	200	40
MOLINE	132	410	340	182	165		169	103	74	256	152	48	153	305		314	92	147	117	262	162	189
PEORIA	40	318	248	90	170	72	129	167	164	153	49	121	213	92	222		130	143	170	70	198
ROCKFORD	136	426	384	186	84	179	44	91	260	48	150	128	309	117	330	143	267		296	196	71
ST. LOUIS, MO	164	169	108	182	300	118	282	337	104	307	219	254	147	262	82	170	133	296		100	328
SPRINGFIELD	64	248	178	85	200	38	182	237	89	207	119	157	154	162	152	70	110	196	100		228

Total mileage through Illinois
55 — 313 miles 80 — 164 miles
70 — 136 miles 90 — 124 miles

MORE MILEAGES — PG. 138

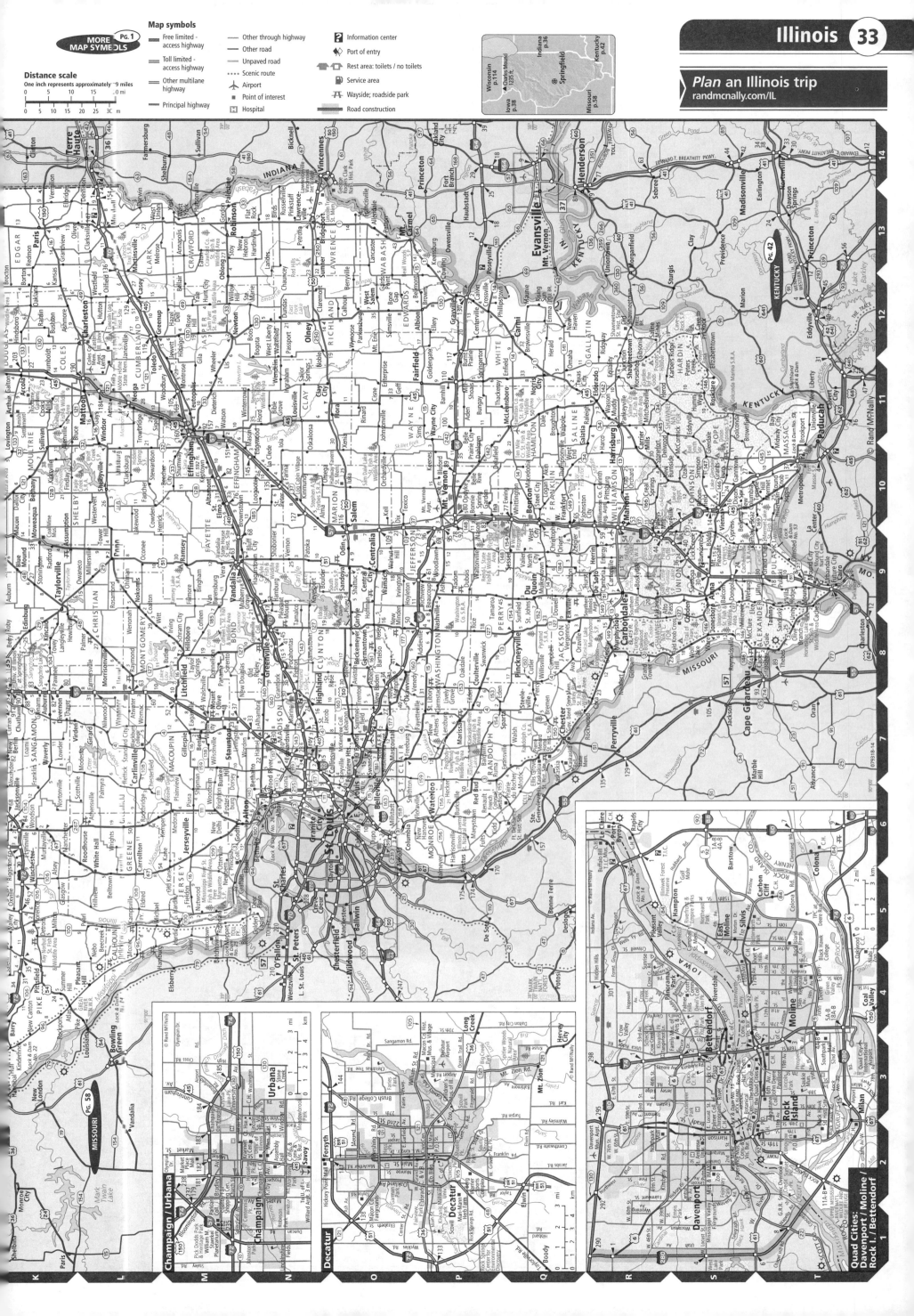

Plan an Illinois trip
randmcnally.com/IL

INDEX OF CITIES PG. 130

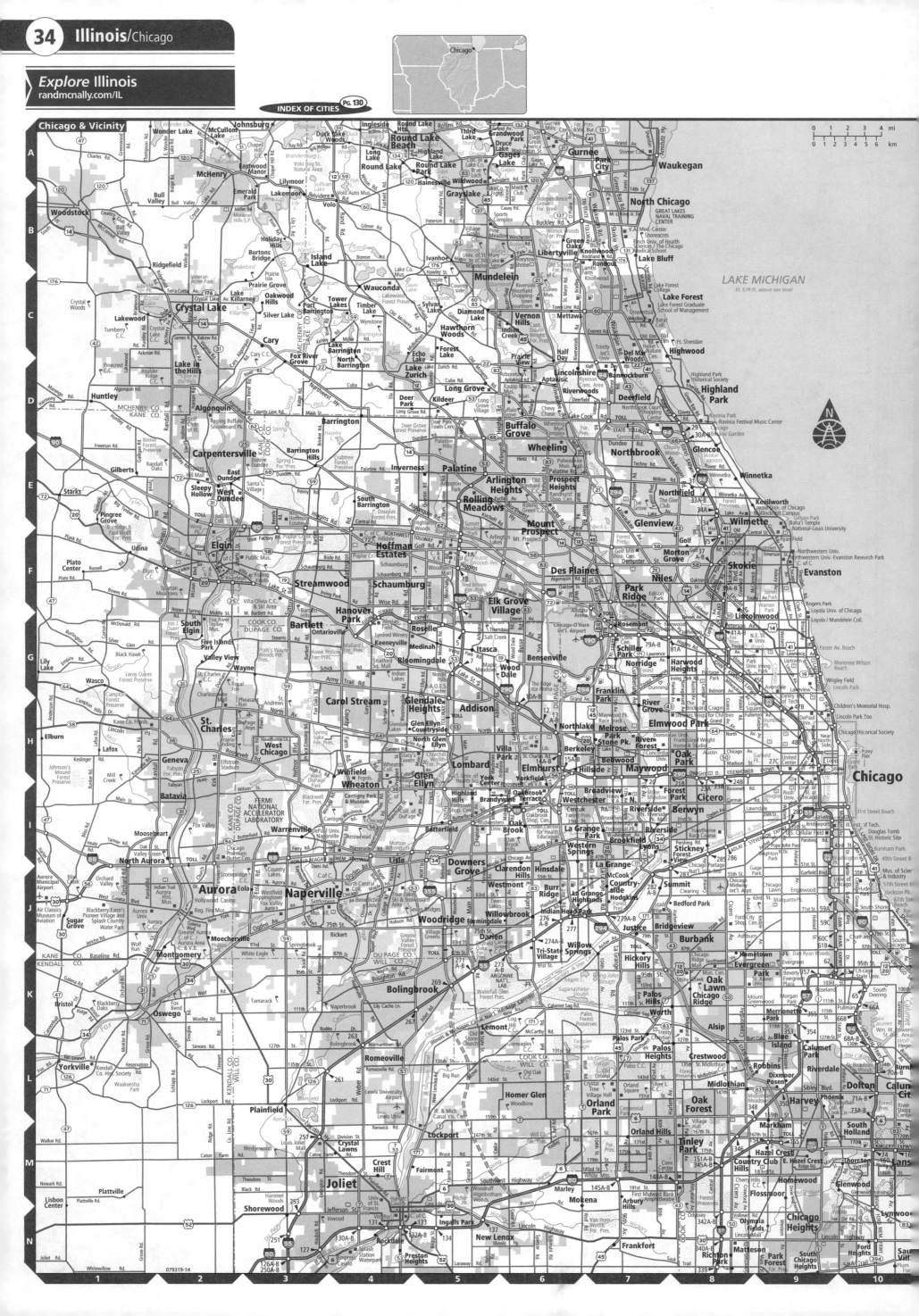

Chicago & Vicinity

LAKE MICHIGAN
El. 579 ft. above sea level

Map symbols

Plan a trip randmcnally.com/IL

Get travel info randmcnally.com/IN

Central Chicago

Peoria

South Bend

Springfield

Fort Wayne

Indianapolis

© Rand McNally

Nickname: The Hoosier State
Land area: 35,867 sq. mi. (rank: 38th)
Population: 6,195,643 (rank: 14th)
Largest city: Indianapolis, 783,438

INDEX OF CITIES (PG. 130)

Mileage between cities	Anderson	Angola	Bloomington	Chicago, Il.	Columbus	Crawfordsville	Danville, Il.	Evansville	Fort Wayne	Greensburg	Indianapolis	Kokomo	Lafayette	Michigan City	New Albany	Richmond	South Bend	Terre Haute	Vincennes
EVANSVILLE	234	353	134	294	179	178	169		319	278	198	186	239	203	298	248	111	259	326	112	54
FORT WAYNE	89	42	180	164	175	168	208	319		135	132	133	90	120	118	85	242	95	92	211	265
GARY	182	135	199	29	202	120	130	278	135		202	150	130	92	126	196	269	221	58	166	224
INDIANAPOLIS	48	167	50	179	48	56	96	186	133	150		50	53	62	170	62	115	73	140	78	132
NEW ALBANY	157	276	89	298	71	166	206	111	242	269	90	115	172	181	289	171		182	259	188	137
RICHMOND	59	140	120	250	115	129	169	259	95	221	67	73	104	133	241	43	182		191	151	205
SOUTH BEND	142	76	198	87	192	133	173	326	92	186	140	91	107	34	141	259	191		218	272
TERRE HAUTE	126	245	57	182	121	57	57	112	211	166	123	78	131	92	186	140	188	151	218		58

Total mileage through Indiana
65 - 261 miles | 74 - 172 miles
70 - 157 miles | 90 - 156 miles

MORE MILEAGES (PG. 138)

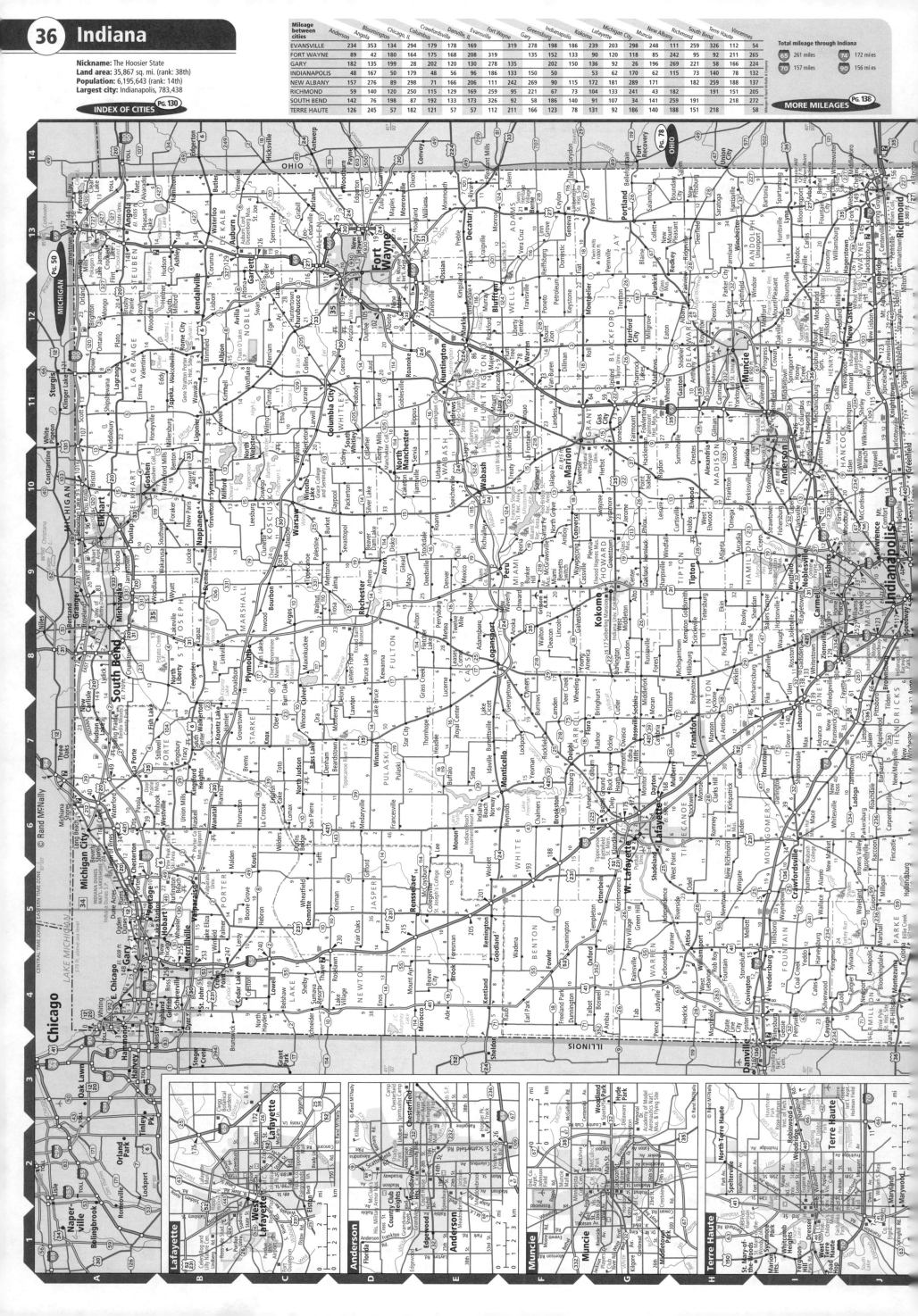

Explore Indiana
randmcnally.com/IN

Nickname: The Hawkeye State
Land area: 55,869 sq. mi. (rank: 23rd)
Population: 2,944,062 (rank: 30th)
Largest city: Des Moines, 196,093

INDEX OF CITIES PG. 131

MORE MILEAGES PG. 138

Mileage between cities	Ames	Burlington	Cedar Rapids	Council Bluffs	Davenport	Decorah	Des Moines	Dubuque	Fort Dodge	Iowa City	Keokuk	Mason City	Ottumwa	Sioux City	Sioux Falls SD	Spirit Lake	Storm Lake	Waterloo
BURLINGTON	208		100	314	79	210	185	151	273	77	42	239	77	386	471	376	331	158
CEDAR RAPIDS	106	100		256	82	110	72	72	174	26	118	129	113	328	360	262	231	58
COUNCIL BLUFFS	162	314	256		296	337	127	329	158	240	332	250	217	95	180	186	128	237
DAVENPORT	190	79	82	296		175	167	70	255	57	121	221	129	368	453	358	313	140
DES MOINES	33	185	72	127	167	208		200	98	111	203	121	90	199	284	201	156	100
DUBUQUE	187	151	72	329	70	105	200		209	85	191	174	186	325	395	297	266	93
SIOUX CITY	176	386	328	95	368	309	199	325	123	312	404	213	289		85	110	75	230
WATERLOO	99	158	58	237	140	79	108	93	114	84	176	81	131	230	302	204	173	

Total mileage through Iowa
29 — 155 miles
35 — 218 miles
80 — 303 miles
218 — 257 miles

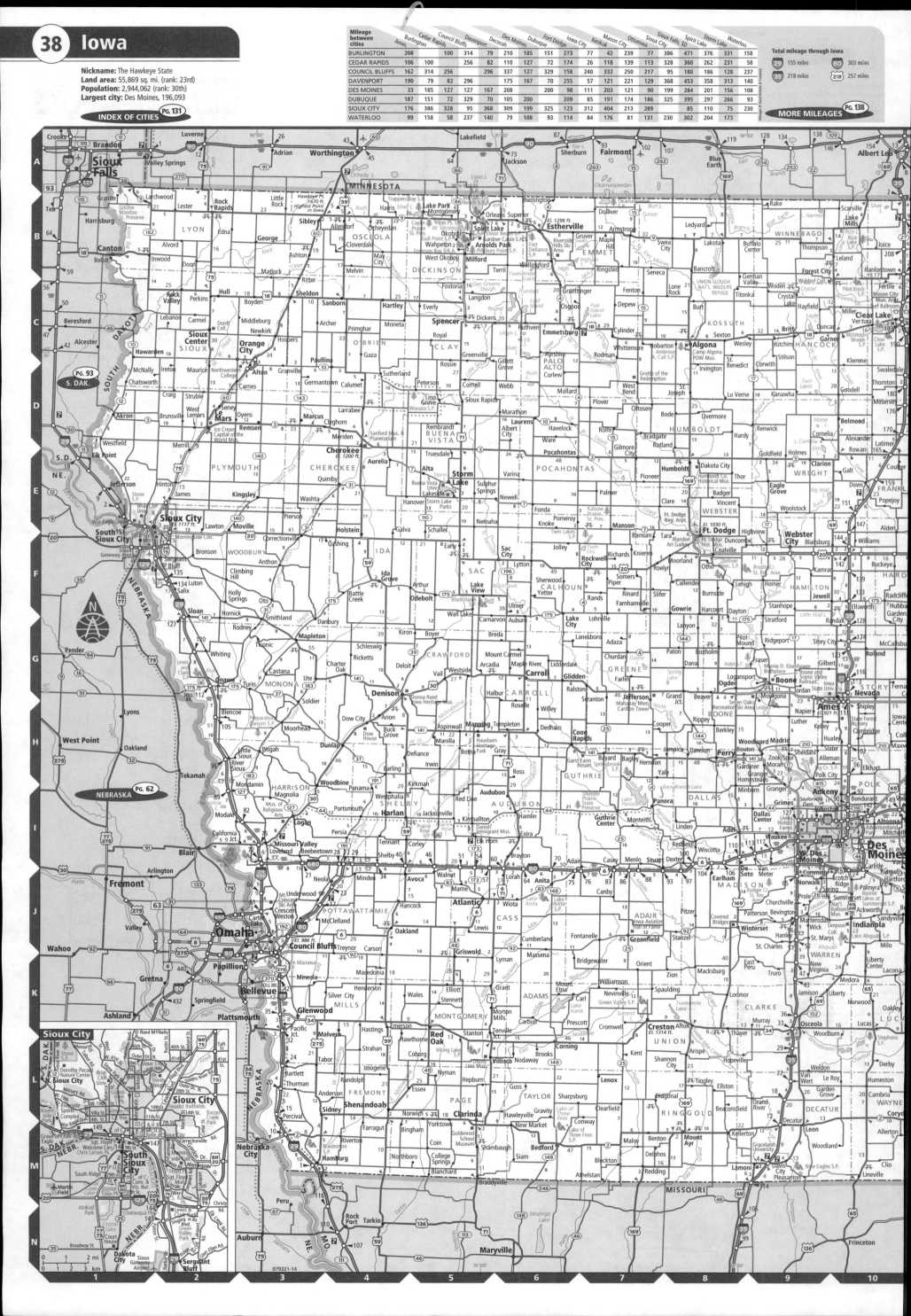

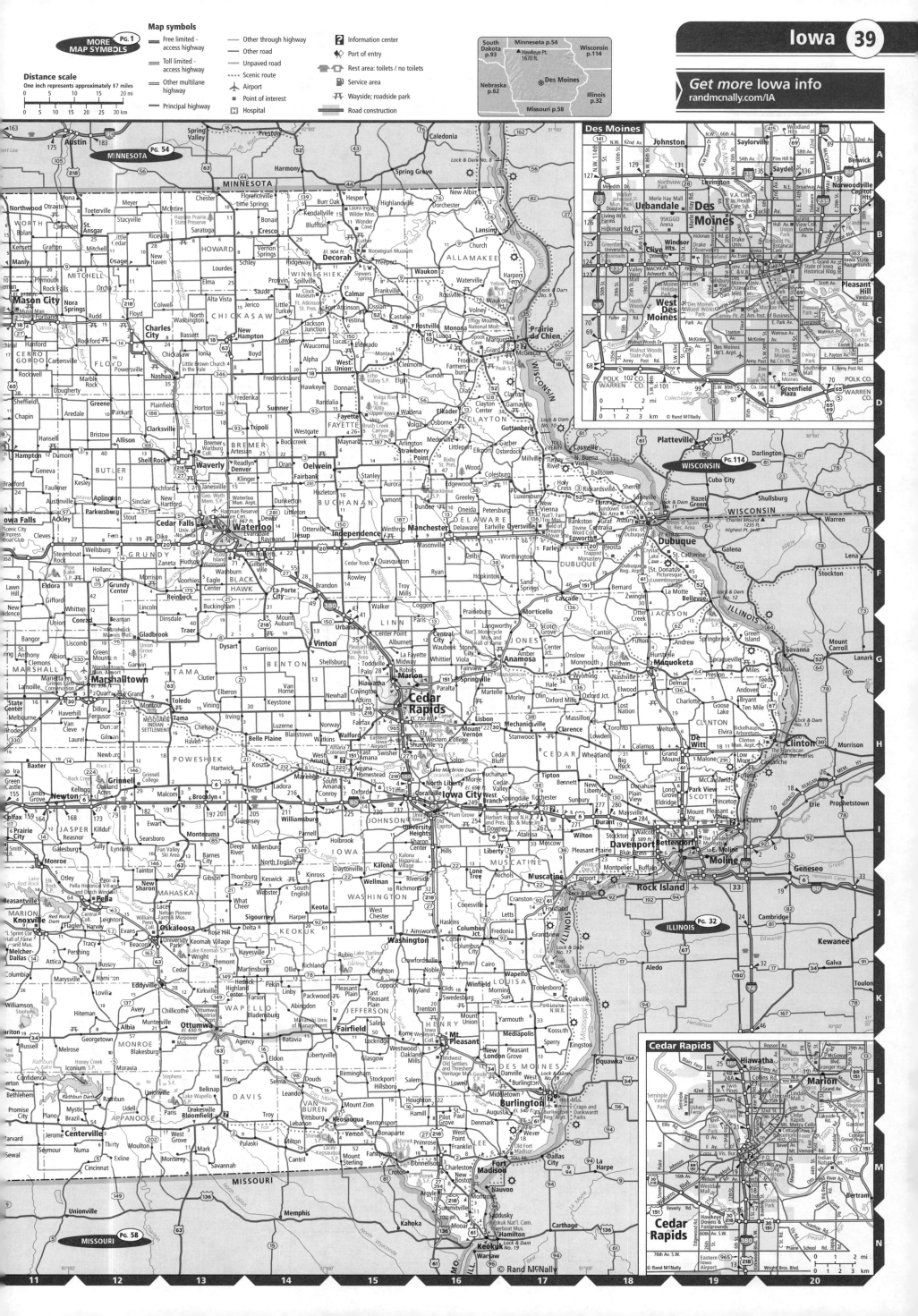

Nickname: The Sunflower State
Land area: 81,815 sq. mi. (rank: 13th)
Population: 2,723,507 (rank: 33rd)
Largest city: Wichita, 354,617

INDEX OF CITIES PG. 131

MORE MILEAGES PG. 138

Mileage between cities	Arkansas City	Atchison	Coffeyville	Dodge City	Emporia	Fort Scott	Goodland	Great Bend	Hays	Hutchinson	Joplin, MO	Kansas City	Liberal	Manhattan	Oakley	Salina	Topeka	Wichita
DODGE CITY	211	328	300		239	306	193	85	104	125	345	338	83	231	134	166	277	154
GOODLAND	385	398	459	193	349	481		268	207	145	268	512	408	208	59	236	347	324
HUTCHINSON	120	235	194	125	109	205	268	63	127		247	212	192	138	211	73	184	59
JOPLIN, MO	157	196	68	345	175	59	512	307	371	247		148	434	251	455	280	193	191
KANSAS CITY	225	54	171	338	103	89	408	253	267	212	148		401	119	351	172	61	188
SALINA	153	162	227	166	117	245	236	81	95	73	280	172	250	65	179		111	92
TOPEKA	177	52	158	277	61	134	347	192	206	184	193	61	353	58	290	111		140
WICHITA	61	192	138	154	85	152	324	119	183	59	191	188	213	129	267	92	140	

Total mileage through Kansas

35	235 miles	56	464 miles
70	424 miles	81	223 miles

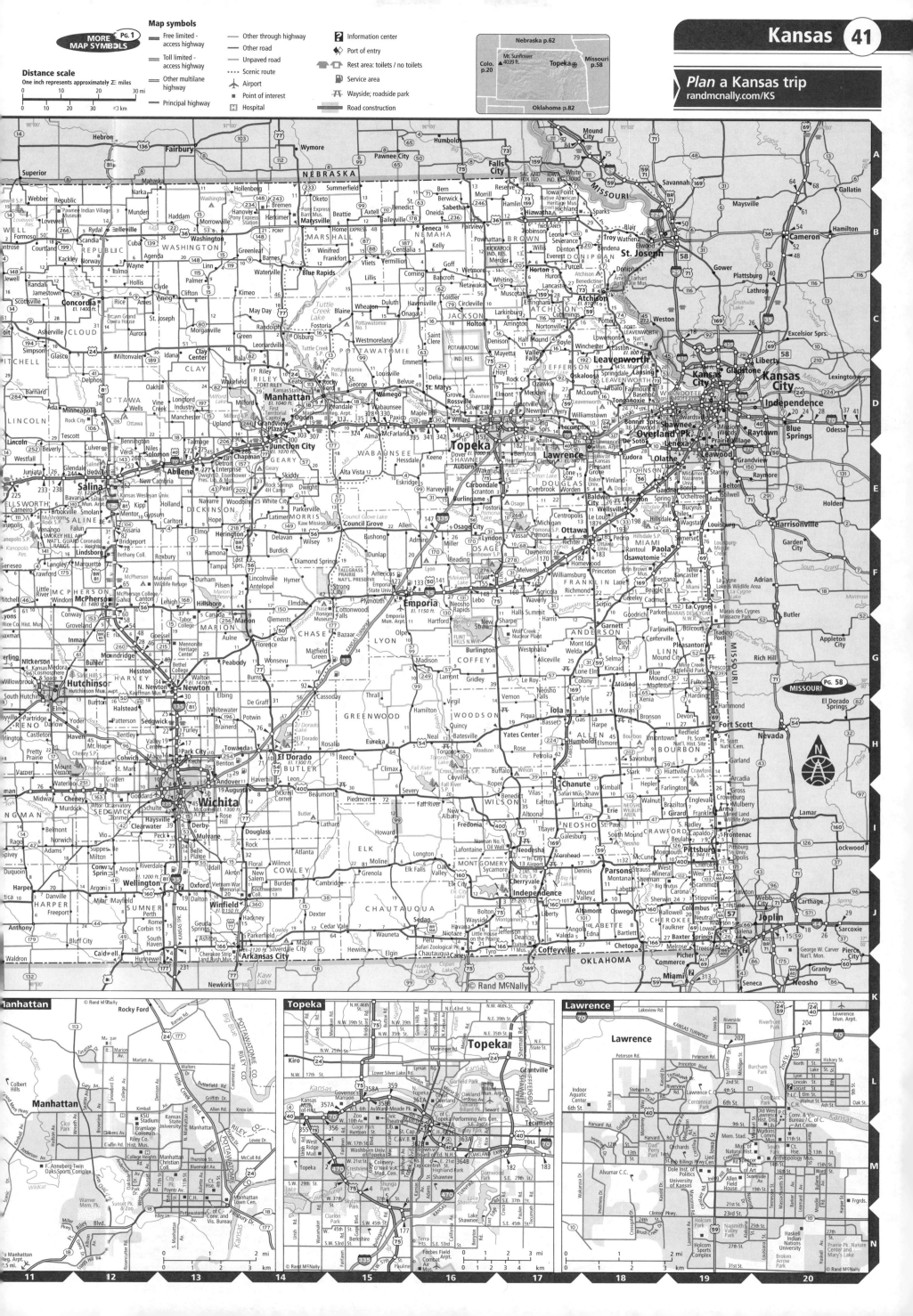

Nickname: The Pelican State
Land area: 43,562 sq. mi. (rank: 33rd)
Population: 4,496,334 (rank: 24th)
Largest city: New Orleans, 469,032

Get travel info
randmcnally.com/LA
INDEX OF CITIES PG. 131

Mileage between cities	Baton Rouge	Beaumont, TX	Bogalusa	De Ridder	El Dorado, AR	Ferriday	Gulfport, MS	Houma	Natchitoches	New Iberia	New Orleans	Shreveport	Vicksburg, MS	Tallulah
ALEXANDRIA	144	160	243	72	147	65	277	211	60	115	223	126	139	156
BATON ROUGE		184	99	168	253	100	133	87	202	67	79	258	162	159
GULFPORT, MS	133	317	68	301	346	223		131	335	200	76	401	225	204
LAFAYETTE	54	134	153	118	241	131	187	110	152	21	133	218	193	213
LAKE CHARLES	126	58	225	48	249	165	259	186	123	97	205	182	239	256
NEW ORLEANS	79	263	69	247	367	186	76	58	281	146		347	246	225
SHREVEPORT	268	195	357	134	95	180	401	328	76	239	347		160	177
VICKSBURG, MS	159	314	180	226	142	79	204	255	171	226	225	177		21

Total mileage through Louisiana

10	274 miles	49 208 miles
20	190 miles	55 66 miles

Distance scale
One inch represents approximately 29 miles

Mileage between cities

Mileage between cities	Bangor	East Millinocket	Eastport	Houlton	Portland	Portsmouth, NH	Rangeley	Waterville
Bangor		63	130	121	132	182	122	57
East Millinocket	63		119	60	193	243	183	118
Eastport	130	119		119	261	311	251	186
Houlton	121	60	119		251	301	241	176
Portland	132	193	261	251		50	120	75
Portsmouth, NH	182	243	311	301	50		168	125
Rangeley	122	183	251	241	120	168		77
Waterville	57	118	186	176	75	125	77	

Total mileage through Maine

- 95 299 miles
- 1 315 miles
- 2 273 miles
- 201 164 miles

MORE MILEAGES PG. 138

Distance scale
One inch represents approximately 21 miles

0 5 10 15 20 mi
0 5 10 15 20 25 30 km

Nickname: The Pine Tree State
Land area: 30,862 sq. mi. (rank: 39th)
Population: 1,305,728 (rank: 40th)
Largest city: Portland, 63,635

Plan a trip
randmcnally.com/ME

INDEX OF CITIES PG. 131

Northern Maine

Lewiston / Auburn

Acadia National Park

Portland

Bangor

Augusta

© Rand McNally

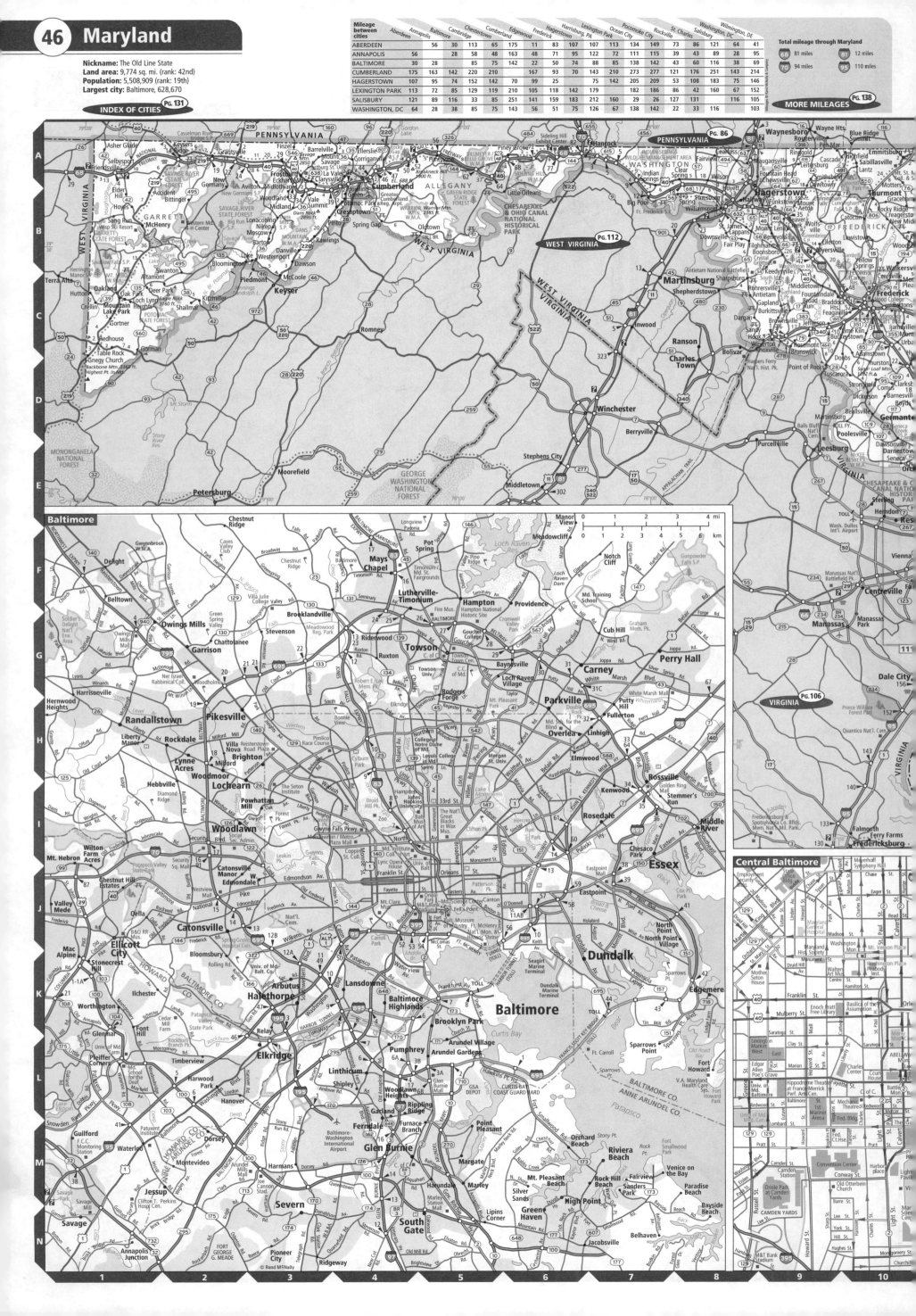

Explore Maryland
randmcnally.com/MD

Map symbols

MORE MAP SYMBOLS PG.1

Free limited - access highway
Toll limited - access highway
Other multilane highway
Principal highway
Other through highway
Other road
Unpaved road
Scenic route
Airport
Point of interest
Hospital

Information center
Port of entry
Rest area: toilets / no toilets
Service area
Wayside; roadside park
Road construction

Distance scale
One inch represents approximately 12 miles

Pennsylvania p.86
West Virginia p.112
Virginia p.106
Annapolis
N.J. p.66
Del. p.24

Cumberland

La Vale • Cumberland
Wiley Ford • Ridgeley
Bowling Green • Carpendale

Columbia

Columbia
Guilford

Hagerstown

Frederick

Annapolis

© Rand McNally

ATLANTIC OCEAN

CHESAPEAKE BAY

DELAWARE

VIRGINIA

PENNSYLVANIA

NEW JERSEY

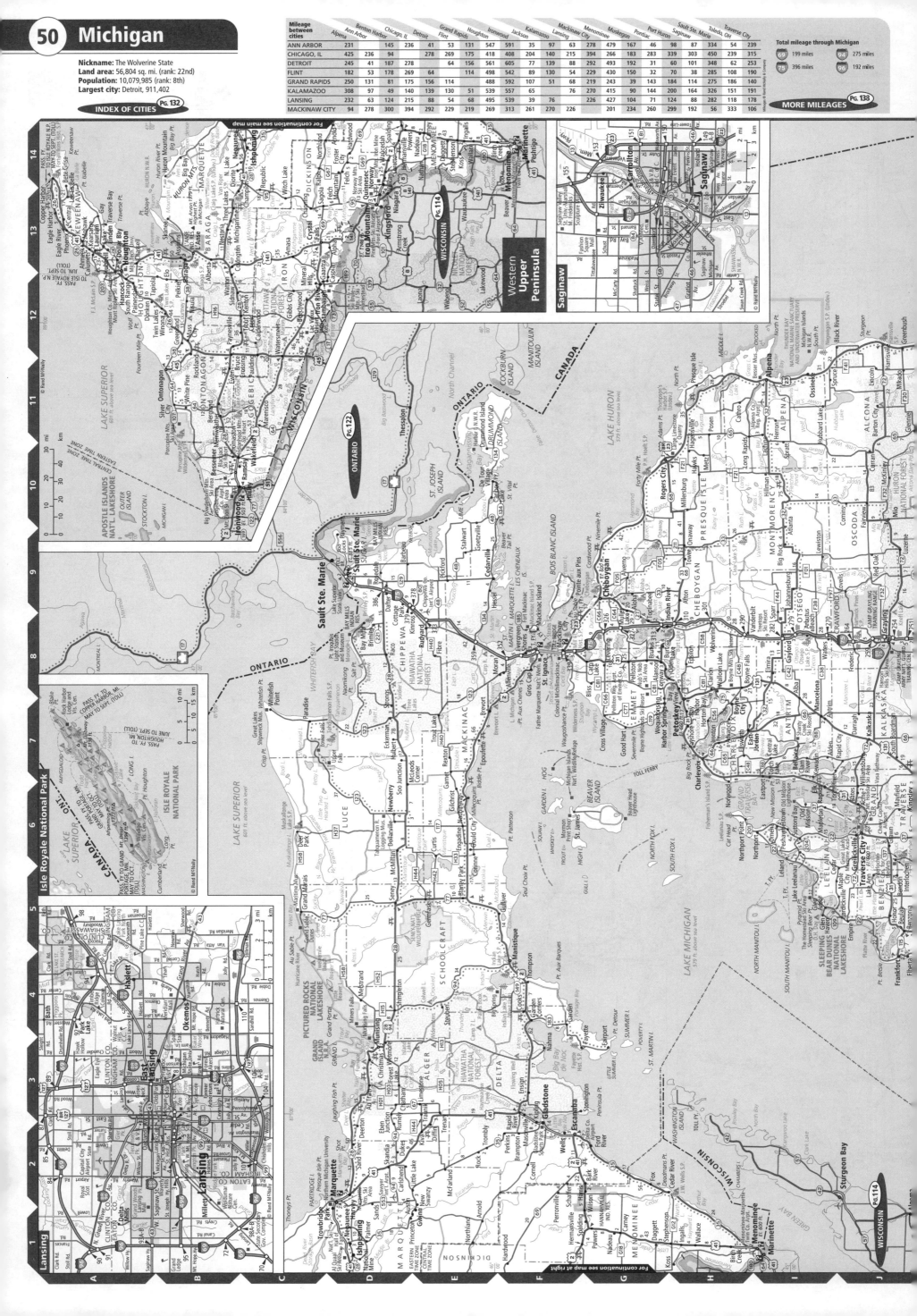

Nickname: The Wolverine State
Land area: 56,804 sq. mi. (rank: 22nd)
Population: 10,079,985 (rank: 8th)
Largest city: Detroit, 911,402

INDEX OF CITIES — PG. 132
MORE MILEAGES — PG. 133

Mileage between cities	Alpena	Ann Arbor	Benton Harbor	Chicago, IL	Detroit	Grand Rapids	Flint	Houghton	Ironwood	Jackson	Kalamazoo	Lansing	Mackinaw City	Menominee	Muskegon	Pontiac	Port Huron	Sault Ste. Marie	Saginaw	Toledo, OH	Traverse City
ANN ARBOR	231		145	236	41	53	131	547	591	35	97	63	278	479	167	46	98	87	334	54	239
CHICAGO, IL	425	236	94		278	269	175	418	408	204	140	215	394	266	183	283	339	303	450	239	315
DETROIT	245	41	187	278		64	156	561	561	77	139	88	293	493	192	31	60	101	348	62	253
FLINT	182	53	178	269	64		114	498	542	89	130	54	229	430	150	32	70	38	285	108	190
GRAND RAPIDS	250	131	81	175	156	114		488	592	107	51	68	219	243	39	143	184	114	275	186	140
KALAMAZOO	308	97	49	140	139	130	51	539	557	65		76	270	415	90	144	200	164	326	151	191
LANSING	232	63	124	215	88	54	68	495	539	39	76		226	427	104	71	124	88	282	118	178
MACKINAW CITY	94	278	300	394	292	229	219	269	313	261	270	226		201	234	260	299	192	56	333	106

Total mileage through Michigan
| 69 | 199 miles | 94 | 275 miles |
| 75 | 396 miles | 96 | 192 miles |

Map symbols

MORE MAP SYMBOLS PG. 1

- —— Free limited - access highway
- === Toll limited - access highway
- —— Other multilane highway
- —— Principal highway
- —— Other through highway
- —— Other road
- —— Unpaved road
- •••• Scenic route
- ✈ Airport
- ■ Point of interest
- Ⓗ Hospital
- ℹ Information center
- ◆ Port of entry
- Rest area: toilets / no toilets
- Service area
- Wayside; roadside park
- Road construction

Distance scale
One inch represents approximately 20 miles

0 5 10 15 20 mi
0 5 10 15 20 25 30 km

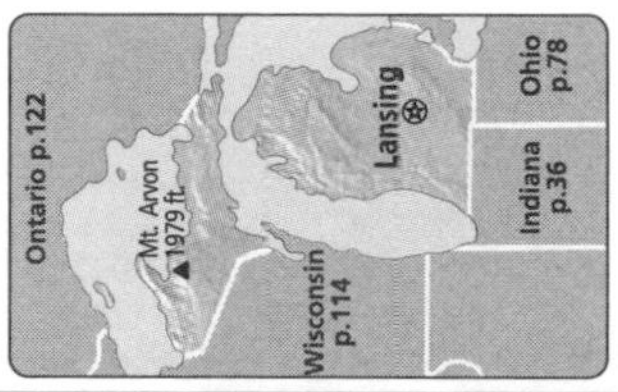

Ontario p.122
Wisconsin p.114
Ohio p.78
Indiana p.36

Get more Michigan info
randmcnally.com/MI

© Rand McNally

LAKE HURON

LAKE MICHIGAN

LAKE ST. CLAIR

LAKE ERIE

CANADA

ONTARIO

INDIANA

OHIO

Detroit

Windsor

Toledo

Lansing

Grand Rapids

Kalamazoo

Flint

Saginaw

Ann Arbor

Jackson

Battle Creek

South Bend

Chicago

Gary

Muskegon

Holland

Portage

Midland

Bay City

Mount Pleasant

Cadillac

Manistee

Ludington

Tecumseh

Monroe

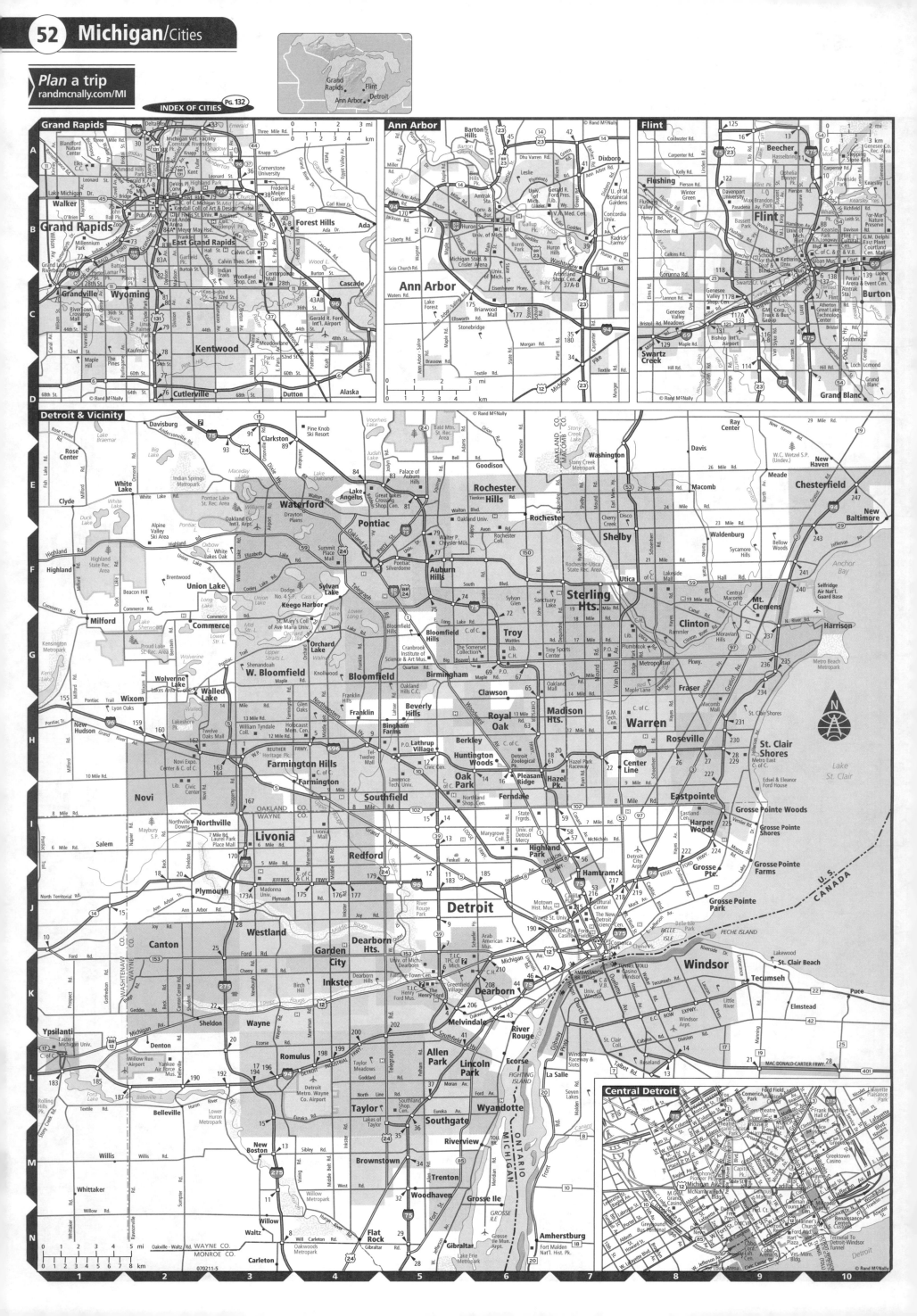

Grand Rapids

Ann Arbor

Flint

Detroit & Vicinity

Central Detroit

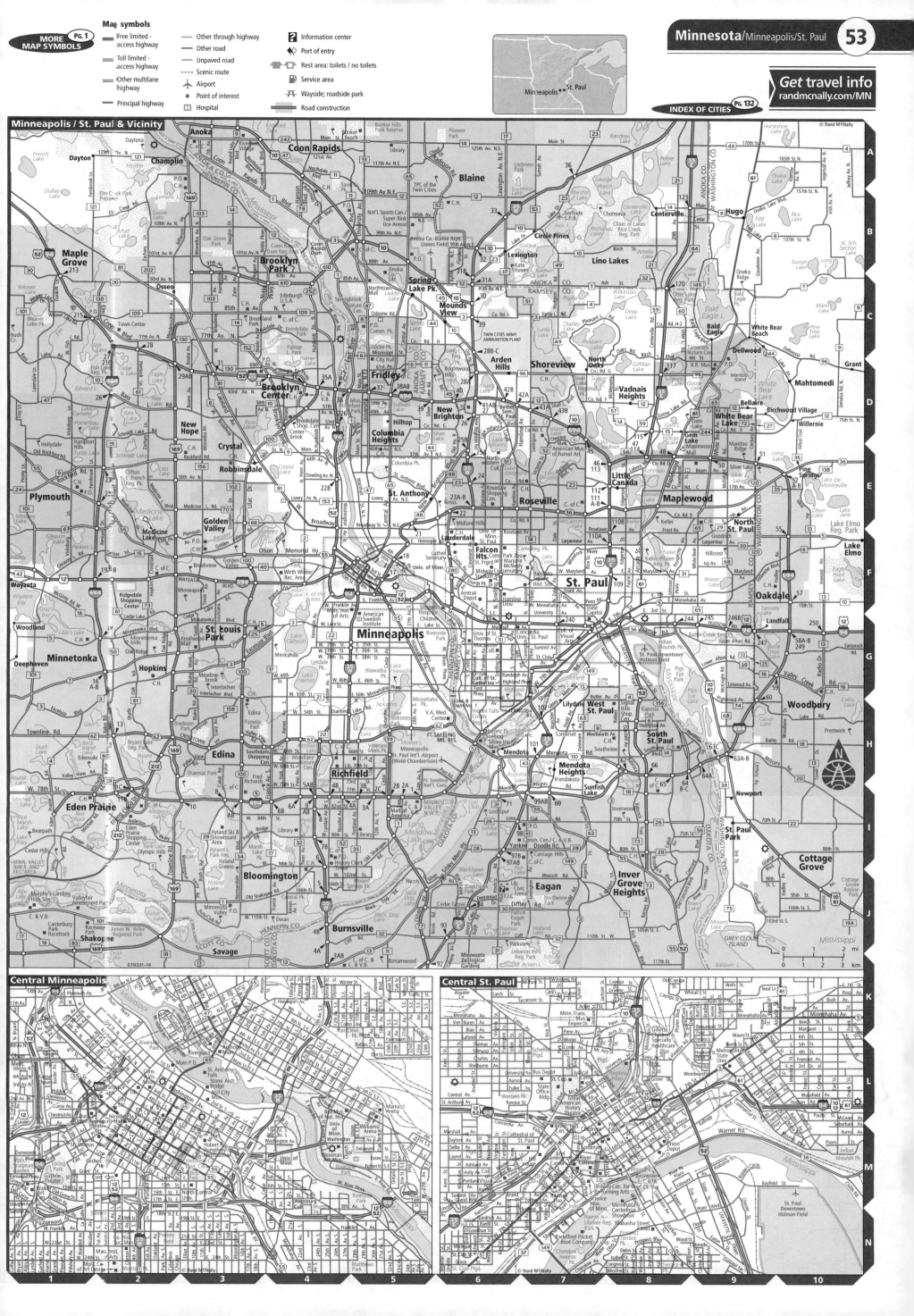

Get travel info
randmcnally.com/MN

INDEX OF CITIES PG. 132

MORE MAP SYMBOLS PG. 1

Map symbols

- Free limited-access highway
- Toll limited-access highway
- Other multilane highway
- Principal highway
- Other through highway
- Other road
- Unpaved road
- Scenic route
- Airport
- Point of interest
- Hospital
- Information center
- Port of entry
- Rest area: toilets / no toilets
- Service area
- Wayside; roadside park
- Road construction

Minneapolis / St. Paul & Vicinity

Central Minneapolis

Central St. Paul

© Rand McNally

Nickname: The North Star State
Land area: 79,610 sq. mi. (rank: 14th)
Population: 5,059,375 (rank: 21st)
Largest city: Minneapolis, 373,188

INDEX OF CITIES PG. 132

MORE MILEAGES PG. 138

Mileage between cities	Albert Lea	Austin	Bemidji	Brainerd	Duluth	Fairmont	Fergus Falls	Grand Forks, ND	Hibbing	International Falls	La Crosse, WI	Mankato	Marshall	Minneapolis	Moorhead	Red Wing	Rochester	St. Cloud	St. Paul	Sioux Falls, SD	Willmar
BEMIDJI	315	319		99	153	296	141	113	119	116	389	272	261	222	142	280	315	150	231	384	194
DULUTH	251	255	153	114		306	211	264	76	164	239	237	276	157	254	198	235	143	151	423	209
MINNEAPOLIS	97	101	222	133	157	152	184	318	194	299	164	80	155		237	60	94	72	10	269	96
MOORHEAD	330	334	142	140	254	357	75	83	216	258	400	283	202	237		295	330	173	246	244	174
ROCHESTER	64	39	315	226	235	119	277	411	274	377	72	82	193	94	330	49		165	84	236	186
ST. CLOUD	165	169	150	61	143	146	120	254	178	250	235	122	133	72	173	130	165		81	221	66
ST. PAUL	100	104	231	142	151	155	193	327	190	293	154	86	161	10	246	50	84	81		272	106
SIOUX FALLS, SD	175	197	384	274	423	121	236	318	462	498	297	155	90	269	244	283	236	221	272		156

Total mileage through Minnesota

35	260 miles	94	260 miles
90	276 miles	2	255 miles

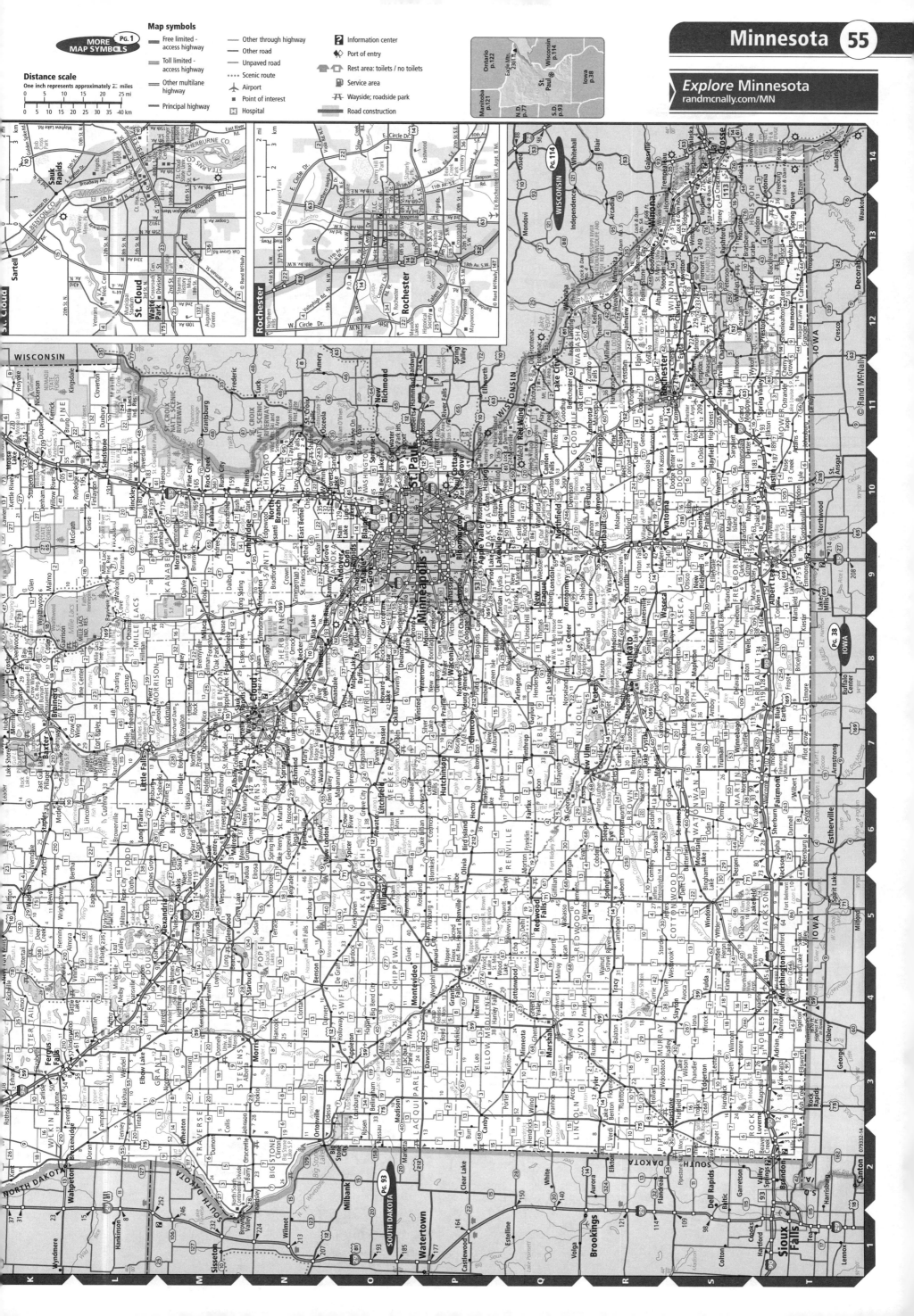

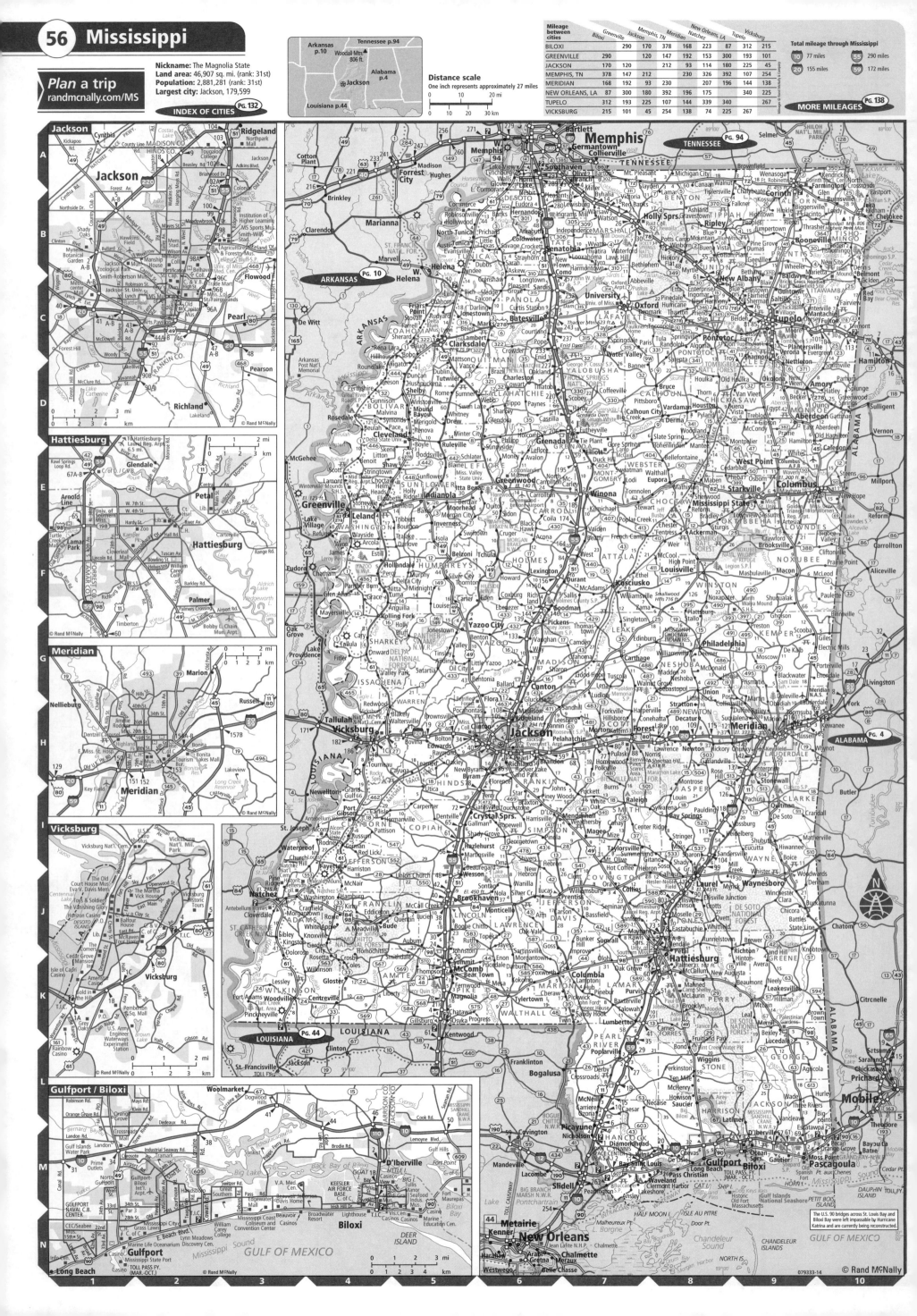

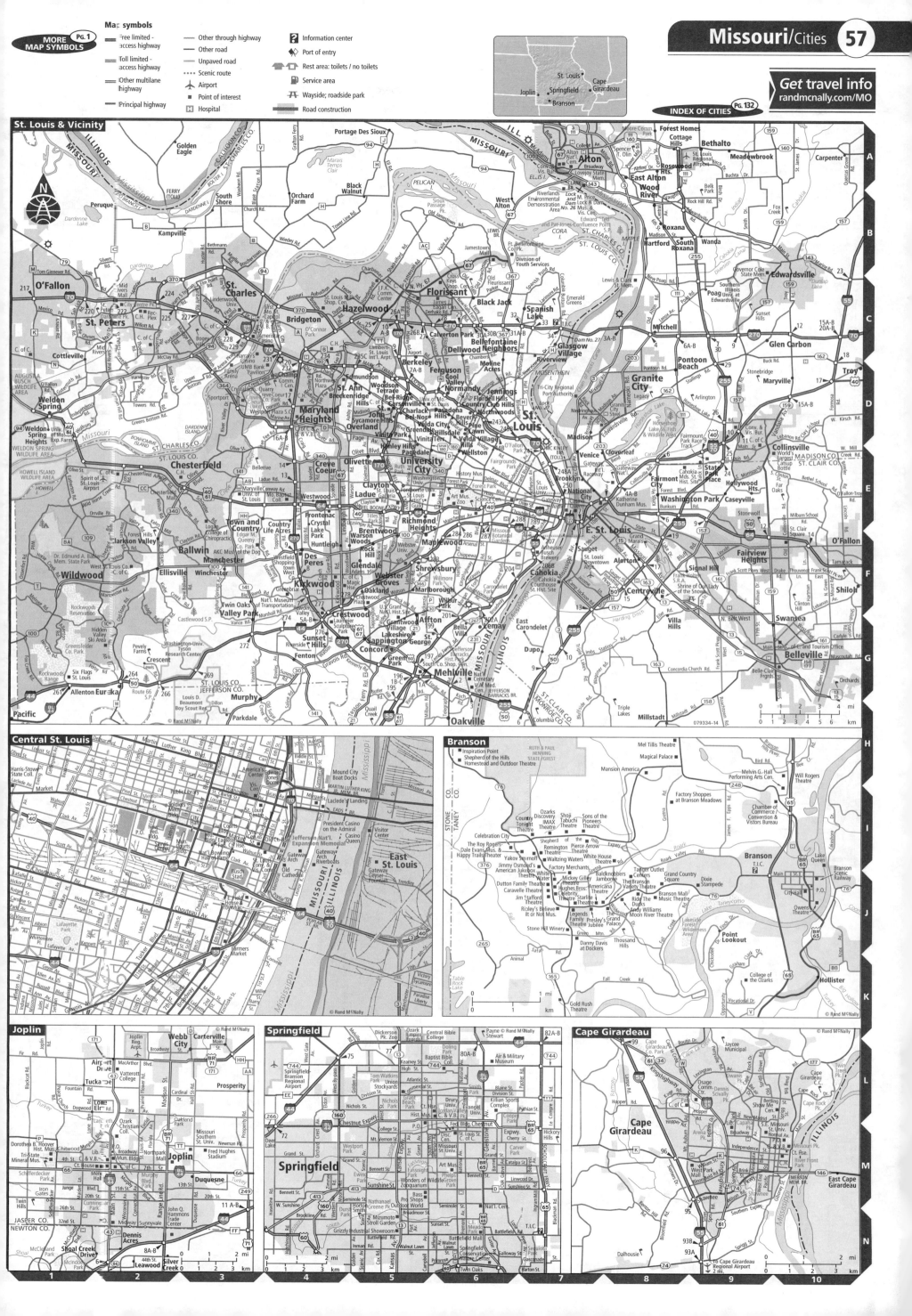

Nickname: The Treasure State
Land area: 145,552 sq. mi. (rank: 4th)
Population: 917,621 (rank: 44th)
Largest city: Billings, 95,220

INDEX OF CITIES PG. 132

Mileage between cities

	Billings	Bozeman	Butte	Dillon	Glasgow	Great Falls	Havre	Helena	Kalispell	Lewistown	Miles City	Missoula	St. Mary	Sheridan, WY	Shelby	West Yellowstone	Sidney
BILLINGS		140	221	254	278	222	249	239	463	126	532	144	340	387	309	127	271	229
BOZEMAN	140		82	115	367	190	305	100	324	286	201	306	271	269	413	89	
BUTTE	221	82		67	431	155	270	65	242	243	311	367	119	271	236	350	494	148
GREAT FALLS	222	190	155	222	276		115	91	233	106	324	327	167	164	86	349	379	269
HELENA	239	100	65	132	367	91		198	195	289	385	111	207	172	368	512	179
KALISPELL	463	324	242	295	425	233	264	198		340	91	609	132	86	160	592	565	390
MILES CITY	144	286	367	400	222	327	385	609		486	492	414	201	129	375		
MISSOULA	340	201	119	172	443	167	282	111	123	274	678		209	227	469	613	267

Total mileage through Montana

15 396 miles	**94** 249 miles	
90 552 miles		

MORE MILEAGES PG. 138

Get more Montana info
randmcnally.com/MT

Map symbols

MORE MAP SYMBOLS PG. 1

- Free limited-access highway
- Toll limited-access highway
- Other multilane highway
- Principal highway
- Other through highway
- Other road
- Unpaved road
- Scenic route
- ✈ Airport
- Point of interest
- Ⓗ Hospital
- ? Information center
- ◆ Port of entry
- Rest area: toilets / no toilets
- Service area
- Wayside; roadside park
- Road construction

Distance scale
One inch represents approximately 30 miles

0 10 20 30 miles
0 10 20 30 40 km

B.C. p.118   Alta. p.119   Saskatchewan p.120
N.D. p.77
Idaho p.31   ● Helena   Granite Peak 2799 ft.   S.D. p.93
Wyoming p.116

CANADA
SASKATCHEWAN   PG. 120

PG. 77 N. DAK.
PG. 93 S. DAK.

116

Missoula

Missoula Int'l. Arpt.
Orchard Homes
Fort Missoula Historic Site

Butte

Walkerville
World Museum of Mining
Montana Tech of the Univ. of Montana
Berkeley Pit Mine & Public Viewing Cen.
Our Lady Of The Rockies
Butte
Timber Butte 6314 ft.

Great Falls

Great Falls
Black Eagle
Montana Expo Park & Frgrds.
Malmstrom Air Force Base
Gibson Flats

Billings

Billings
Billings Heights
Lockwood

Nickname: The Cornhusker State
Land area: 76,872 sq. mi. (rank: 15th)
Population: 1,739,291 (rank: 38th)
Largest city: Omaha, 404,267

INDEX OF CITIES PG. 132

MORE MILEAGES PG. 138

Mileage between cities	Alliance	Beatrice	Cheyenne, WY	Columbus	Grand Island	Kearney	Lincoln	McCook	Nebraska City	Norfolk	North Platte	Ogallala	Omaha	O'Neill	Scottsbluff	Sioux City, IA	Valentine
GRAND ISLAND	321	134	379	365	63		51	97	155	145	109	147	198	152	111	320	179	211
LINCOLN	400	40	458	444	78	97	130		234	49	124	226	277	58	207	399	155	306
NORFOLK	329	161	324	474	46	109	160	124	264		154		256	307	112	75	429	74	186
NORTH PLATTE	177	263	235	221	210	147	226	68	274	256		54	281	194	176	378	131	
OGALLALA	123	314	169	169	261	198	151	277	118	325	307	54		332	248	122	429	185
OMAHA	455	98	513	499	88	152	185	58	289	44	112	281	332		188	454	98	299
SCOTTSBLUFF	57	436	99	109	383	320	273	399	240	447	429	176	122	454		329	453	218
VALENTINE	164	343	138	352	232	211	195	306	190	354	186	131	185	299	111	218	235	

Total mileage through Nebraska
- 80: 455 miles
- 81: 219 miles
- 83: 226 miles
- 84: 436 miles

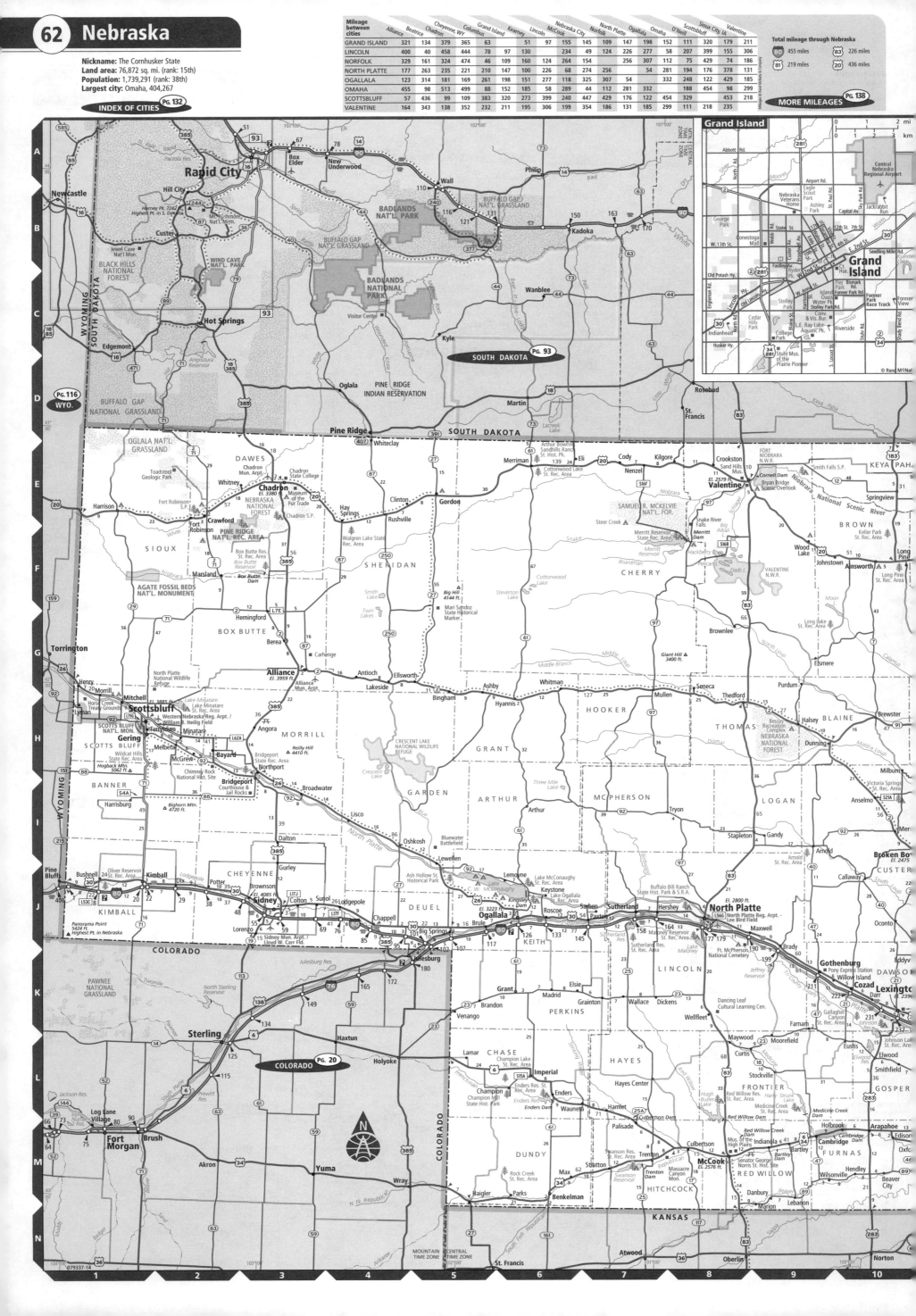

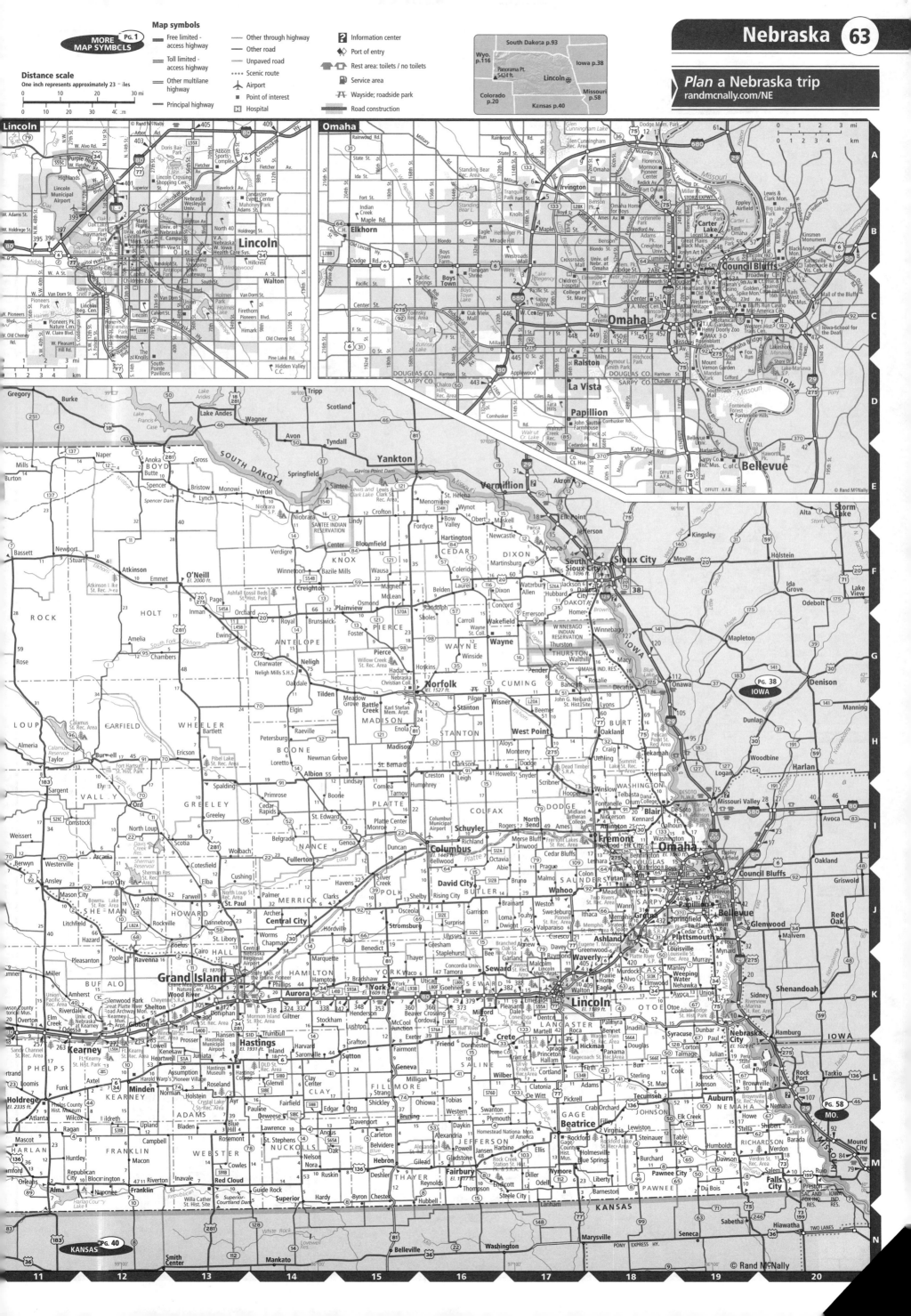

Get travel info
randmcnally.com/NV

Nickname: The Silver State
Land area: 109,826 sq. mi. (rank: 7th)
Population: 2,241,154 (rank: 35th)
Largest city: Las Vegas, 517,017

INDEX OF CITIES   PG. 132

Mileage between cities	Battle Mountain Austin	Boulder City Beatty	Carson City	Elko	Ely	Fallon	Hawthorne	Jackpot	Las Vegas	McDermitt	Panaca	Reno	Winnemucca
ELKO	160	71	368	462	306		190	253	325	119	436	199	307	289	276	125
ELY	146	217	259	273	318		190	256	271	200	247	245	345	120	317	161	271
LAS VEGAS	324	413	116	26	435	436	245	384	312	453		540	165	445	208	466
RENO	171	217	329	473	32	289	317	61	133	408	445	238	437		237	164
S. LAKE TAHOE, CA	200	262	468	28	334	346	90	136	453	442	283	444	60	240	209
TONOPAH	116	205	92	234	227	276	167	176	104	395	208	332	204	237	258
WENDOVER, UT	271	182	381	393	417	111	125	271	364	436	120	367	310	238	489	236
WINNEMUCCA	142	53	350	492	181	125	271	128	200	244	466	74	391	164	258

Total mileage through Nevada
One inch represents approximately 38 miles

15	124 miles	6	307 miles
80	411 miles	95	652 miles

Distance scale
One inch represents approximately 38 miles

0 10 20 30 mi
0 10 20 30 40 km

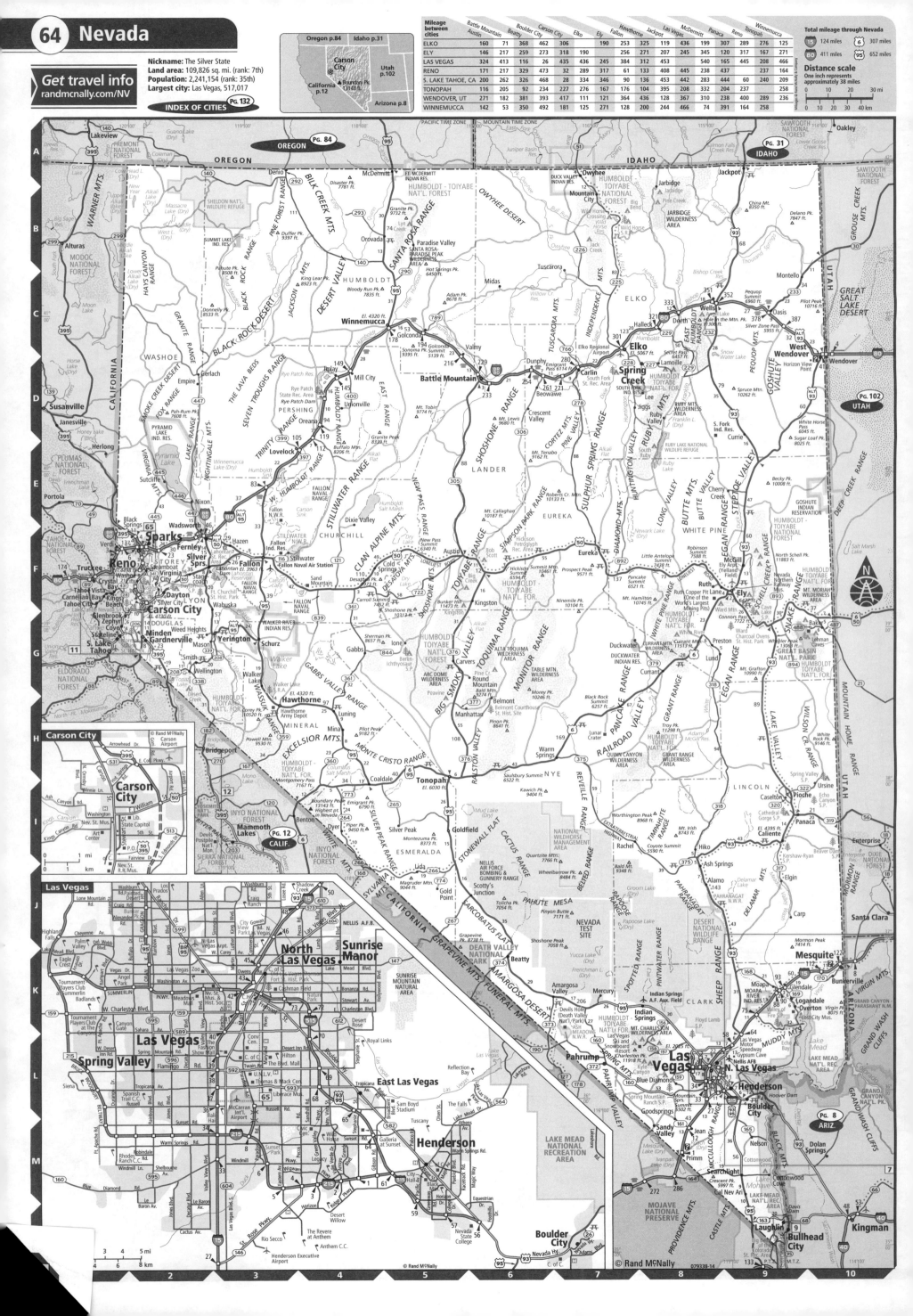

© Rand McNally
079338-14

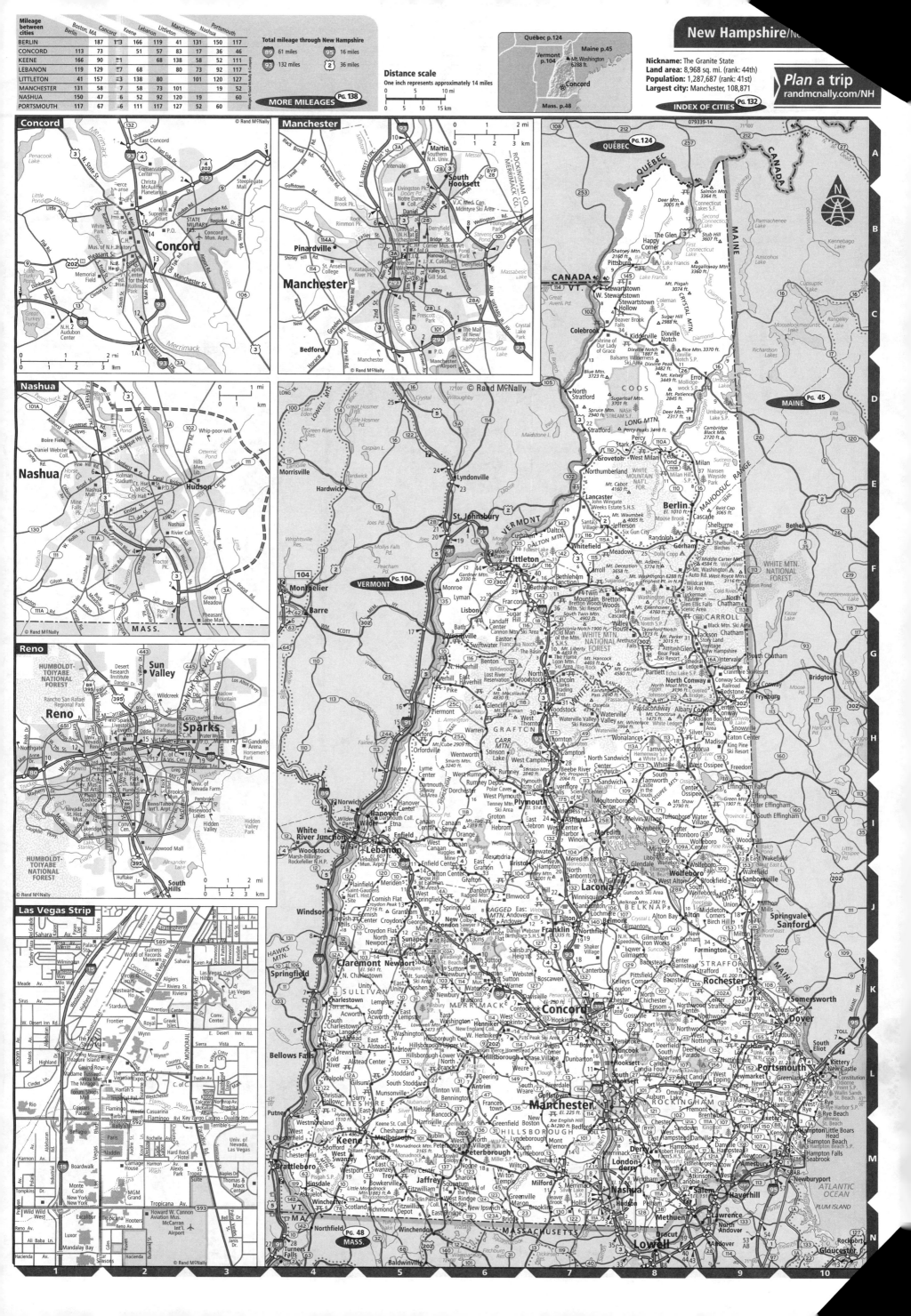

New Jersey
Garden State
...,7 sq. mi. (rank: 46th)
...,638,396 (rank: 10th)
...: Newark, 277,911
INDEX OF CITIES Pg. 132
65

Mileage between cities	Atlantic City	Camden	Cape May	Cherry Hill	Elizabeth	Jersey City	Long Branch	Newark	New Brunswick	New York, NY	Paterson	Phillipsburg	Point Pleasant	Port Jervis, NY	Princeton	Somerville	Toms River	Trenton	Vineland	Wilmington, DE
ATLANTIC CITY		60	49	55	114	122	81	117	95	140	129	145	64	182	93	119	51	81	37	70	86
CAMDEN	60		93	6	79	87	77	82	63	97	94	85	71	147	48	70	55	37	38	14	36
NEWARK	117	82	151	78	5	5	46		25	15	19	63	56	75	41	34	66	55	115	68	117
NEW BRUNSWICK	95	63	129	59	22	30	33	25		40	37	52	38	90	18	14	44	36	96	49	98
PATERSON	129	94	163	90	22	15	58	19	37	31		66	68	54	58	43	78	67	127	80	129
PHILLIPSBURG	145	85	178	91	63	68	63	52	78	66		96	76	56	39	106	57	23	70	100
TRENTON	81	37	114	33	52	60	50	55	36	70	67	57	44	107	12	31	46		70	20	68
WILMINGTON, DE	86	36	93	43	114	122	112	117	98	132	129	100	106	162	79	101	88	68	44	51

Total mileage through New Jersey

78	68 miles	95	98 miles
80	68 miles		

MORE MILEAGES Pg. 138

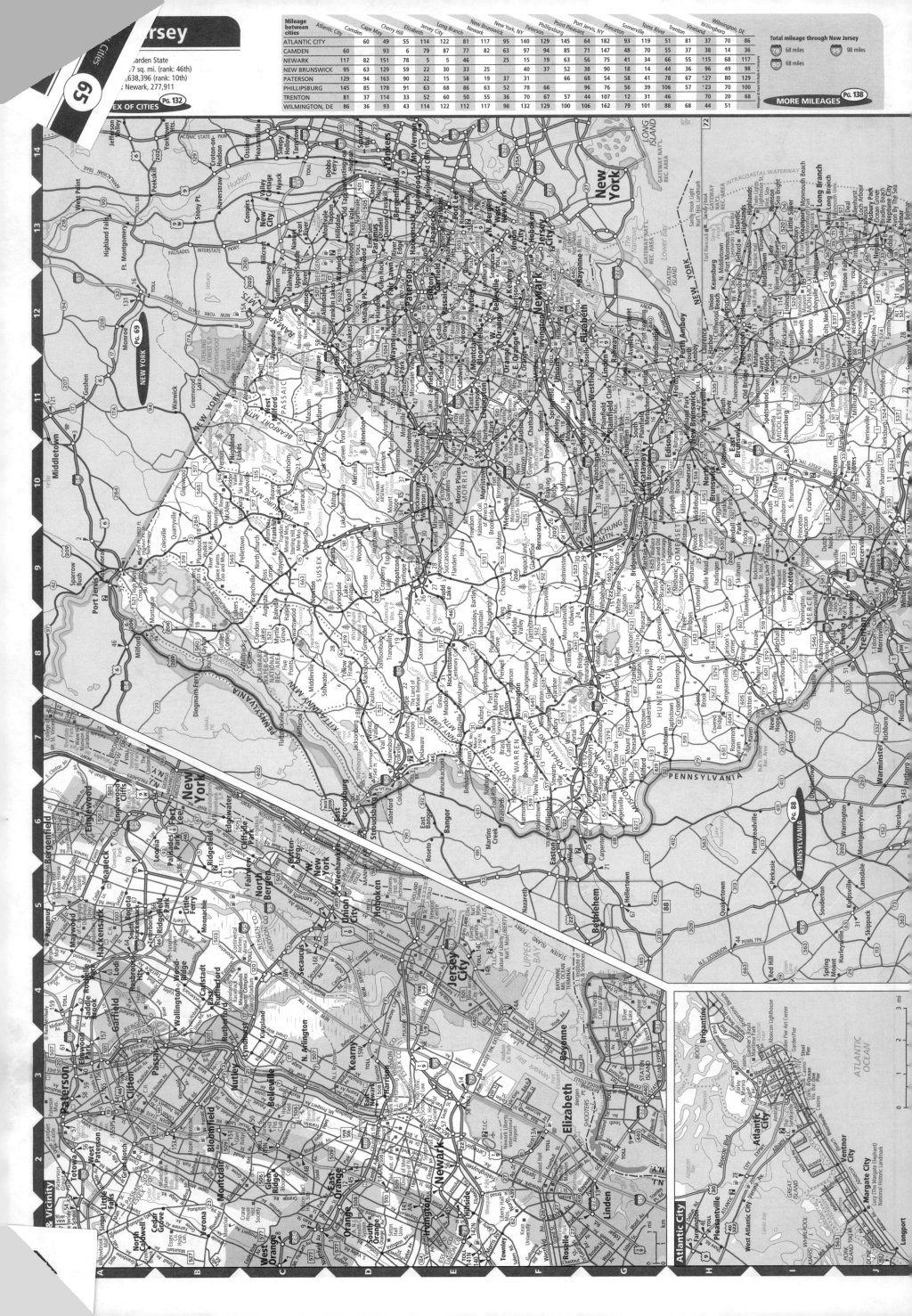

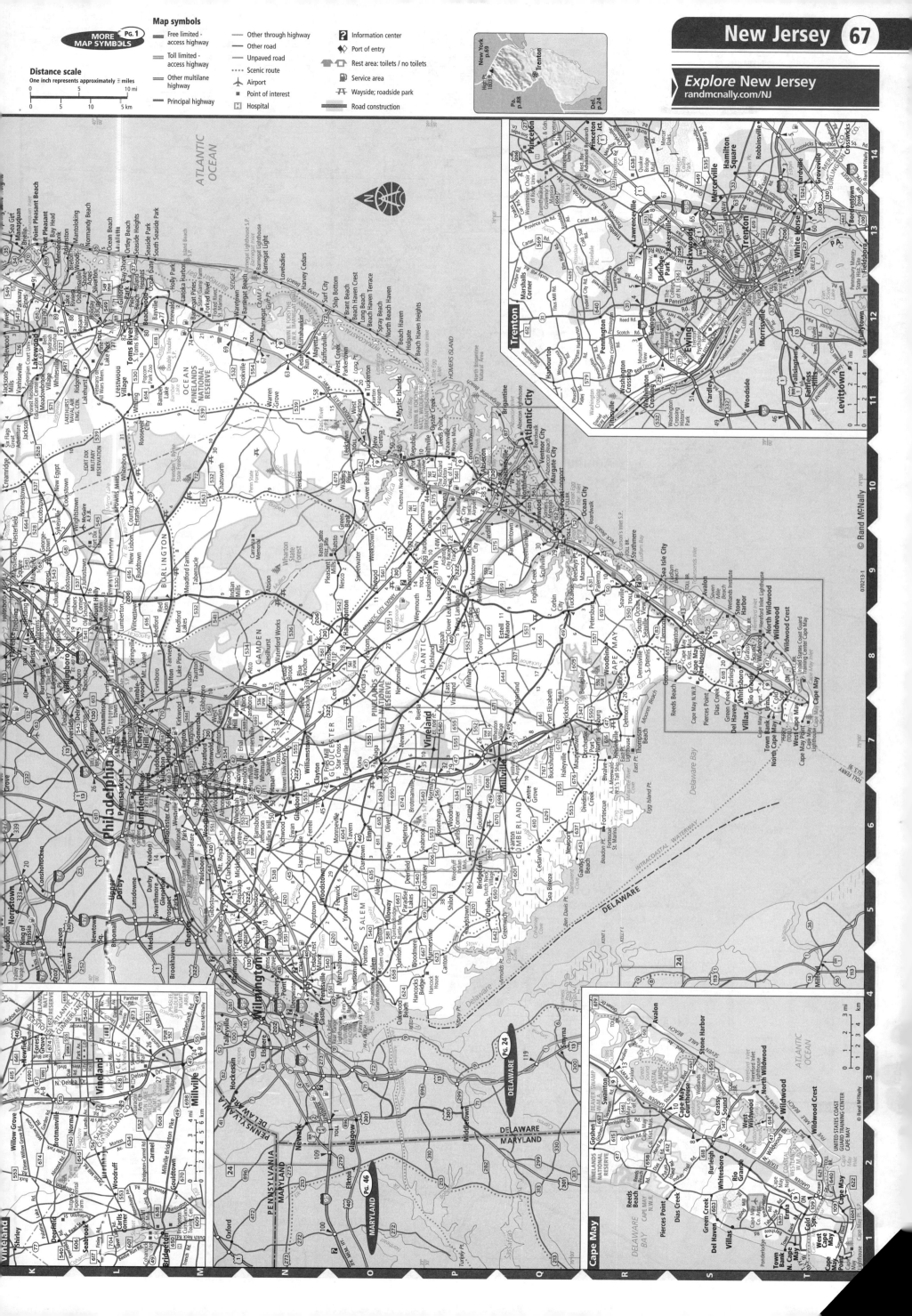

Get travel info
randmcnally.com/NM

Nickname: Land of Enchantment
Land area: 121,356 sq. mi. (rank: 5th)
Population: 1,874,614 (rank: 36th)
Largest city: Albuquerque, 471,856

INDEX OF CITIES PG. 133

Mileage between cities	Alamogordo	Albuquerque	Carlsbad	Clovis	El Paso, TX	Grants	Las Cruces	Las Vegas	Lordsburg	Raton	Santa Fe	Socorro	Taos	Truth or Consequences	Tucumcari
ALBUQUERQUE	210		275	217	267	79	315	224	118	294	224	58	78	126	150	174
CARLSBAD	146	275		179	165	354	70	208	253	324	359	267	240	328	280	242
CLOVIS	229	217	179		314	296	127	208	165	416	233	209	246	240	318	82
GALLUP	324	139	414	356	381	61	414	338	257	303	363	197	192	265	264	313
LAS CRUCES	69	224	208	240	46	278		257		342	118	448	282	146	350	75	305
SANTA FE	217	58	267	209	325	137	307	282	63	352	169		116	69	208	166
TRINIDAD, CO	345	246	381	255	430	325	468	470	128	446	324	118	396		199
TUCUMCARI	236	174	242	82	321	253	200	305	122	468	177	166	252	197	324	

Total mileage through New Mexico
10: 164 miles 40: 374 miles
25: 462 miles

Distance scale
One inch represents approximately 38 miles
0 10 20 30 mi
0 10 20 30 40 km

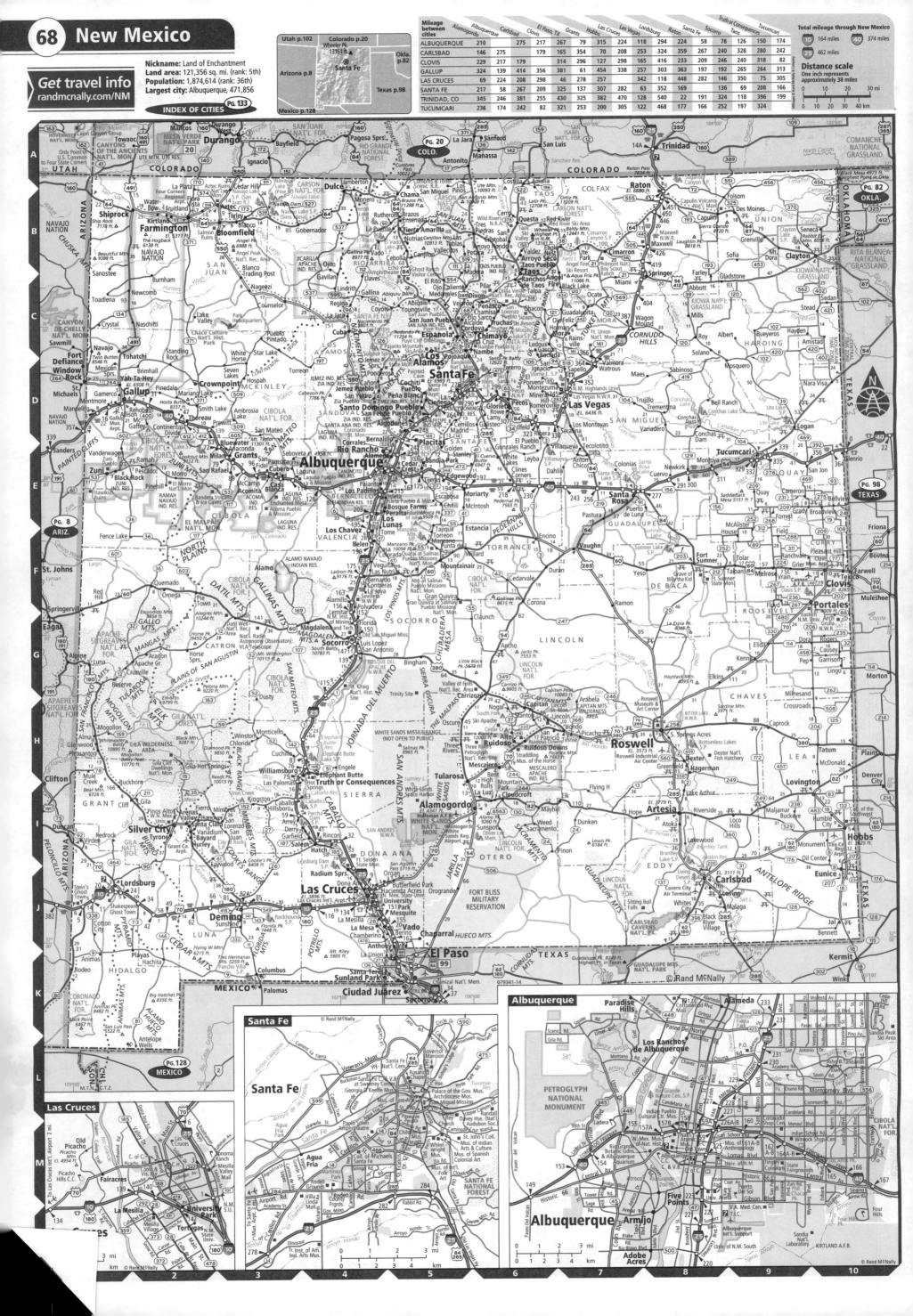

© Rand McNally
079341-14

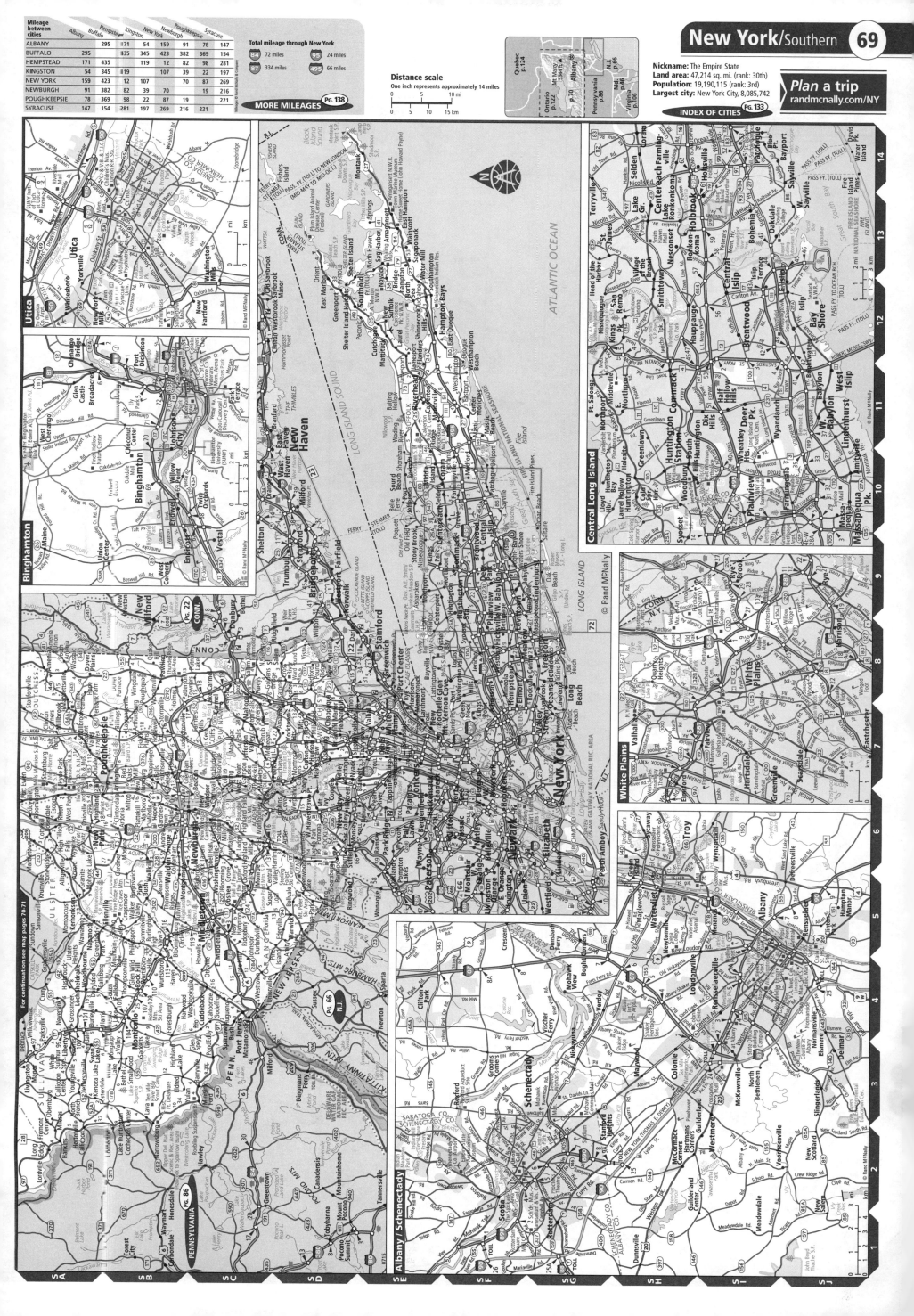

Nickname: The Empire State
Land area: 47,214 sq. mi. (rank: 30th)
Population: 19,190,115 (rank: 3rd)
Largest city: New York City, 8,085,742

Plan a trip
randmcnally.com/NY

INDEX OF CITIES — PG. 133

Mileage between cities	Albany	Buffalo	Hempstead	Kingston	New York	Newburgh	Poughkeepsie	Syracuse
ALBANY		295	171	54	159	91	78	147
BUFFALO	295		435	345	423	382	369	154
HEMPSTEAD	171	435		119	12	82	98	281
KINGSTON	54	345	119		107	39	22	197
NEW YORK	159	423	12	107		70	87	269
NEWBURGH	91	382	82	39	70		19	216
POUGHKEEPSIE	78	369	98	22	87	19		221
SYRACUSE	147	154	281	197	269	216	221	

Total mileage through New York

84	72 miles	95	24 miles
87	334 miles	495	66 miles

MORE MILEAGES — PG. 138

Distance scale
One inch represents approximately 14 miles

0   5   10 mi
0   5   10   15 km

Nickname: The Empire State
Land area: 47,214 sq. mi. (rank: 30th)
Population: 19,190,115 (rank: 3rd)
Largest city: New York City, 8,085,742

INDEX OF CITIES Pg. 133

MORE MILEAGES Pg. 138

Total mileage through New York
81 184 miles · 87 334 miles · 86 176 miles · 90 385 miles

Mileage between cities	Albany	Auburn	Binghamton	Buffalo	Elmira	Glens Falls	Ithaca	Jamestown	Kingston	Lake Placid	Massena	New York	Niagara Falls	Olean	Oneonta	Oswego	Plattsburgh	Rochester	Syracuse	Utica	Watertown
ALBANY		176	134	295	192	58	176	357	54	142	221	159	309	304	80	176	161	231	147	95	208
BINGHAMTON	134	90		230	59	179	51	224	134	263	242	199	244	171	56	111	282	166	76	93	148
BUFFALO	295	128	230		148	313	154	71	345	347	312	417	22	77	277	159	378	78	154	204	218
JAMESTOWN	357	193	224	71	166	402	191		356	412	377	417	93	56	279	224	505	143	219	269	283
PLATTSBURGH	161	259	282	378	340	110	287	505	214	87	49	319	392	452	228	259		314	230	188	170
ROCHESTER	231	64	166	78	121	249	90	143	281	283	248	359	92	118	213	77	314		90	140	154
SYRACUSE	147	27	76	154	92	165	58	219	197	201	166	269	149	161	58	191	123	40	230		56
UTICA	95	85	93	204	147	113	113	269	145	164	161	250	218	241	62	85	188	140	56		84

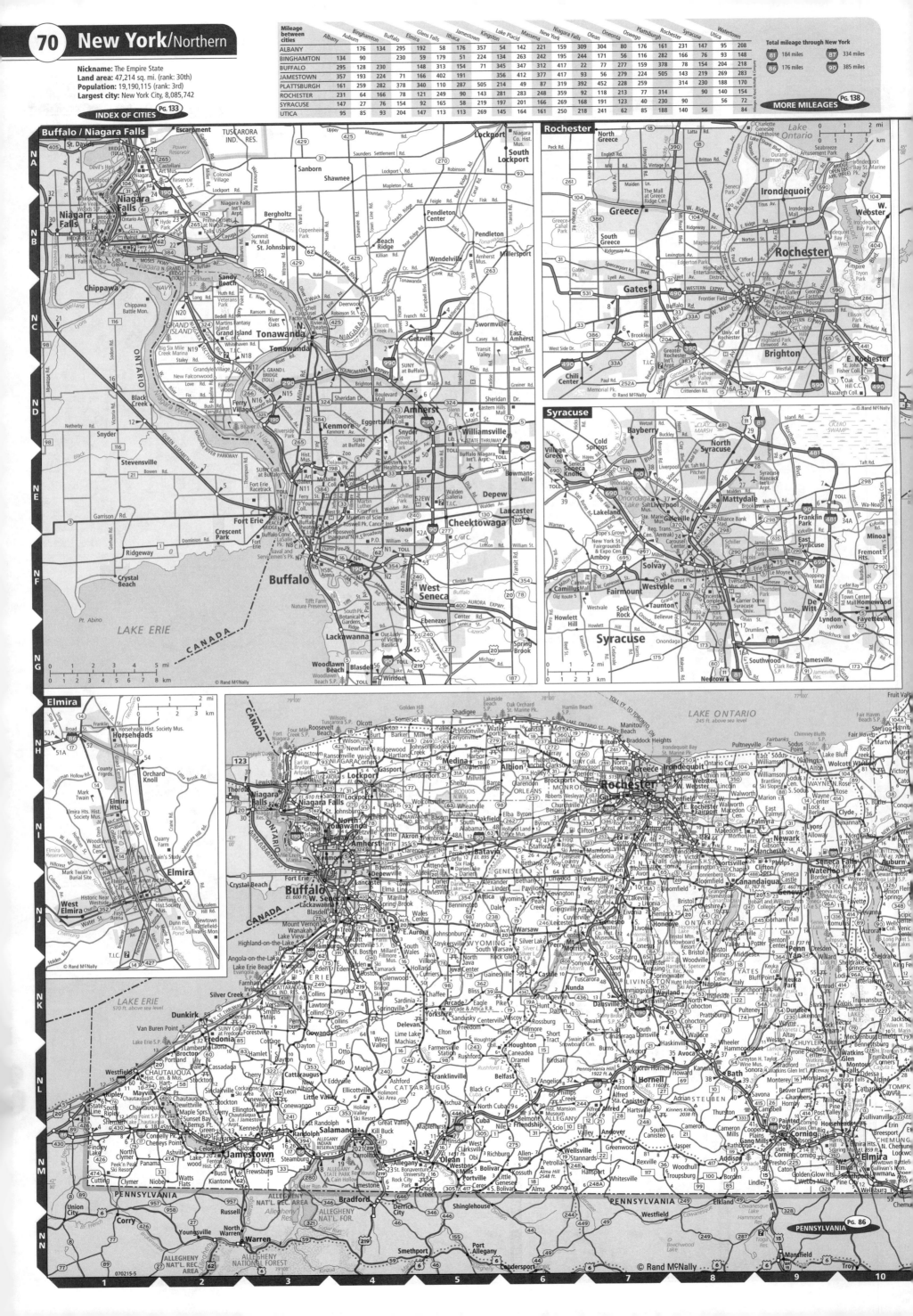

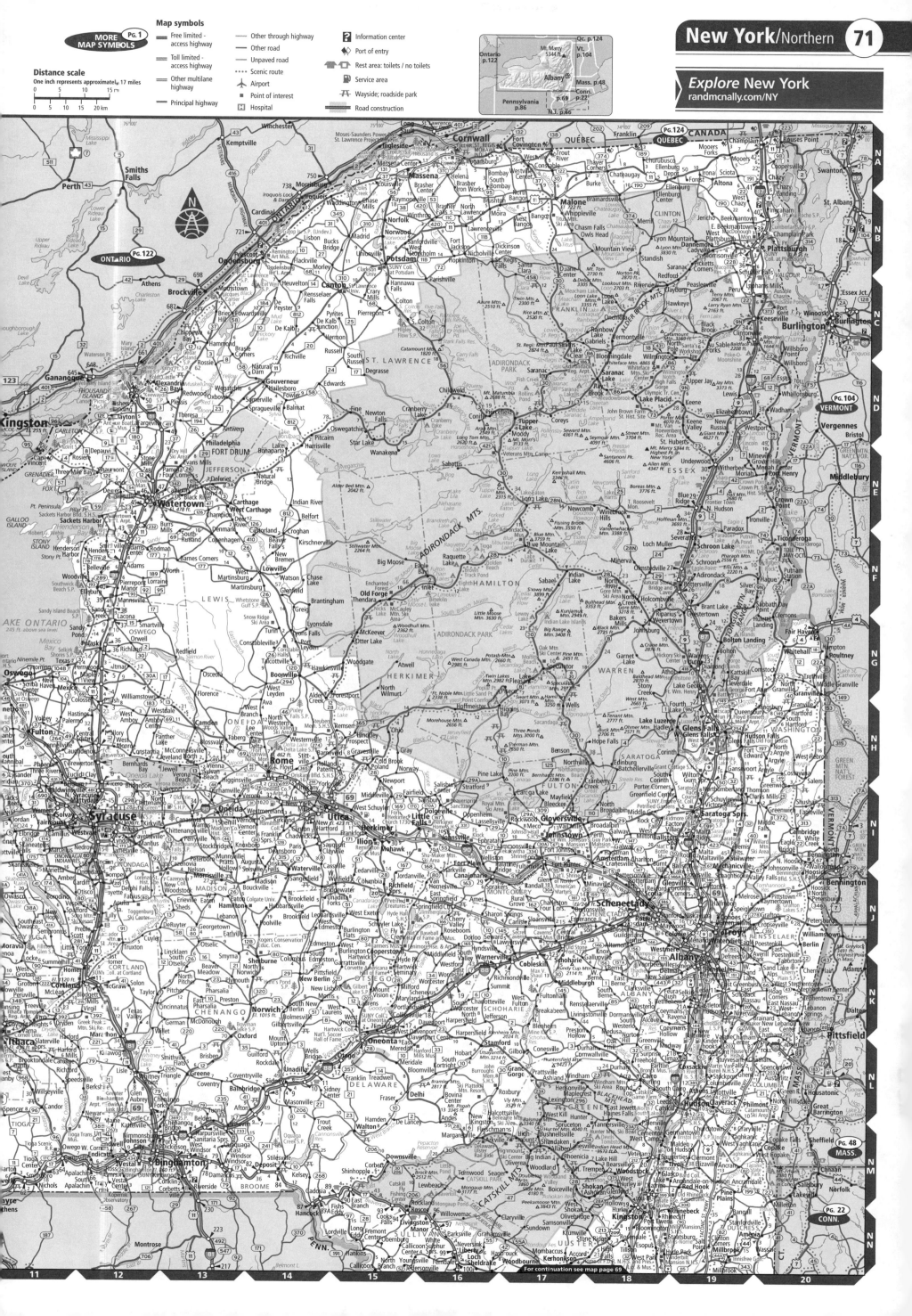

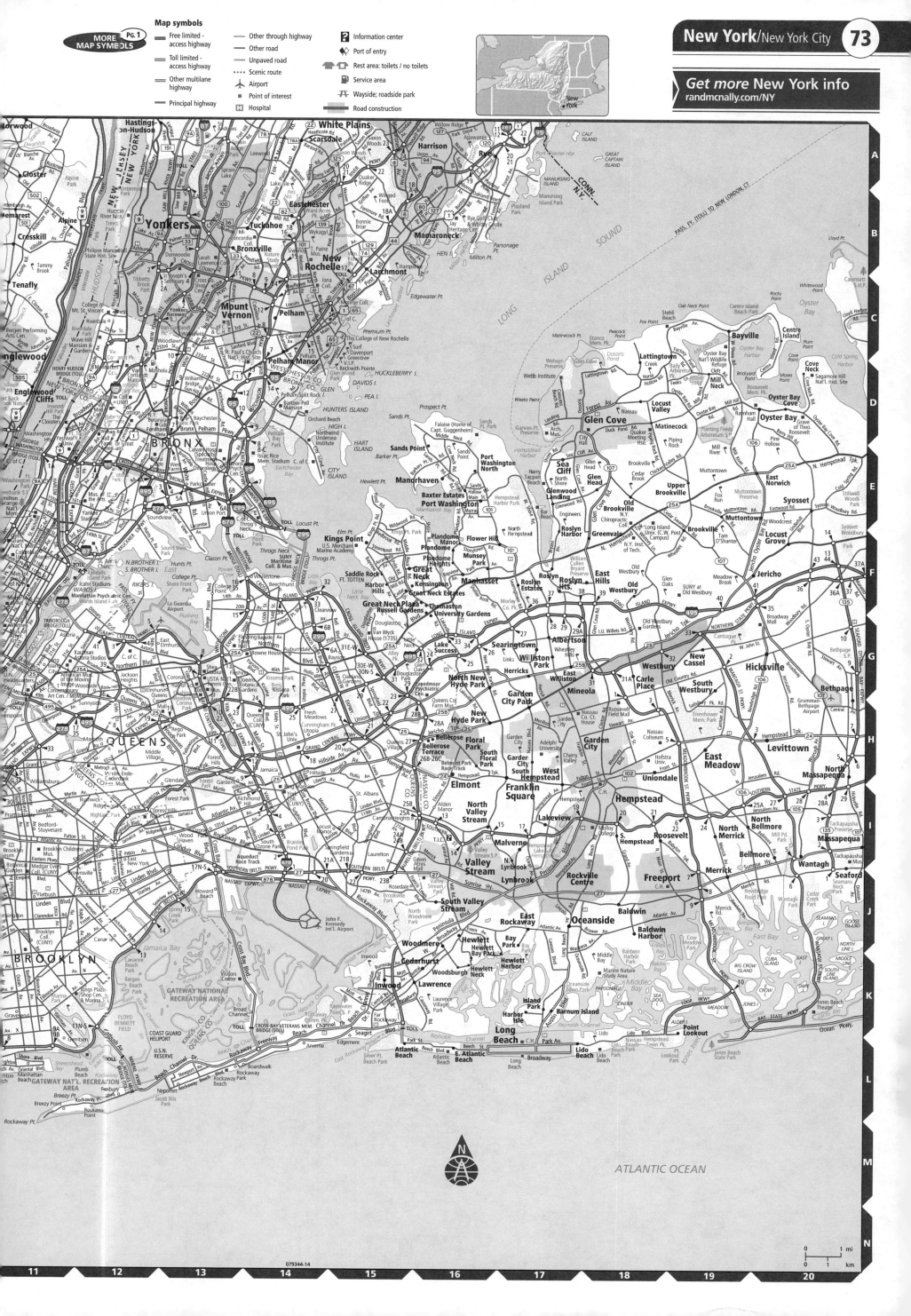

Nickname: The Tar Heel State
Land area: 48,711 sq. mi. (rank: 29th)
Population: 8,407,248 (rank: 11th)
Largest city: Charlotte, 584,658

INDEX OF CITIES Pg. 133

Mileage between cities	Asheville	Boone	Charlotte	Elizabeth City	Durham	Fayetteville	Greensboro	Greenville	Hickory	Knoxville, TN	Nags Head	New Bern	Roanoke Rapids	Raleigh	Rockingham	Rocky Mt.	Wilmington	Winston-Salem
ASHEVILLE		85	126	221	409	261	168	325	73	115	444	358	247	306	199	299	328	144
CHARLOTTE	126	118		143	331	139	97	247	63	229	366	280	169	228	75	221	204	83
FAYETTEVILLE	261	206	139	92	206		98	109	192	373	241	130	66	128	64	96	118	121
GREENSBORO	168	113	97	53	241	98		157	99	280	276	190	79	138	90	131	208	28
GREENVILLE	325	270	247	105	96	109	157		256	437	131	46	80	174	38	137	185	
RALEIGH	247	192	169	27	164	66	79	80	178	359	199	112	86		97	54	130	107
WILMINGTON	328	321	204	156	213	118	208	137	307	431	239	90	130	192	129	160		236
WINSTON-SALEM	144	89	83	81	269	121	28	185	75	256	304	218	107	166	109	159	236	

Total mileage through North Carolina

40 — 419 miles	85 — 233 miles
77 — 102 miles	95 — 182 miles

MORE MILEAGES Pg. 138

VIRGINIA Pg. 106
TENN. Pg. 94
S. CAROLINA Pg. 92
S. CAR. Pg. 92
GA. Pg. 28

Western North Carolina

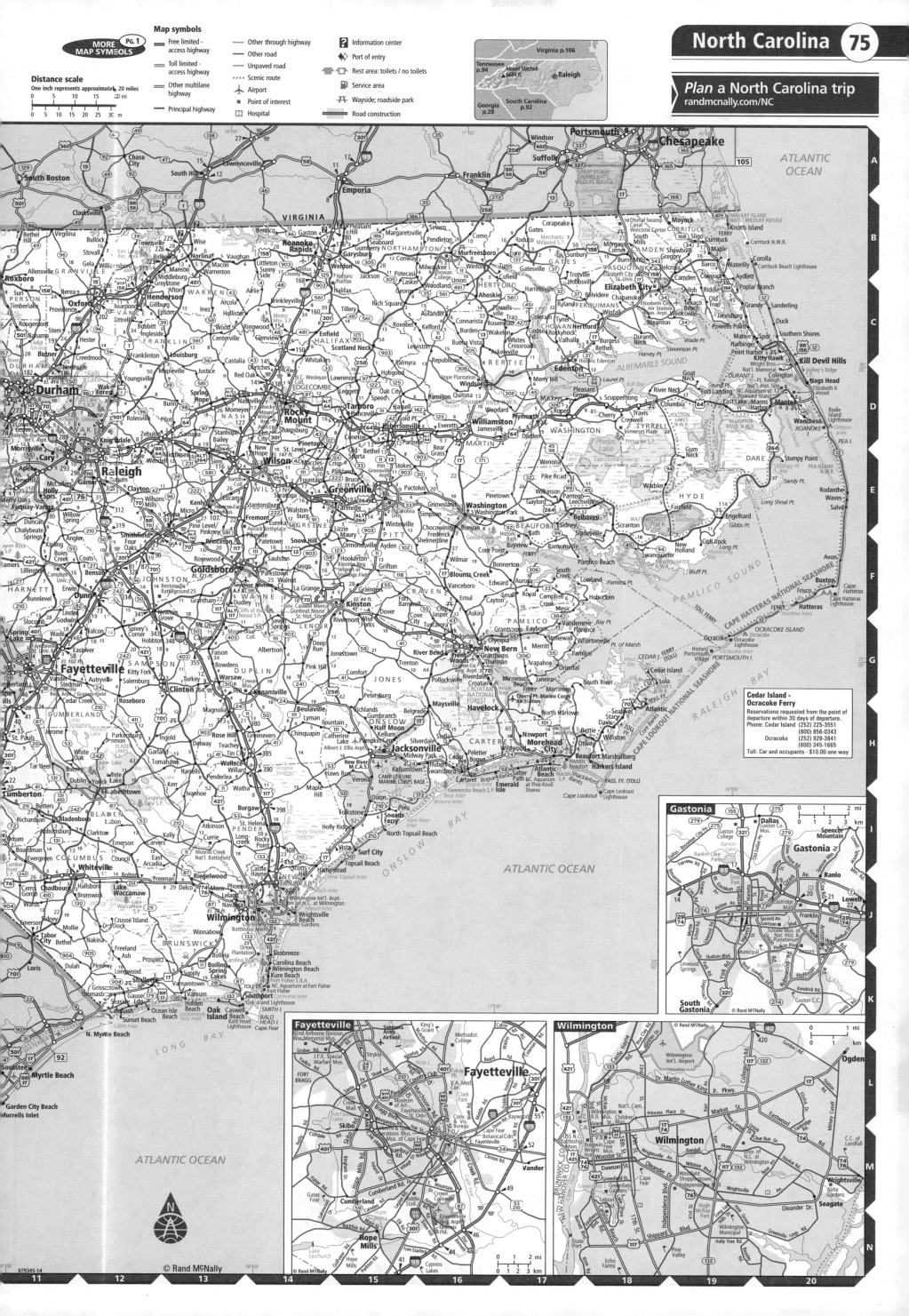

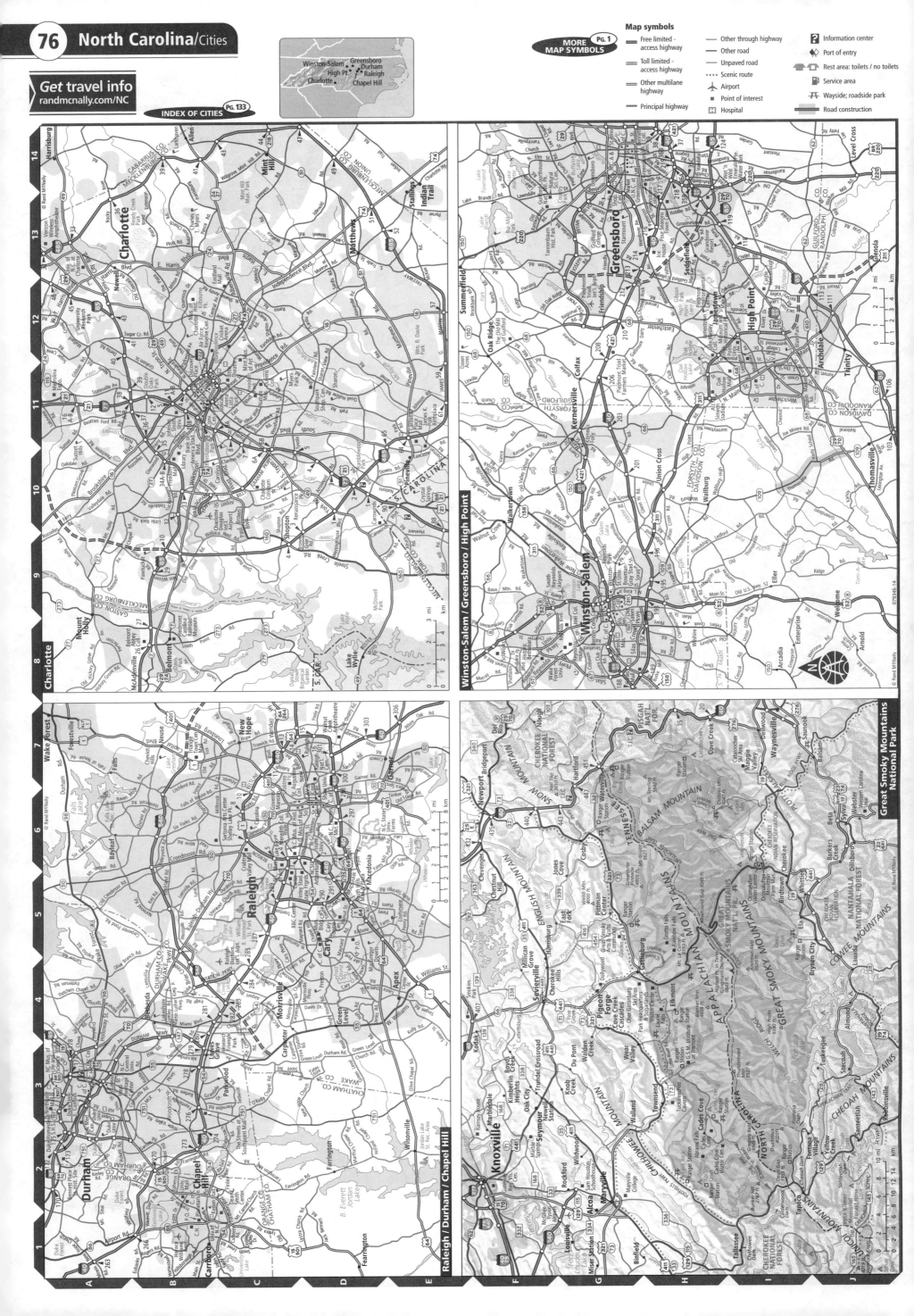

Get travel info
randmcnally.com/NC

INDEX OF CITIES PG. 133

MORE PG. 1
MAP SYMBOLS

Map symbols

Free limited-access highway
Toll limited-access highway
Other multilane highway
Principal highway
Other through highway
Other road
Unpaved road
Scenic route
Airport
Point of interest
Hospital

Information center
Port of entry
Rest area: toilets / no toilets
Service area
Wayside; roadside park
Road construction

Winston-Salem / Greensboro / High Point

Charlotte

Raleigh / Durham / Chapel Hill

Great Smoky Mountains National Park

Nickname: The Peace Garden State
Land area: 68,976 sq. mi. (rank: 17th)
Population: 633,837 (rank: 48th)
Largest city: Fargo, 91,484

Plan a trip
randmcnally.com/ND

Mileage between cities	Bismarck	Devils Lake	Dickinson	Fargo	Garrison	Grand Forks	Minot	Williston
BISMARCK		179	99	193	76	269	111	230
DEVILS LAKE	179		275	163	168	89	121	249
DICKINSON	99	275		289	148	365	183	131
FARGO	193	163	289		266	78	263	420
GARRISON	76	168	148	266		257	47	141
GRAND FORKS	269	89	365	78	257		210	338
MINOT	111	121	183	263	47	210		126
WILLISTON	230	249	131	420	141	338	126	

Total mileage through North Dakota
29 218 miles   2 359 miles
94 352 miles   83 265 miles

Distance scale
One inch represents approximately 30 miles
0   10   20 mi
0   10   20   30 km

MORE MILEAGES Pg. 138

INDEX OF CITIES Pg. 133

Manitoba p.121
Minn. p.54
Sask. p.120
Mont. p.60
South Dakota p.93

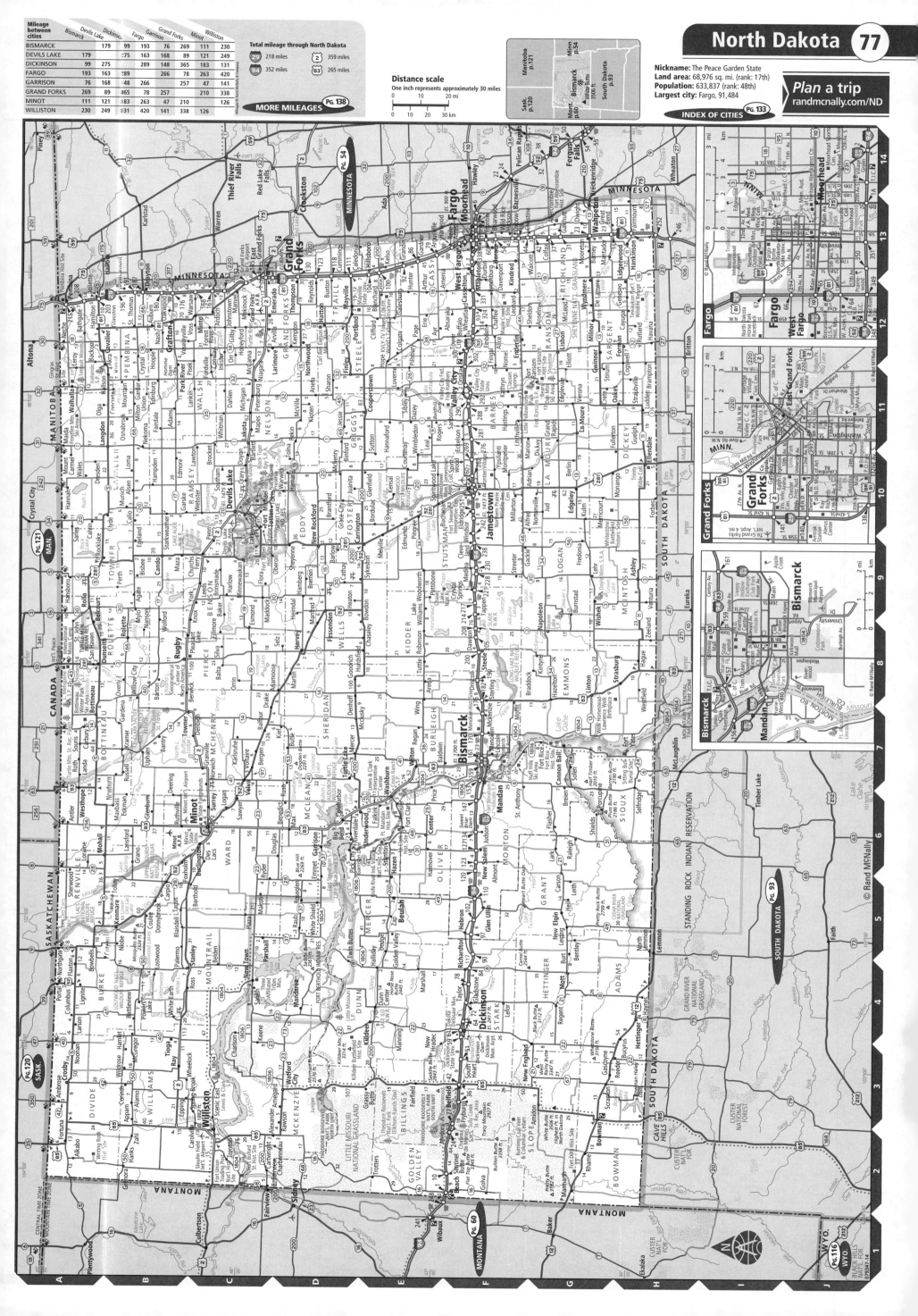

Nickname: The Buckeye State
Land area: 40,948 sq. mi. (rank: 35th)
Population: 11,435,798 (rank: 7th)
Largest city: Columbus, 728,432

INDEX OF CITIES — Pg. 133

MORE MILEAGES — Pg. 138

Mileage between cities

	Akron	Ashtabula	Canton	Cincinnati	Cleveland	Columbus	Defiance	Findlay	Lima	Mansfield	New Philadelphia	Pittsburgh, PA	Sandusky	Steubenville, OH	Toledo	Wheeling, WV	Youngstown
AKRON		84	20	238	39	128	184	133	152	66	104	45	107	85	137	101	48
CLEVELAND	39	59	58	252		142	162	124	157	80	118	83	62	135	115	139	76
COLUMBUS	128	198	127	111	142		150	98	93	66	120	183	113	150	142	125	176
FINDLAY	133	183	132	157	124	98	51		33	69	138	240	63	192	43	194	181
LIMA	152	216	151	126	157	93	42	33		88	157	259	96	211	74	219	200
MANSFIELD	66	136	65	176	80	66	121	69	88		71	173	54	125	103	127	114
TOLEDO	137	174	156	198	115	142	59	43	74	103	92	157	60	233		230	174
YOUNGSTOWN	48	59	68	286	76	221	181	200	114	152	93	70	122	70	213	97	

Total mileage through Ohio

Route	Miles
71	248 miles
80	237 miles
75	211 miles
77	245 miles

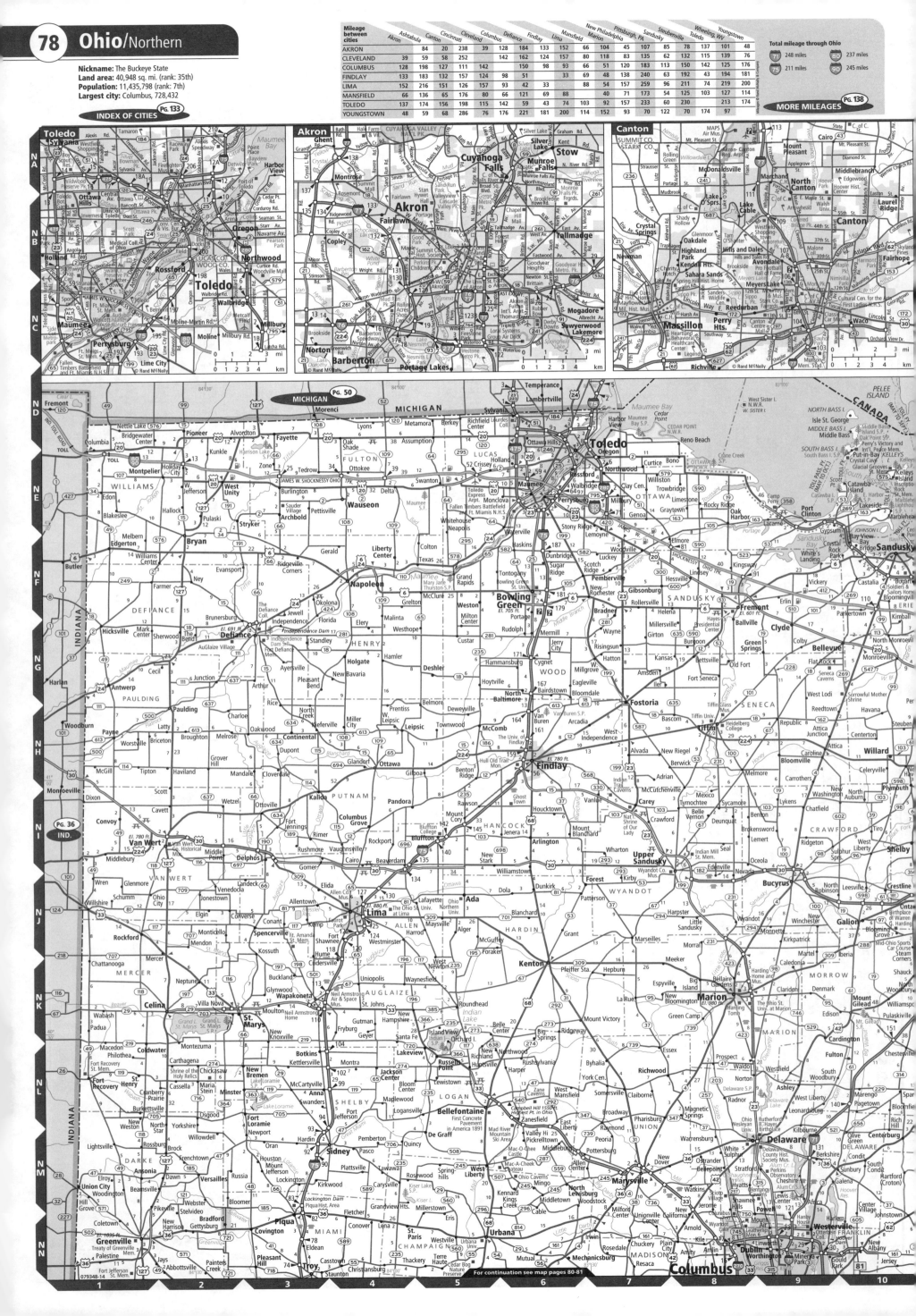

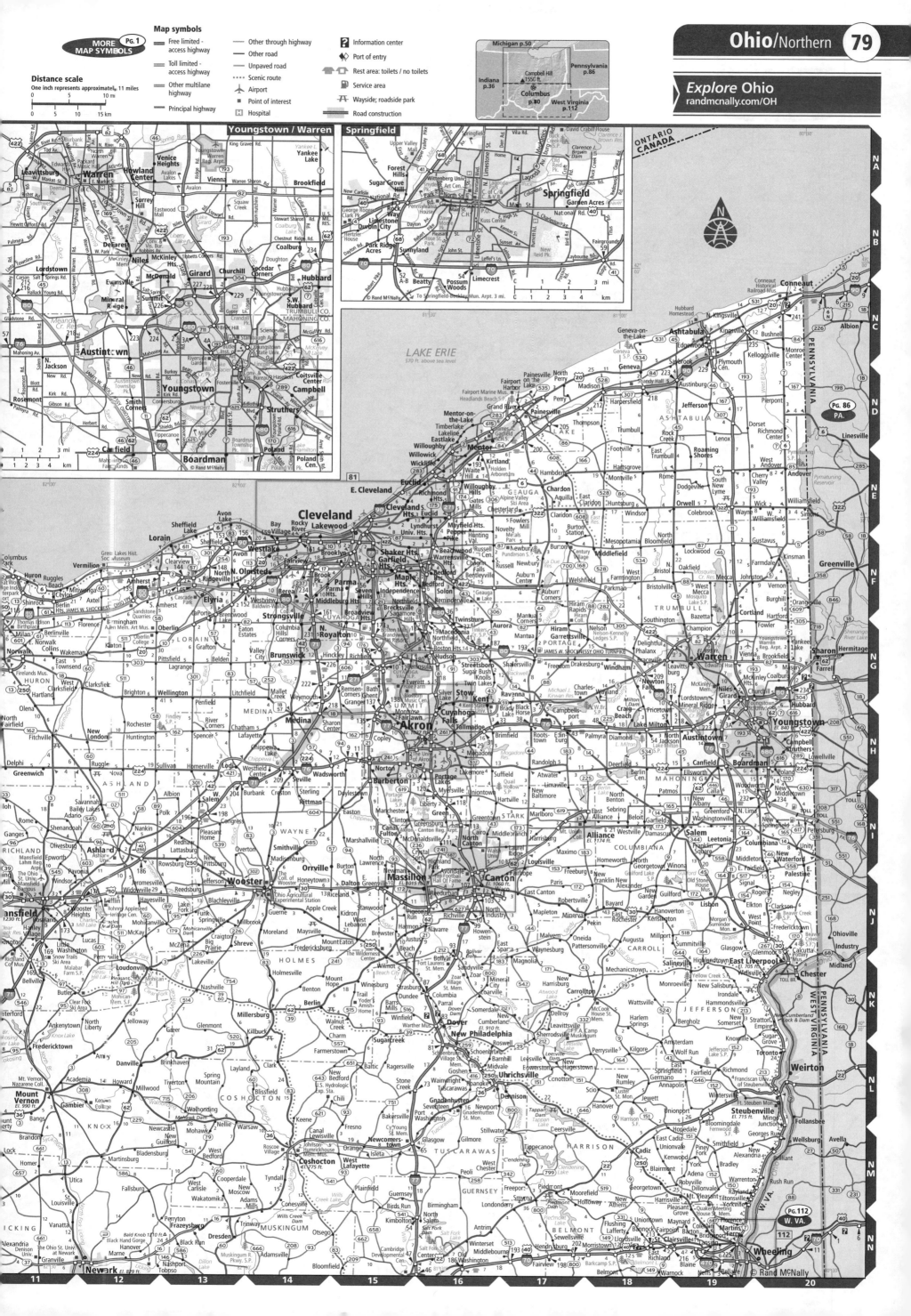

Explore Ohio
randmcnally.com/OH

Nickname: The Buckeye State
Land area: 40,948 sq. mi. (rank: 35th)
Population: 11,435,798 (rank: 7th)
Largest city: Columbus, 728,432

INDEX OF CITIES Pg. 133

Mileage between cities	Athens	Cambridge	Chillicothe	Cincinnati	Cleveland	Columbus	Dayton	Gallipolis	Huntington, WV	Jackson	Lancaster	Marietta	Portsmouth	Springfield	Washington C.H.	Wheeling, WV	Wilmington	Zanesville
CINCINNATI	164	185	112		252	111	54	154	141	124	135	232	121	80	81	232	54	162
COLUMBUS	74	78	48	111	142		73	108	138	77	30	125	91	45	41	125	64	55
DAYTON	148	152	82	52	214	73		144	174	113	104	199	127	28	51	199	37	129
GALLIPOLIS	48	121	63	154	249	108	144		36	32	85	70	54	148	95	163	115	106
MARIETTA	44	50	114	106	232	166	125	199	70	137	86	83		131	171	138	92	185	70
PORTSMOUTH	87	161	43	121	232	91	127	54	47	47	86	131		131	79	208	98	138
SPRINGFIELD	120	124	74	80	186	45	28	148	178	117	76	171	131		43	171	39	101
ZANESVILLE	58	23	95	162	144	55	129	106	205	89	45	70	138	101	92	70	115	

Total mileage through Ohio

70	225 miles	75	211 miles
71	248 miles	77	160 miles

MORE MILEAGES Pg. 138

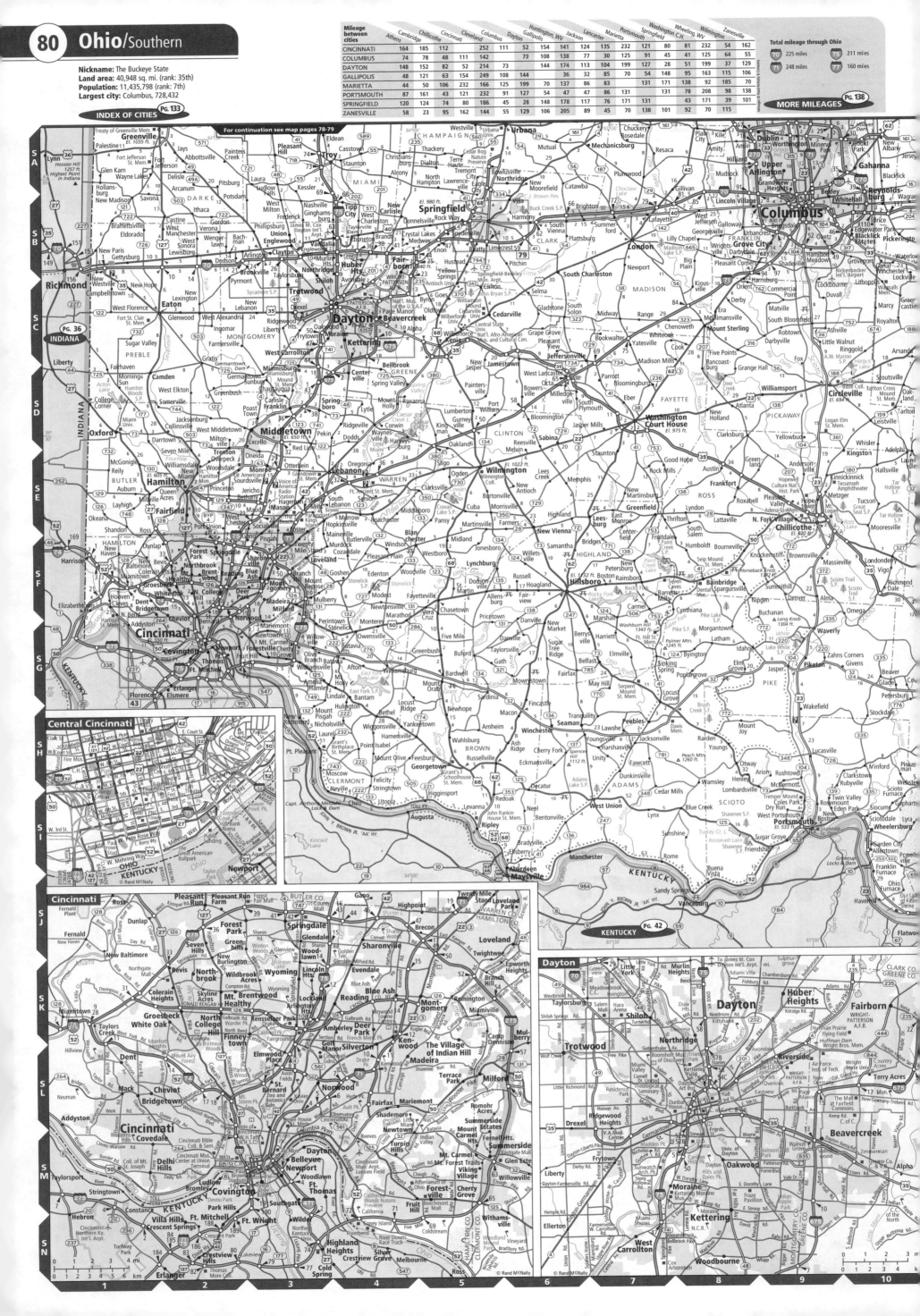

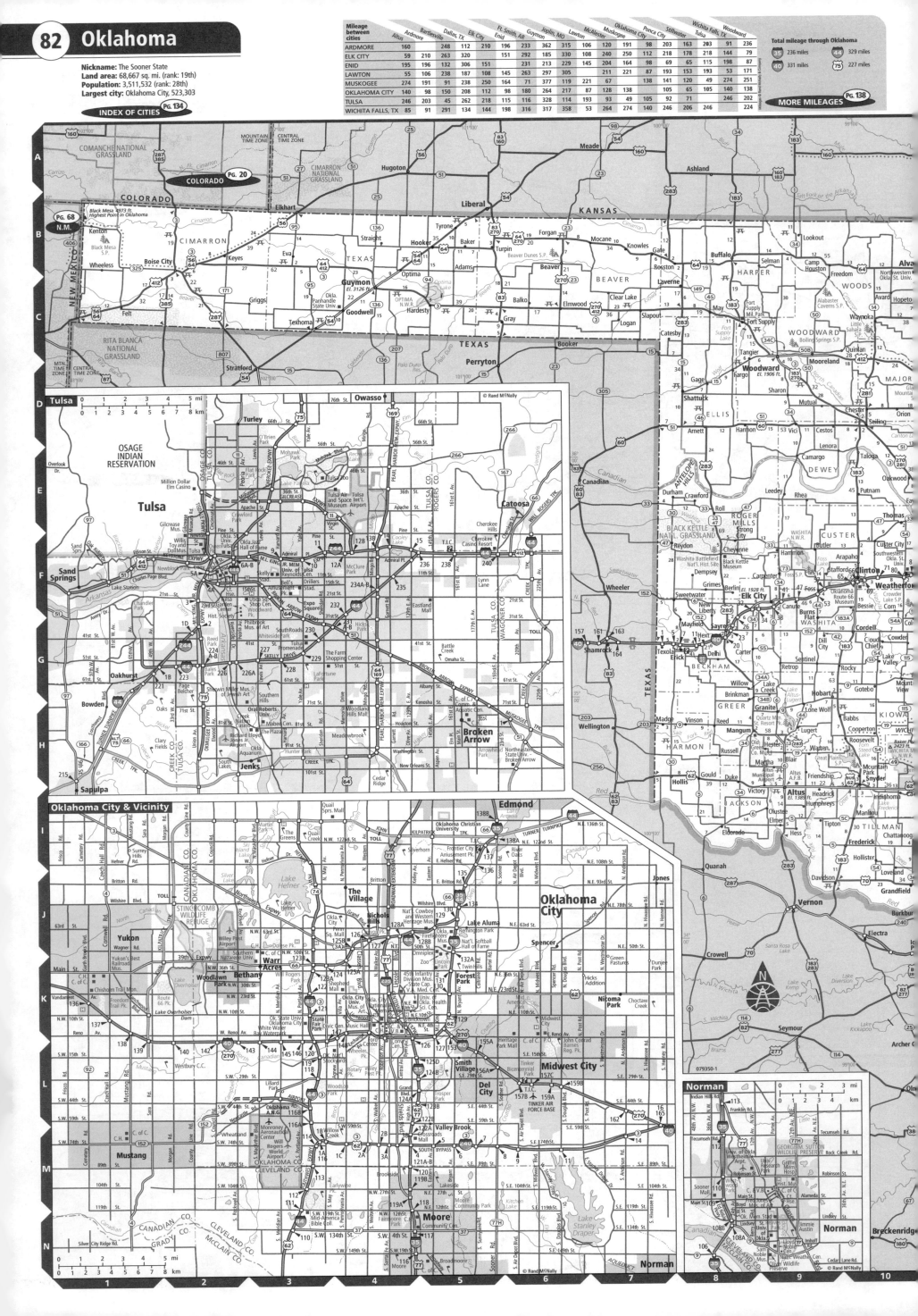

82 Oklahoma

Nickname: The Sooner State
Land area: 68,667 sq. mi. (rank: 19th)
Population: 3,511,532 (rank: 28th)
Largest city: Oklahoma City, 523,303

INDEX OF CITIES PG. 134

Mileage between cities	Altus	Ardmore	Bartlesville	Dallas, TX	Elk City	Enid	Ft. Smith, AR	Guymon	Joplin, MO	Lawton	McAlester	Muskogee	Oklahoma City	Ponca City	Stillwater	Tulsa	Wichita Falls, TX	Woodward
ARDMORE	160		248	112	210	196	233	362	315	106	120	191	98	203	163	203	91	236
ELK CITY	59	210	263	320		151	292	185	330	108	240	250	112	218	178	218	144	79
ENID	195	196	132	306	151		231	213	229	145	204	164	98	69	65	115	198	87
LAWTON	55	106	238	187	108	145	263	297	305		211	221	87	191	153	193	53	171
MUSKOGEE	274	191	91	238	250	164	71	377	119	221	67		138	141	120	49	274	251
OKLAHOMA CITY	140	98	150	208	112	98	180	264	217	87	128	138		105	65	105	140	138
TULSA	246	203	45	262	218	115	116	328	114	193	93	49	105		92	71	246	202
WICHITA FALLS, TX	85	91	291	134	144	198	316	317	358	53	264	274	140	246	206	246		224

Total mileage through Oklahoma
35 236 miles
40 331 miles
44 329 miles
75 227 miles

MORE MILEAGES PG. 138

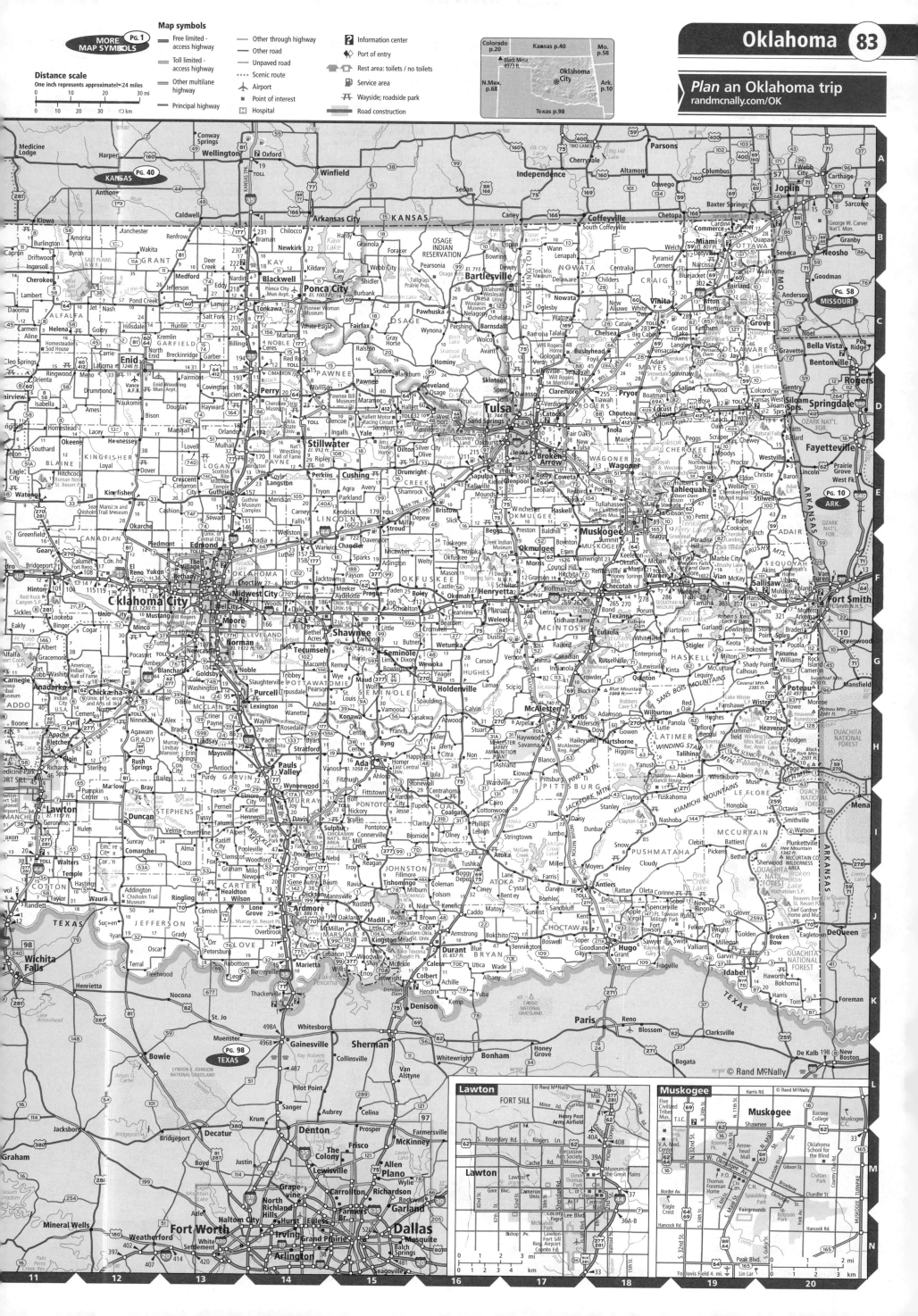

Nickname: The Beaver State
Land area: 95,997 sq. mi. (rank: 10th)
Population: 3,559,596 (rank: 27th)
Largest city: Portland, 538,544

INDEX OF CITIES PG. 134

MORE MILEAGES PG. 138

Mileage between cities	Astoria	Bend	Brookings	Burns	Coos Bay	Crater Lake Np	Eugene	Grants Pass	John Day	Klamath Falls	Lakeview	Medford	Ontario	Pendleton	Portland	Salem	The Dalles
BEND	257		296	130	222	128	106	115	194	153	139	175	175	261	243	161	132	133
BURNS	387	130	426		352	258	236	245	324	70	236	140	305	131	199	291	262	263
CORVALLIS	177	128	227	258	120		183	45	263	216	303	208	389	288	81	36	165
EUGENE	205	115	214	245	107	45	142		141	250	175	263	167	376	316	109	64	193
MEDFORD	368	170	79	328	79	167	27	328	78	172		436	418	272	227	356
ONTARIO	466	261	557	131	483	389	367	376	455	133	367	271	436		164	371	418	287
PENDLETON	302	243	515	199	469	288	349	316	453	129	382	339	418	164		207	254	123
PORTLAND	100	161	308	291	201	81	247	109	246	265	280	336	272	371	207		47	84

Total mileage through Oregon
- I-5: 308 miles
- I-84: 375 miles
- I-82: 11 miles
- US 101: 348 miles

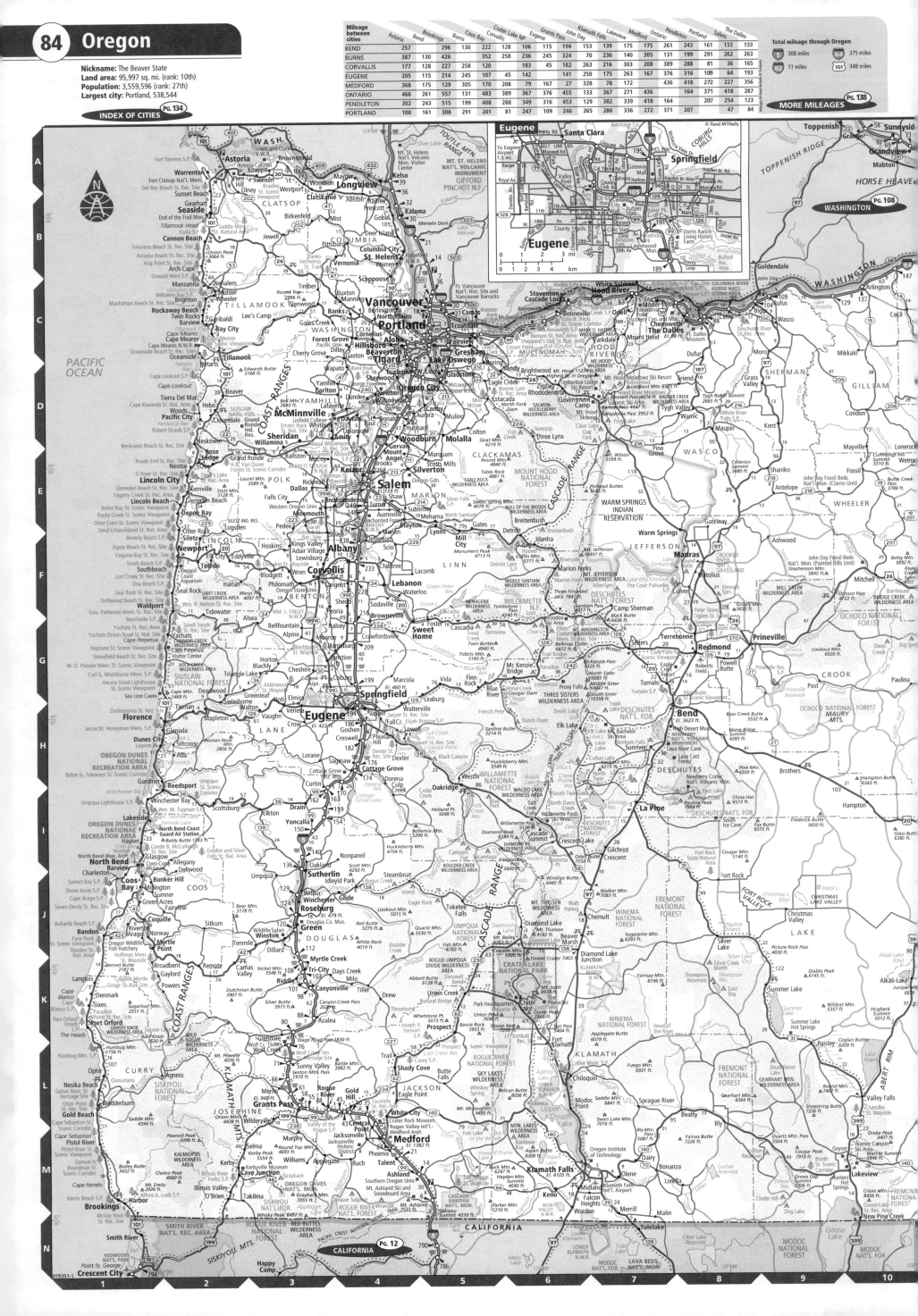

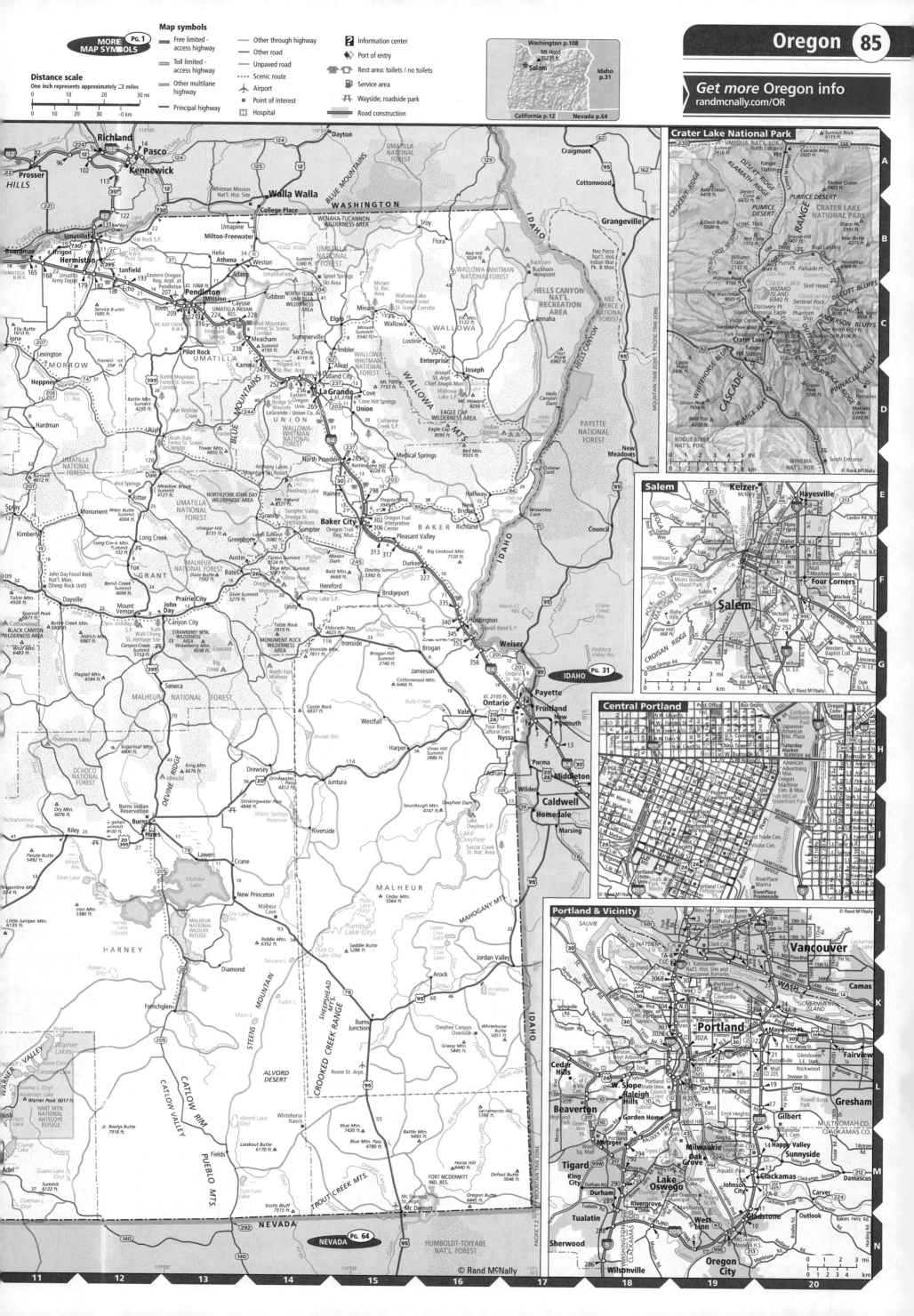

Nickname: The Keystone State
Land area: 44,817 sq. mi. (rank: 32nd)
Population: 12,365,455 (rank: 6th)
Largest city: Philadelphia, 1,479,339

INDEX OF CITIES PG. 134

For continuation see map pages 88-89

MORE MILEAGES PG. 138

Mileage between cities	Altoona	Beaver Falls	Bedford	Chambersburg	Du Bois	Erie	Greensburg	Harrisburg	Indiana	Johnstown	Kittanning	Meadville	New Castle	Philadelphia	Pittsburgh	State College	Uniontown	Warren	Washington	Williamsport	Youngstown, OH
ALTOONA		132	35	92	73	203	73	112	45	78	168	144	238	95	43	112	133	127	105	160
ERIE	203	117	230	283	150		156	300	154	191	123	43	98	426	127	209	184	69	150	261	100
HARRISBURG	134	239	105	54	151	300	181		178	140	204	265	355	114	204	89	185	211	212	89	267
JOHNSTOWN	45	105	41	98	87	191	46	140	29		55	156	117	244	68	87	157	108	149	133
NEW CASTLE	144	22	156	209	110	98	82	251	82	110	51	63		355	54	169	110	74	221	16
PITTSBURGH	95	40	109	162	110	98	127	33	204	60	68	42	92	54	308		137	47	147	29	199	70
STATE COLLEGE	43	174	77	135	60	209	115	89	94	87	120	174	169	199	137		154	120	169	66	171
WILLIAMSPORT	105	240	139	135	112	261	177	89	156	149	172	226	221	184	199	66	216	172	231		223

Total mileage through Pennsylvania

| 70 | 168 miles | 76 | 183 miles |
| 80 | 311 miles | 90 | 46 miles |

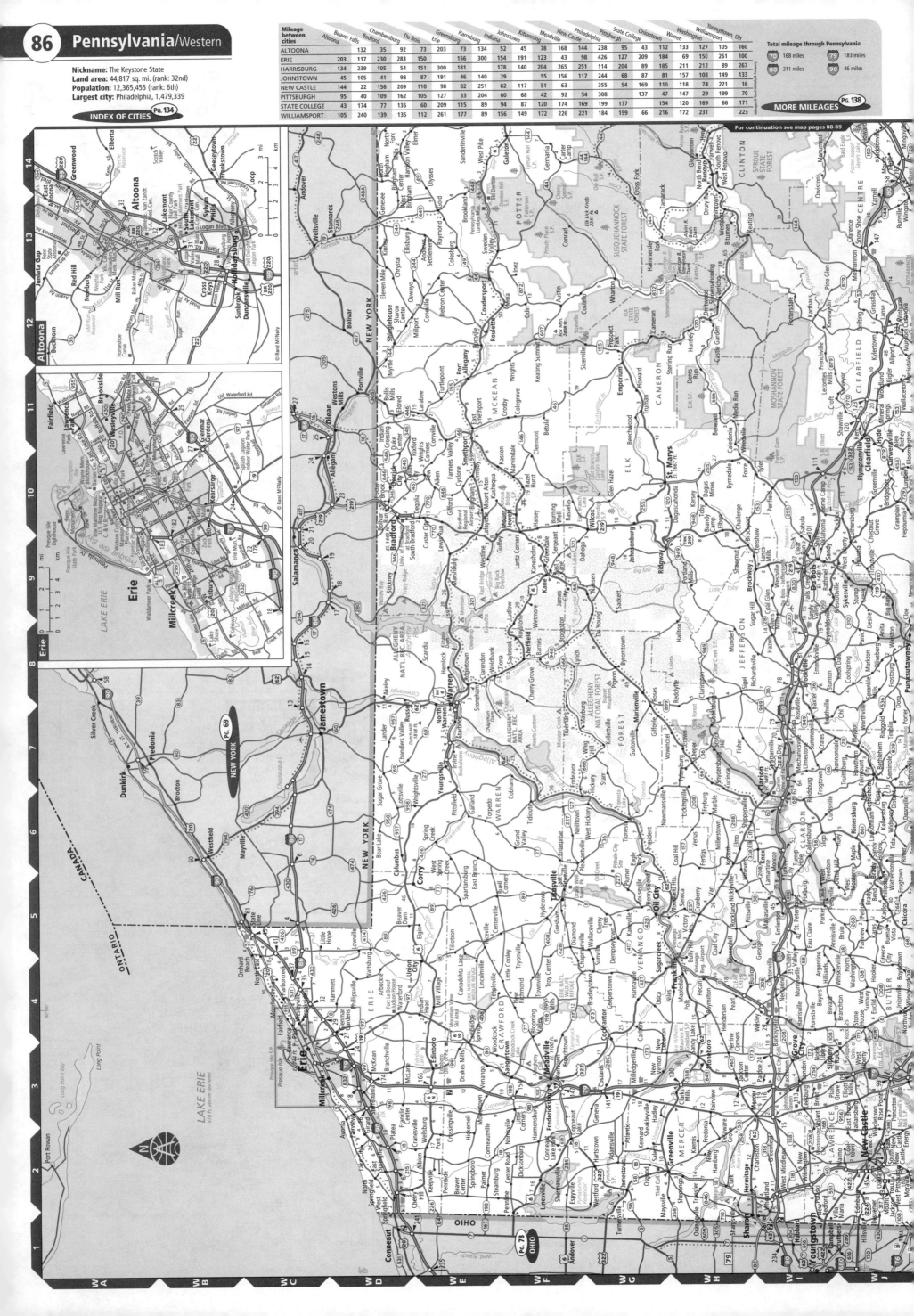

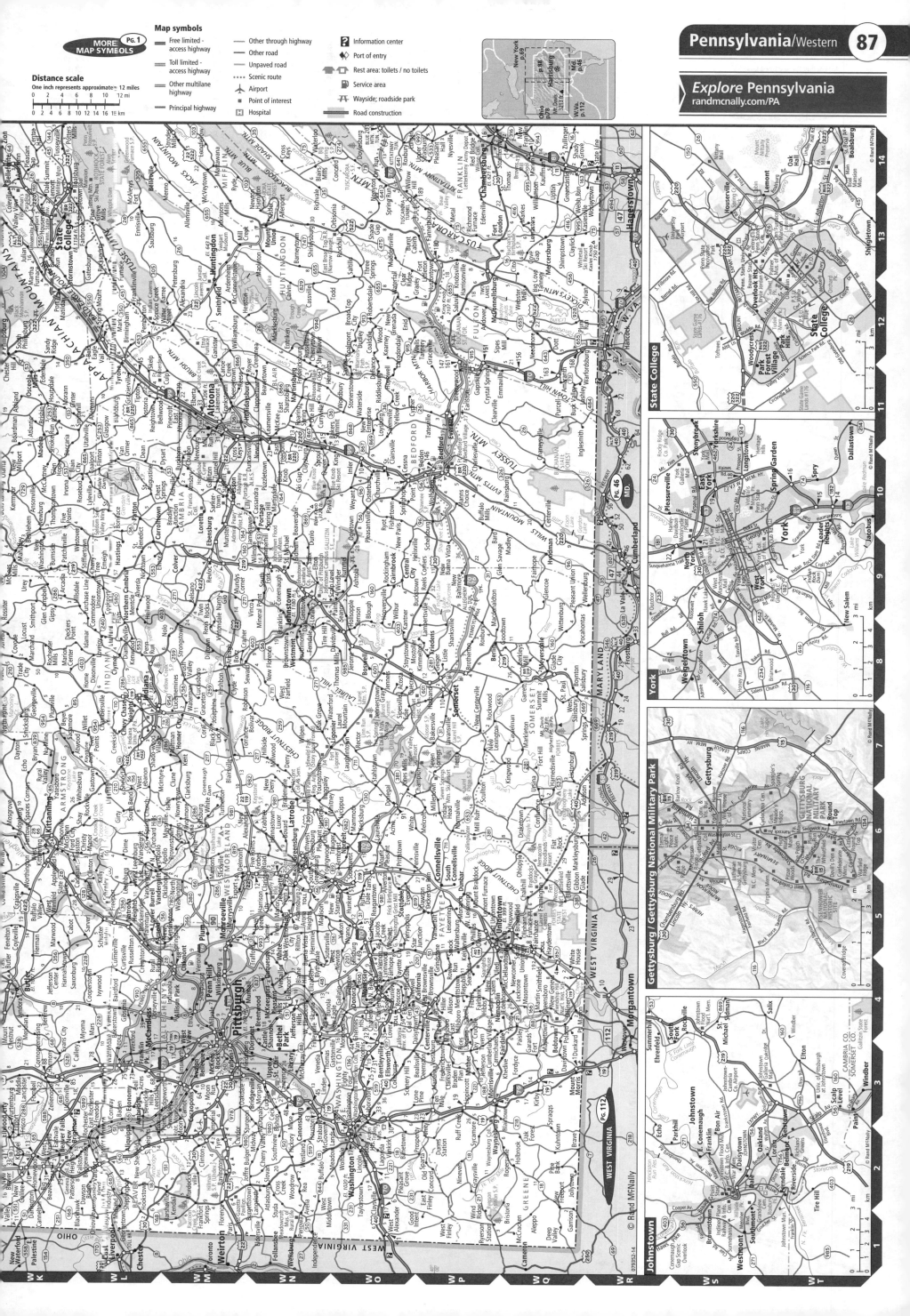

Explore Pennsylvania
randmcnally.com/PA

Nickname: The Keystone State
Land area: 44,817 sq. mi. (rank: 32nd)
Population: 12,365,455 (rank: 6th)
Largest city: Philadelphia, 1,479,339

PG. 134 INDEX OF CITIES

Mileage between cities	Allentown	Altoona	Baltimore MD	Binghamton, NY	Chambersburg	Easton	Gettysburg	Harrisburg	Hazleton	Lancaster	Mansfield	Philadelphia	Pittsburgh	Port Jervis, NY	Reading	Scranton	State College	Trenton, NJ	Wilkes-Barre	Williamsport	York
ALLENTOWN		214	162	134	134	19	123	84	49	72	183	66	284	83	34	76	169	78	62	134	110
CHAMBERSBURG	134	92	97	234		149	25	54	129	88	188	158	162	231	111	170	135	177	156	135	71
HARRISBURG	84	134	88	184	54	99	39		79	44	138	114	204	181	67	120	89	133	106	89	36
PHILADELPHIA	66	238	102	184	158	81	143	114	99	83	233		308	145	65	126	199	35	112	184	109
READING	34	191	112	158	112	53	96	67	53	34	163	65	261	119		100	152	84	86	114	60
SCRANTON	76	192	198	59	170	68	159	120	47	154	104	126	286	61	100		153	138	16	106	146
STATE COLLEGE	169	43	173	217	135	190	126	89	128	129	111	199	137	214	152	153		218	139	66	121
WILLIAMSPORT	134	105	173	125	135	143	126	89	81	129	49	184	199	167	114	106	66	196	70		121

Total mileage through Pennsylvania

76	350 miles
80	311 miles
81	232 miles
95	51 miles

PG. 138 MORE MILEAGES

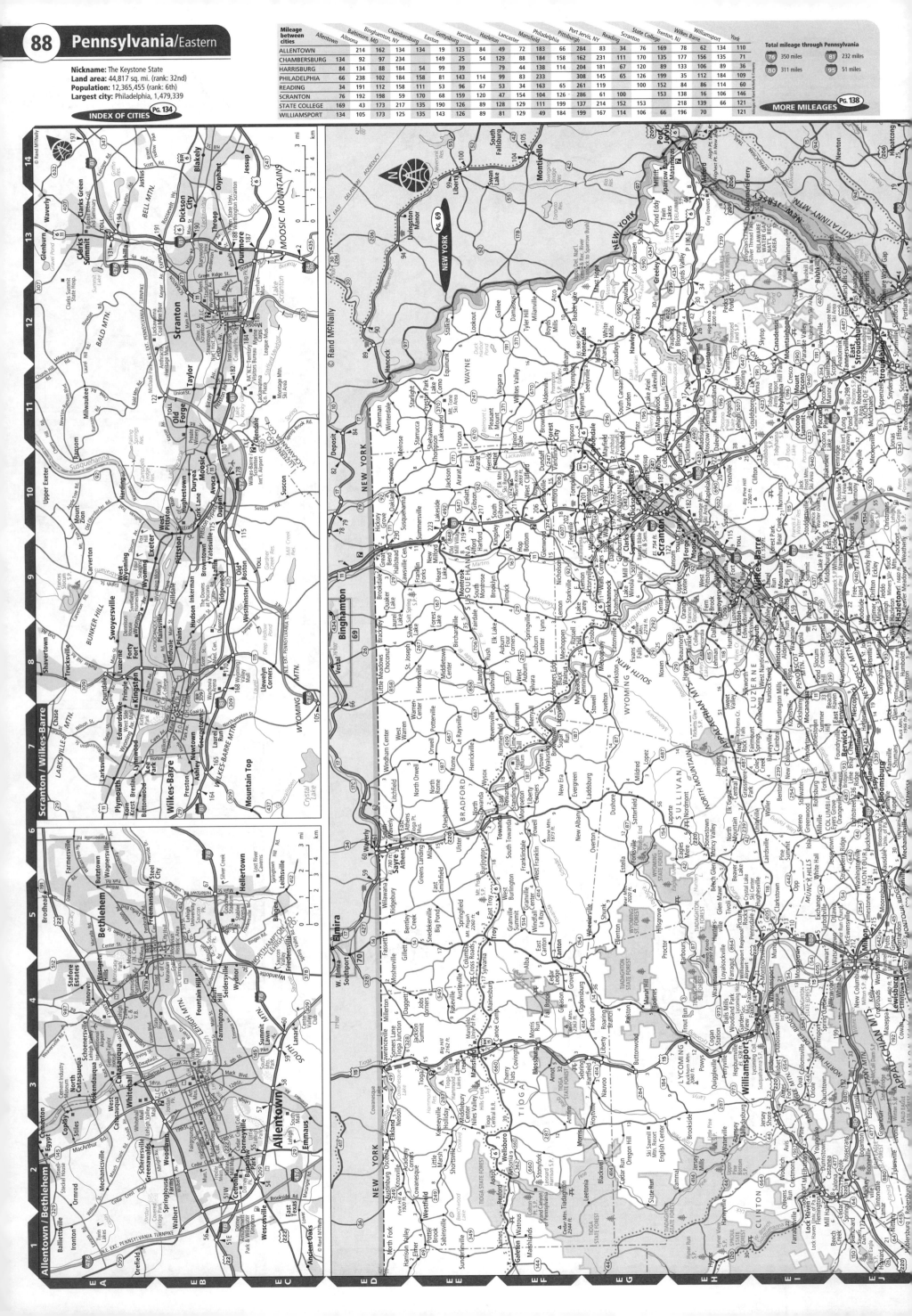

Plan a Pennsylvania trip
randmcnally.com/PA

Map symbols

Free limited - access highway
Toll limited - access highway
Other multilane highway
Principal highway
Other through highway
Other road
Unpaved road
Scenic route
Airport
Point of interest
Hospital

Information center
Port of entry
Rest area: toilets / no toilets
Service area
Wayside; roadside park
Road construction

MORE MAP SYMBOLS PG. 1

Distance scale
One inch represents approximately 2 miles

Reading

Lancaster

Harrisburg

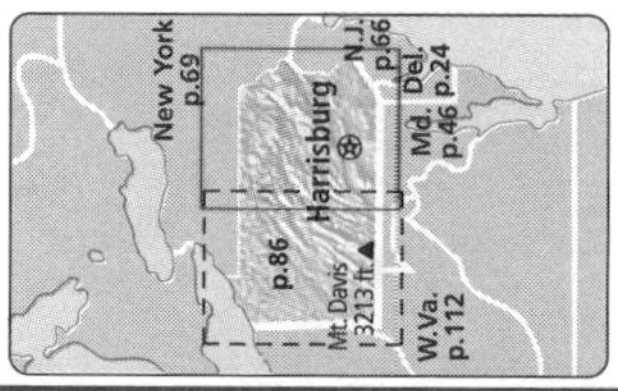

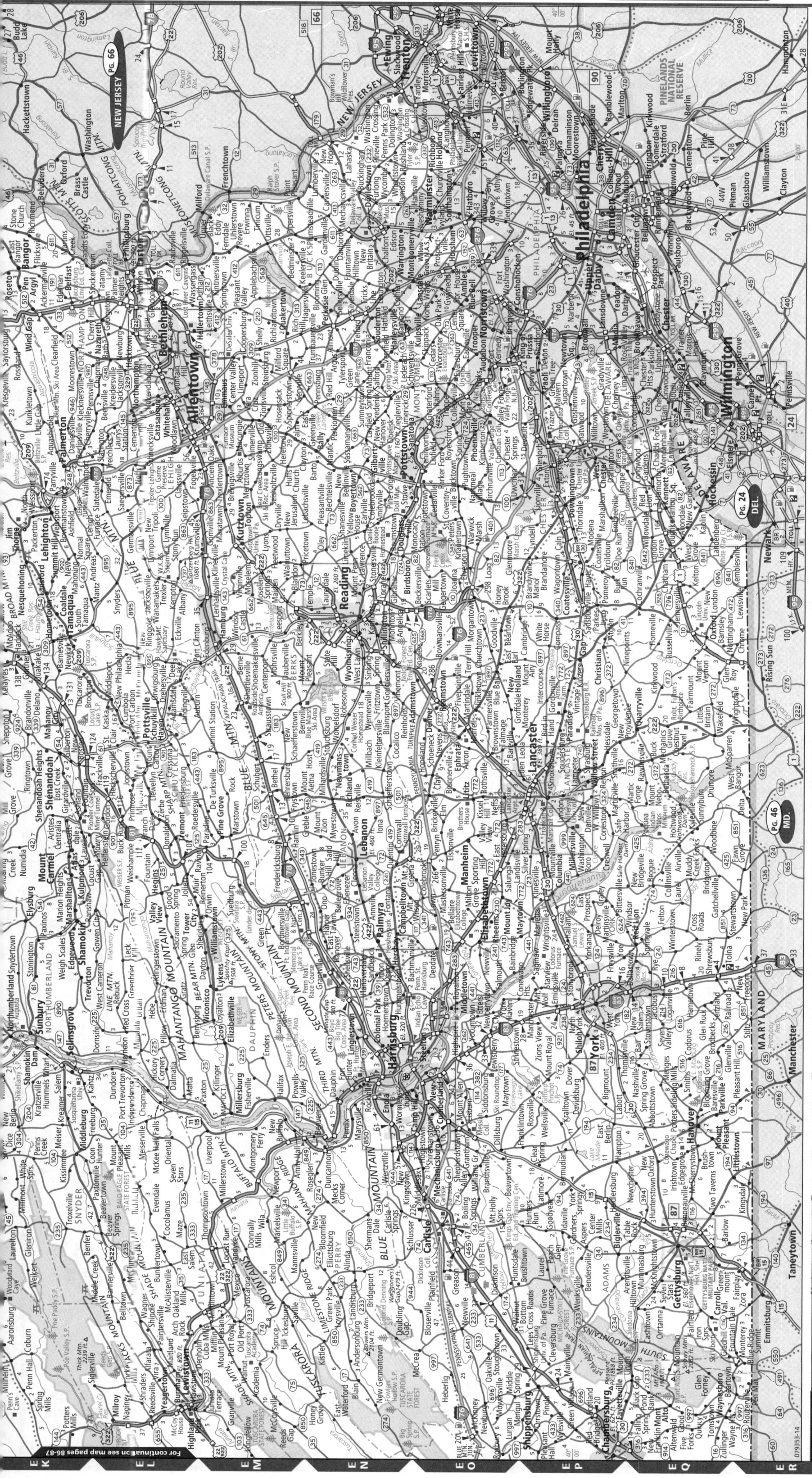

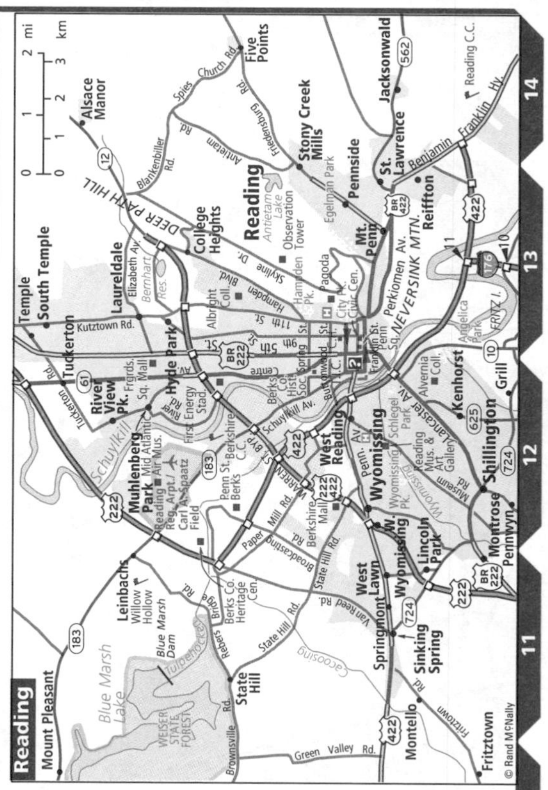

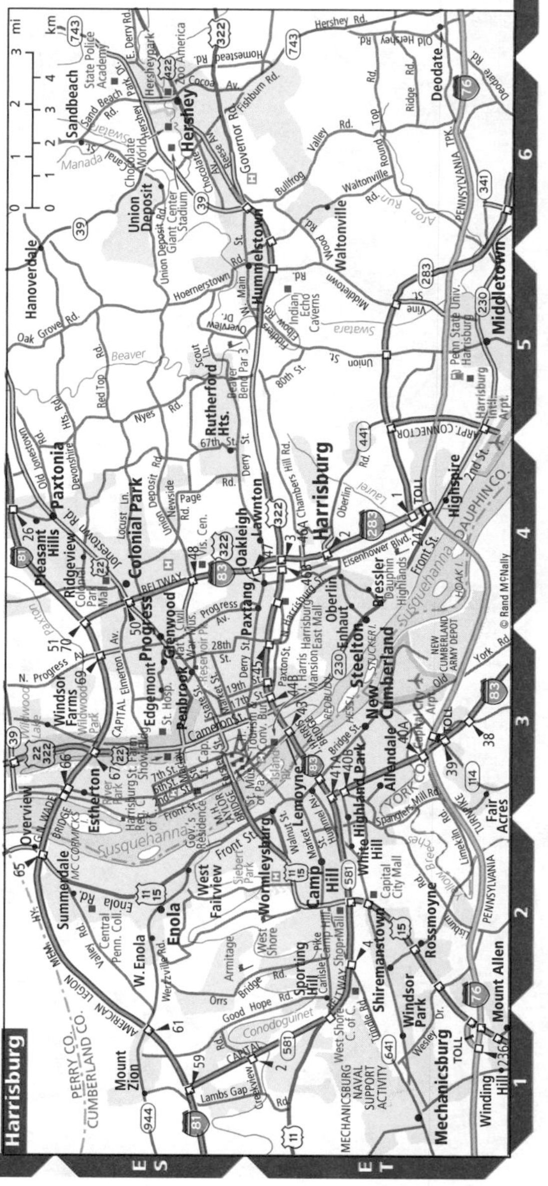

For continuation see map pages 86-87

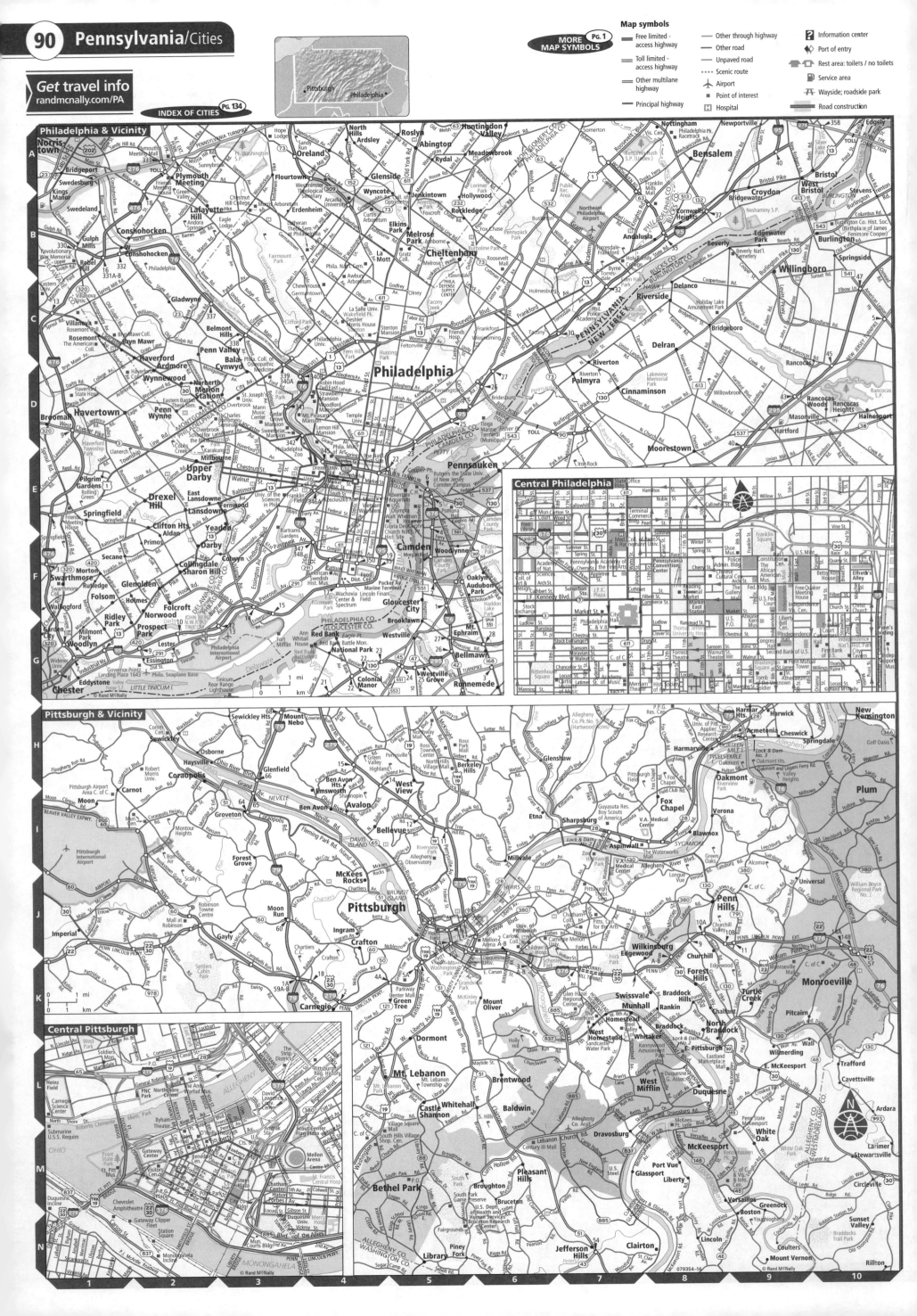

Nickname: The Ocean State
Land area: 1,045 sq. mi. (rank: 50th)
Population: 1,076,164 (rank: 43rd)
Largest city: Providence, 176,365

Plan a trip
randmcnally.com/RI

Mileage between cities	Chepachet	Fall River, MA	Kingston	Newport	Providence	Warwick	Westerly	Woonsocket	Worcester, MA
FALL RIVER, MA	36		37	23	16	26	58	32	59
KINGSTON	44	37		16	30	25	24	47	74
NEWPORT	46	23	16		32	27	37	49	76
PROVIDENCE	20	16	30	32		10	42	16	43
WARWICK	27	26	25	27	10		37	26	53
WESTERLY	56	58	24	37	42	37		59	70
WOONSOCKET	17	32	47	49	16	26	59		32
WORCESTER, MA	37	59	74	76	43	53	70	32	

Total mileage through Rhode Island
95: 42 miles   6: 31 miles
1: 60 miles

Distance scale
One inch represents approximately 6 miles
0 1 2 3 4 mi
0 1 2 3 4 5 6 km

MORE MILEAGES Pg. 138

Massachusetts p.48
Jerimoth Hill
812 ft.
Providence
Connecticut p.22

INDEX OF CITIES Pg. 134

© Rand McNally
079355-14
© Rand McNally

Nickname: The Palmetto State
Land area: 30,109 sq. mi. (rank: 40th)
Population: 4,147,152 (rank: 25th)
Largest city: Columbia, 117,357

Get travel info
randmcnally.com/SC

INDEX OF CITIES   PG. 134

Mileage between cities	Anderson	Augusta, GA	Beaufort	Charleston	Charlotte, NC	Columbia	Fayetteville, NC	Georgetown	Greenwood	Myrtle Beach	Orangeburg	Savannah, GA	Spartanburg	Sumter
AUGUSTA, GA	104		122	176	158	68	233	212	59	214	85	140	120	116
CHARLESTON	223	176	69		207	113	217	59	196	95	77	105	202	99
CHARLOTTE, NC	134	158	229	207		91	139	190	123	173	136	249	75	115
COLUMBIA	114	68	135	113	91		166	128	87	147	42	155	93	44
FLORENCE	189	146	152	130	105	79	91	85	162	68	92	172	168	45
MYRTLE BEACH	257	214	170	95	173	147	127	36	230		144	206	236	97
SAVANNAH, GA	265	140	39	105	249	155	259	170	204	206	119		244	141
SPARTANBURG	60	120	224	202	75	93	255	238	64	236	131	244		137

Total mileage through South Carolina

26 — 142 miles	85 — 106 miles
20 — 221 miles	95 — 199 miles

Distance scale
One inch represents approximately 23 miles

0 5 10 15 20 mi
0 5 10 15 20 25 30 km

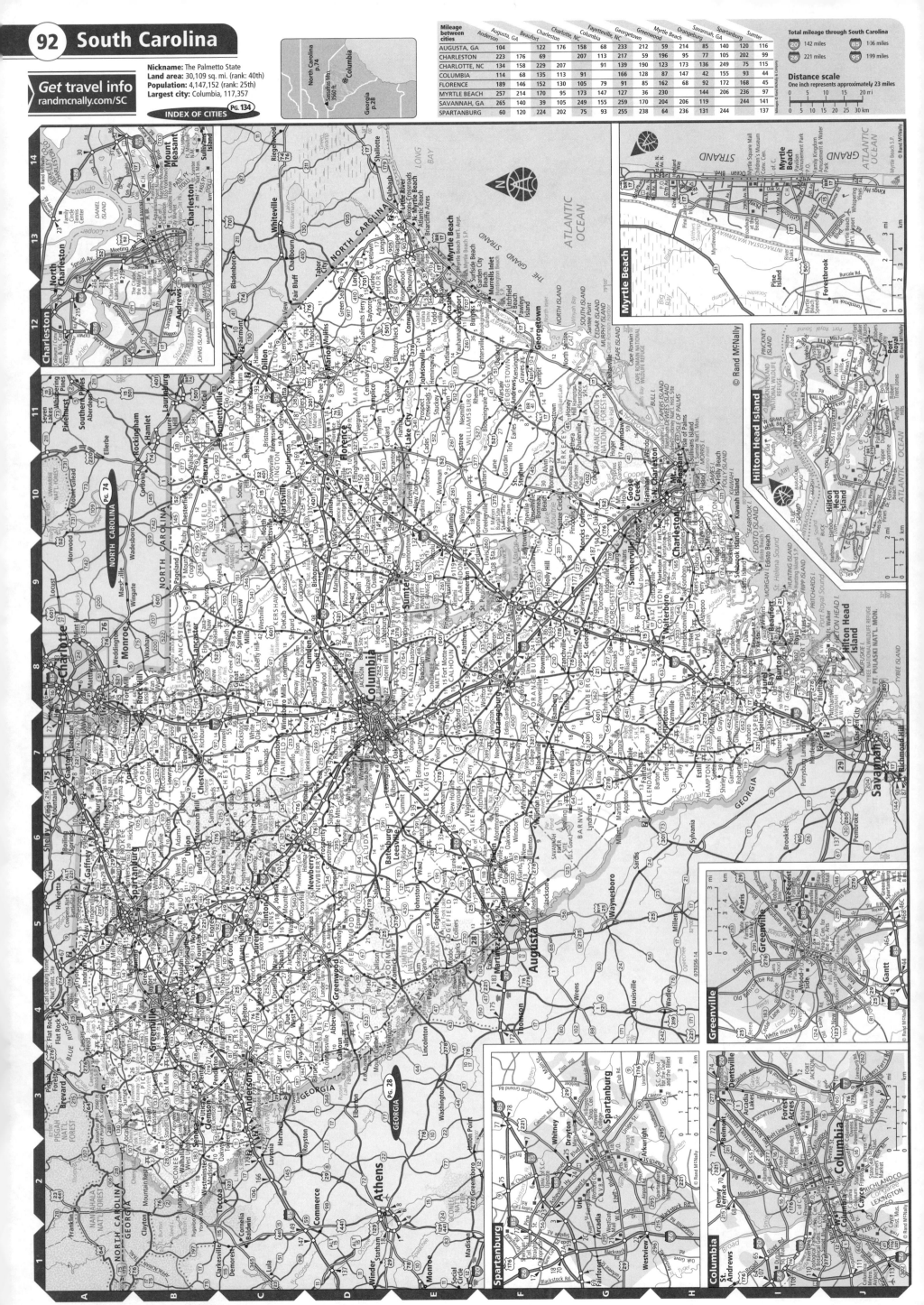

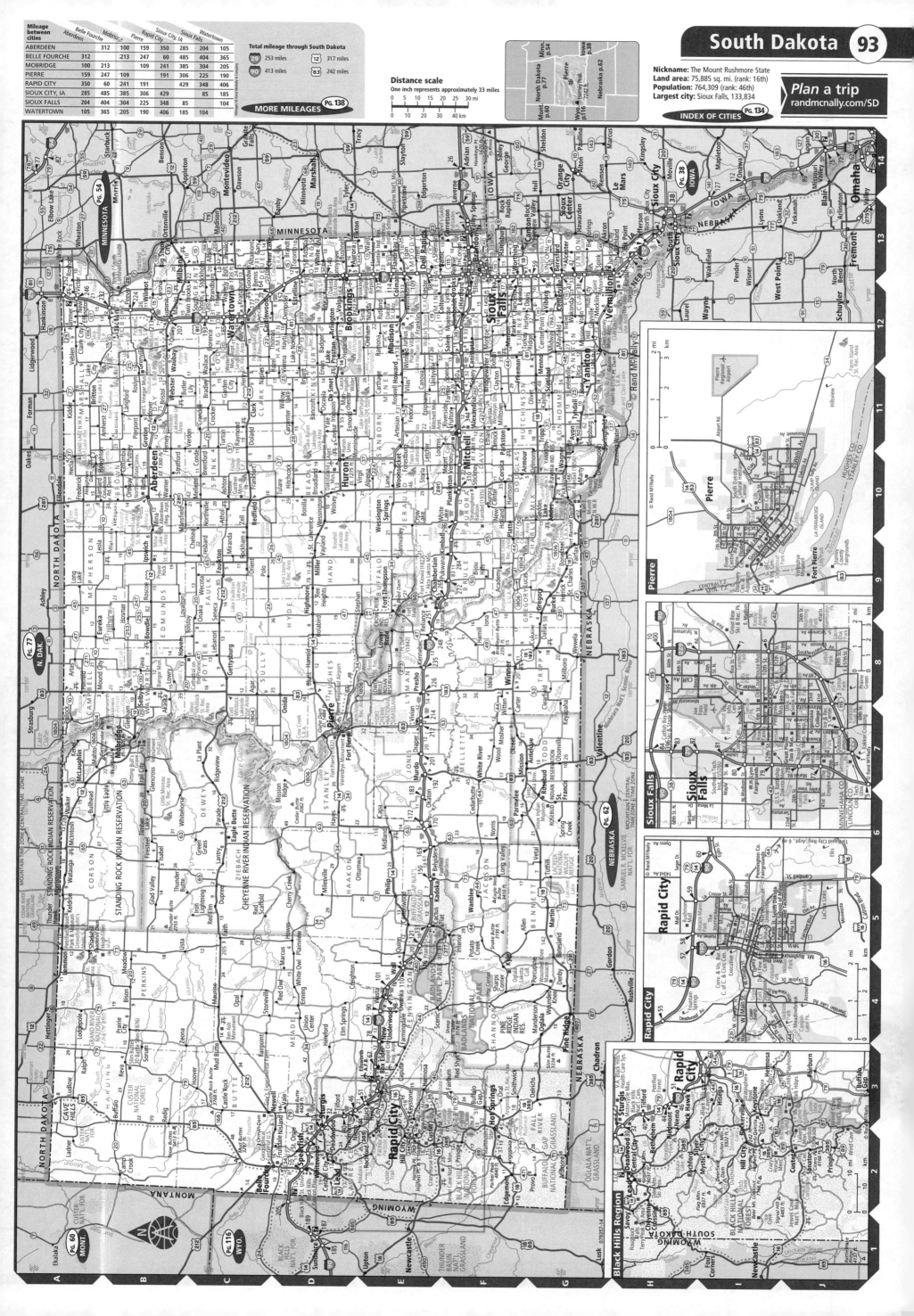

Mileage between cities	Aberdeen	Belle Fourche	Mobridge	Pierre	Rapid City	Sioux City IA	Sioux Falls	Watertown
ABERDEEN		312	100	159	350	285	204	105
BELLE FOURCHE	312		213	247	60	485	404	365
MOBRIDGE	100	213		109	241	385	304	205
PIERRE	159	247	109		191	306	225	190
RAPID CITY	350	60	241	191		429	348	406
SIOUX CITY, IA	285	485	385	306	429		85	185
SIOUX FALLS	204	404	304	225	348	85		104
WATERTOWN	105	365	205	190	406	185	104	

Total mileage through South Dakota

29: 253 miles   12: 317 miles
90: 413 miles   83: 242 miles

MORE MILEAGES PG. 138

Distance scale
One inch represents approximately 33 miles

0 5 10 15 20 25 30 mi
0 10 20 30 40 km

Nickname: The Mount Rushmore State
Land area: 75,885 sq. mi. (rank: 16th)
Population: 764,309 (rank: 46th)
Largest city: Sioux Falls, 133,834

Plan a trip
randmcnally.com/SD

INDEX OF CITIES PG. 134

94 Tennessee

Nickname: The Volunteer State
Land area: 41,217 sq. mi. (rank: 34th)
Population: 5,841,748 (rank: 16th)
Largest city: Memphis, 645,978

INDEX OF CITIES PG. 134

Mileage between cities	Atlanta, GA	Bristol	Chattanooga	Clarksville	Cookeville	Dyersburg	Fayetteville	Gatlinburg	Johnson City	Kingsport	Knoxville	La Follette	Memphis	Morristown	Nashville	Oak Ridge	Union City
CHATTANOOGA	115	227		172	100	297	97	154	255	221	213	114	151	335	161	127	114	310
CLARKSVILLE	287	336	172		124	174	137	263	132	330	322	223	260	212	270	47	207	139
DYERSBURG	412	463	297	174		251	242	390	49	457	449	350	387	76	397	173	334	35
FAYETTEVILLE	212	324	97	137	109	242		251	200	318	310	211	248	252	258	90	190	232
JOHNSON CITY	268	25	221	330	457	318		109	415	24	107	143	495	72	285	132	468
KNOXVILLE	215	113	114	223	103	350	211	40	308	107	99		39	388	47	178	25	361
MEMPHIS	393	501	335	212	289	76	252	428	87	495	487	388		425	435	215	372	113
NASHVILLE	242	291	127	47	79	173	90	218	131	285	277	178	215	211		225	162	185

Total mileage through Tennessee

(40) 455 miles		(75) 161 miles	
(65) 121 miles		(81) 76 miles	

MORE MILEAGES PG. 138

Memphis & Vicinity

Nashville

079358-14

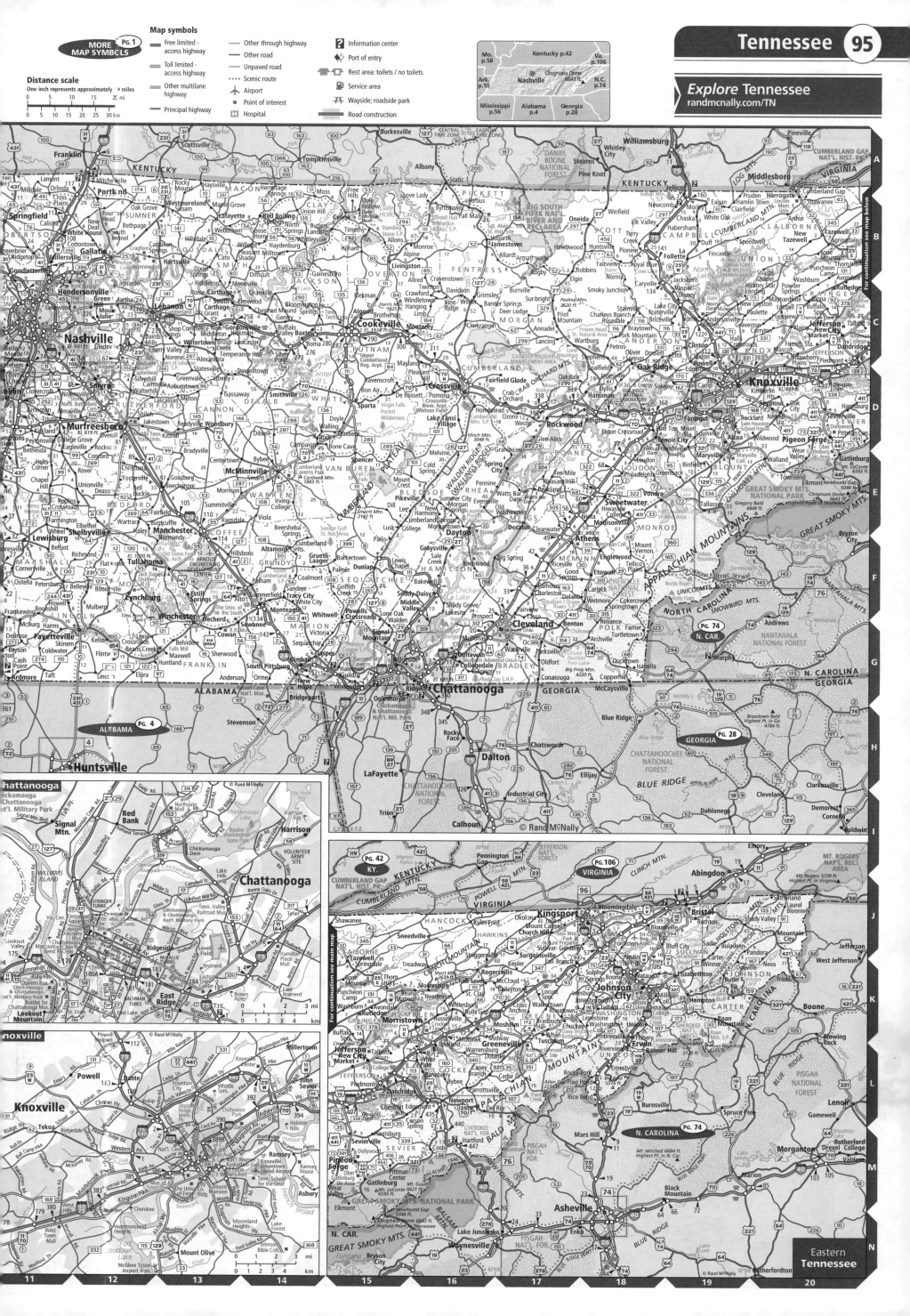

Explore Tennessee
randmcnally.com/TN

Plan a trip
randmcnally.com/TN

Get travel info
randmcnally.com/TX

INDEX OF CITIES PG. 135

Houston & Vicinity

Galveston

Tri-Cities: Johnson City / Kingsport / Bristol

Central Houston

© Rand McNally

INDEX OF CITIES PG. 135

Nickname: The Lone Star State
Land area: 261,797 sq. mi. (rank: 2nd)
Population: 22,118,509 (rank: 2nd)
Largest city: Houston, 2,009,690

INDEX OF CITIES **Pg. 135**

Mileage between cities	Abilene	Amarillo	Big Bend NP	Big Spring	Carlsbad NM	Childress	Clovis, NM	Dallas	Del Rio	Eagle Pass	El Paso	Fort Stockton	Houston	Lubbock	Midland	Odessa	Pecos	Perryton	San Angelo	San Antonio	Van Horn
ABILENE		283	379	108	276	155	269	185	247	302	447	252	347	165	147	168	242	307	92	261	328
AMARILLO	283		469	225	296	117	103	359	449	504	432	342	605	118	235	258	332	121	300	512	418
DALLAS	185	359	565	294	462	242	455		416	416	633	438	247	351	428	396	262	277	514		
EL PASO	447	432	324	340	165	556	314	633	424	479		238	753	344	301	281	207	524	402	558	115
LUBBOCK	165	118	351	107	179	147	104	351	331	386	344	224	519		117	140	214	239	182	394	300
ODESSA	168	258	213	61	139	277	203	354	250	305	281	84	546	140	22		76	379	131	351	162
SAN ANGELO	92	300	290	86	255	226	286	262	155	210	402	163	363	182	111	131	205	378		213	283
SAN ANTONIO	261	512	446	299	458	417	498	277	151	139	558	319	199	394	331	351	374	569	213		439

Total mileage through Texas

10	881 miles		40	177 miles
20	636 miles			

MORE MILEAGES **Pg. 138**

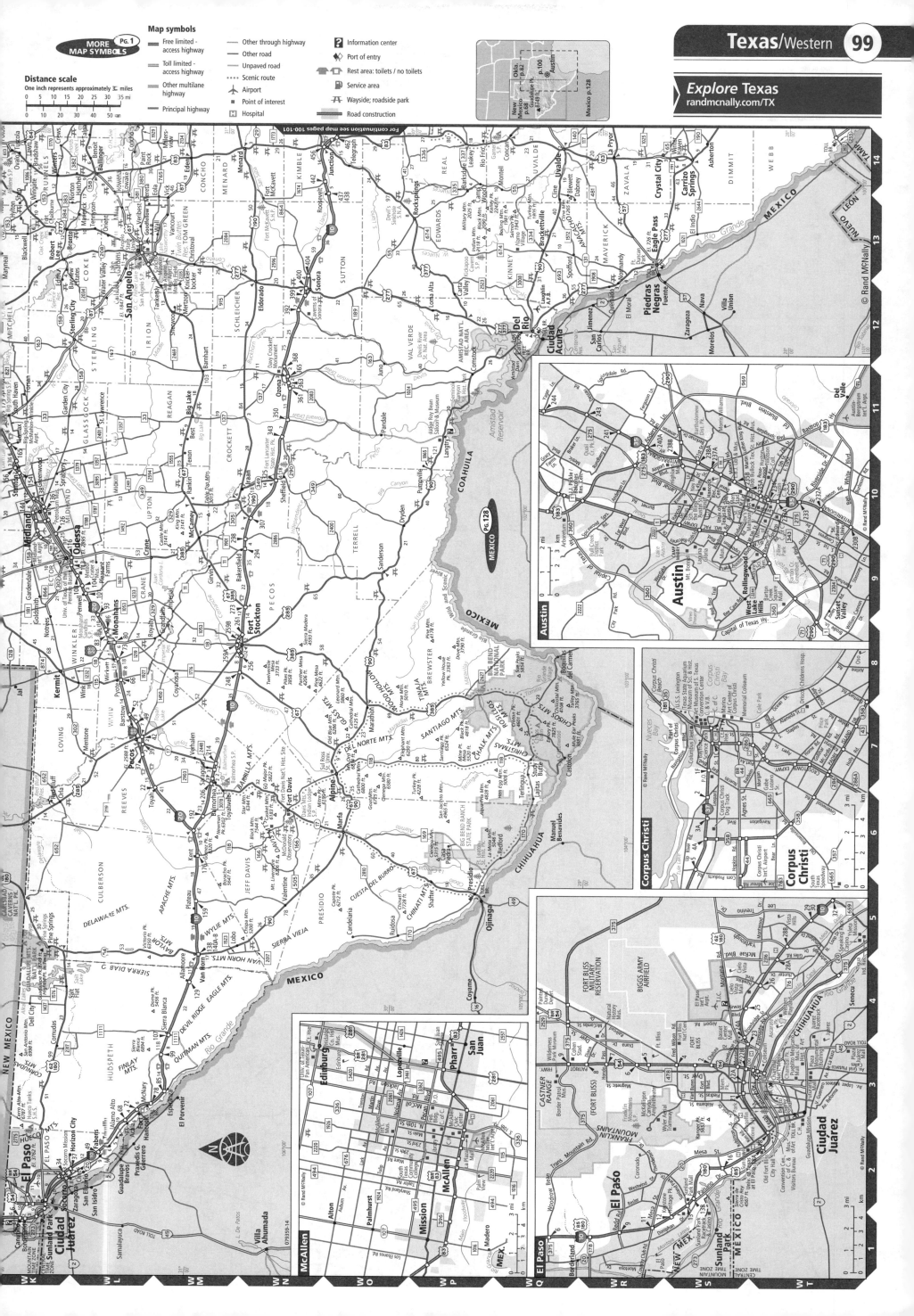

Explore Texas
randmcnally.com/TX

Nickname: The Lone Star State
Land area: 261,797 sq. mi. (rank: 2nd)
Population: 22,118,509 (rank: 2nd)
Largest city: Houston, 2,009,690

INDEX OF CITIES Pg. 135

Mileage between cities	Abilene	Austin	Beaumont	Brownsville	Corpus Christi	Dallas	Fort Worth	Galveston	Houston	Laredo	Lufkin	McAllen	Paris	San Angelo	San Antonio	Shreveport, LA	Texarkana	Tyler	Victoria	Waco	Wichita Falls
ABILENE		230	467	539	405	186	155	394	347	409	359	497	294	92	261	373	362	285	352	191	141
AUSTIN	230		246	352	218	195	190	209	162	232	222	310	304	206	82	327	372	228	124	99	303
BROWNSVILLE	539	352	443		159	547	542	386	355	203	473	60	656	691	278	593	646	580	231	451	655
CORPUS CHRISTI	405	218	303	159		413	408	232	215	141	333	152	522	357	144	453	506	446	94	317	521
DALLAS	186	195	294	547	413		30	294	247	427	182	505	109	262	277	186	177	98	307	96	134
HOUSTON	347	162	88	355	215	247	267	47		349	119	348	310	363	199	239	292	206	127	188	380
SAN ANTONIO	261	82	283	278	144	277	272	246	199	150	313	236	386	213		409	454	310	117	181	385
SHREVEPORT, LA	373	327	195	593	453	186	216	286	239	559	119	586	150	420	409		71	99	365	228	320

Total mileage through Texas		
10	811 miles	30	223 miles
20	636 miles	35	504 miles

MORE MILEAGES Pg. 138

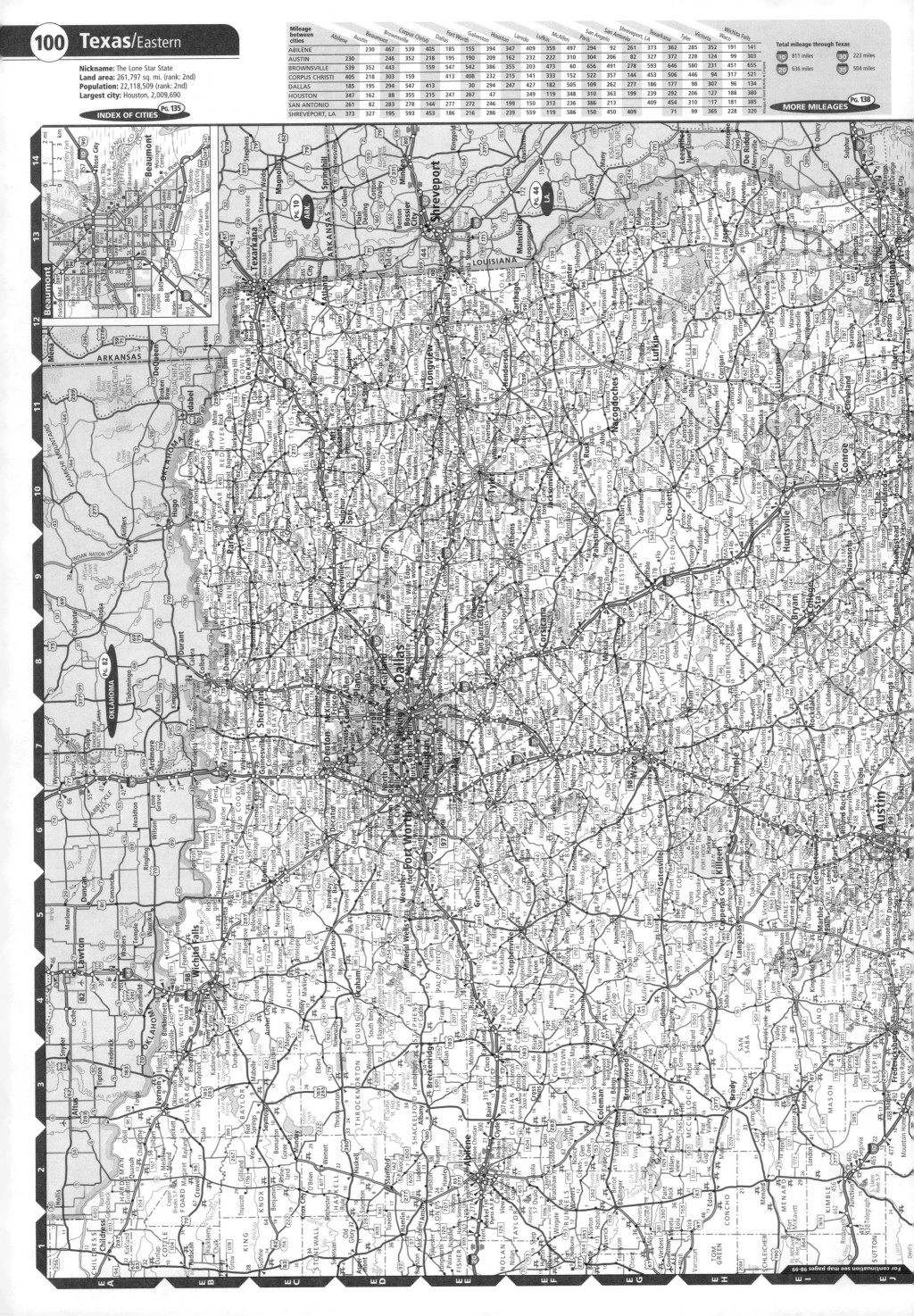

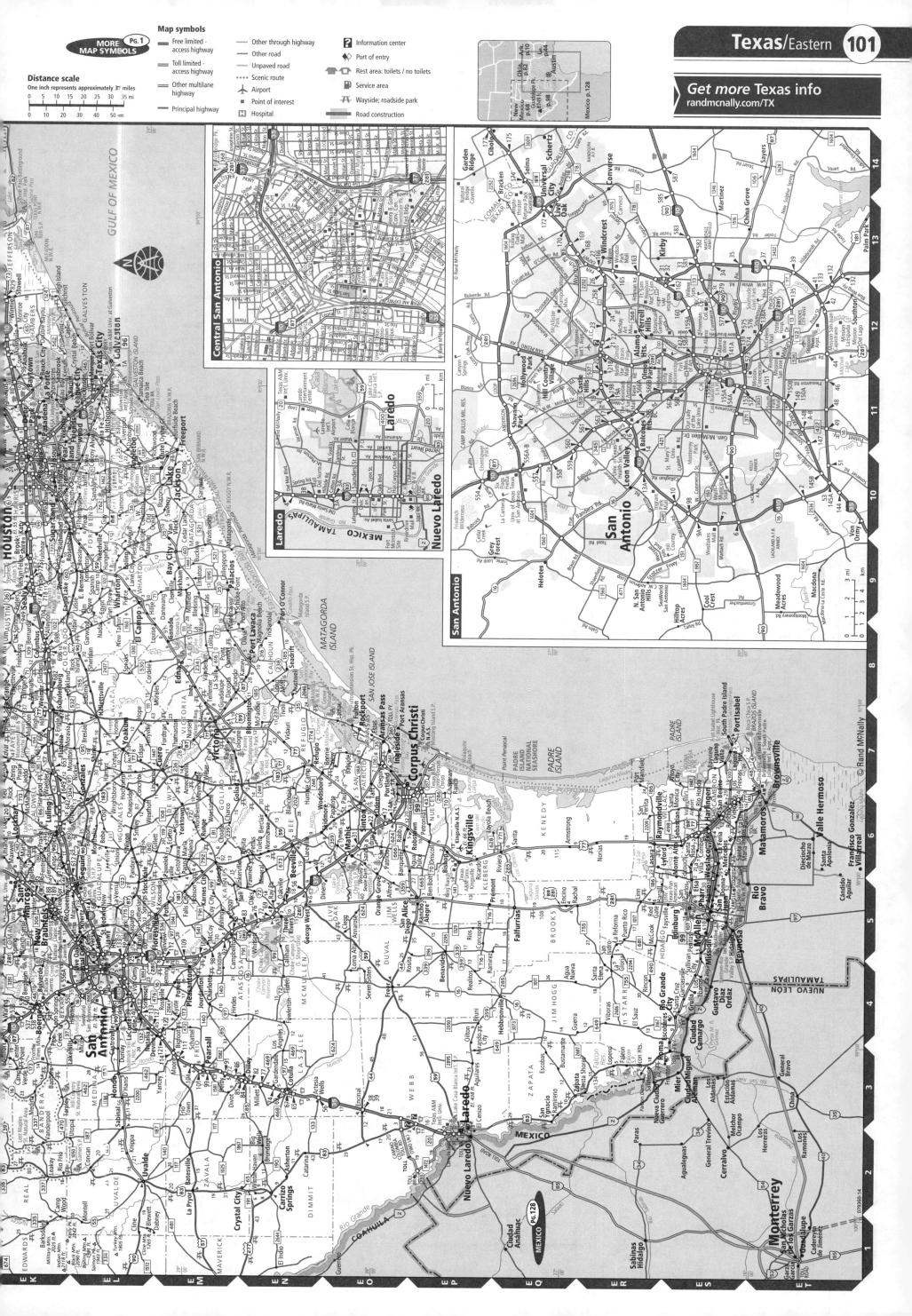

Nickname: The Beehive State
Land area: 82,144 sq. mi. (rank: 12th)
Population: 2,351,467 (rank: 34th)
Largest city: Salt Lake City, 179,894

INDEX OF CITIES — PG. 135

Mileage between cities	Bicknell	Blanding	Cedar City	Evanston, WY	Grand Jct., CO	Las Vegas, NV	Logan	Moab	Ogden	Page, AZ	Park City	Price	Provo	Richfield	St. George	Salt Lake City	Vernal	Wendover
GRAND JCT., CO	217	186	332	287		505	361	112	321	375	288	165	243	224	385	286	141	403
LOGAN	274	387	318	115	361	491		313	42	458	110	197	118	232	371	74	249	192
MOAB	169	74	284	295	112	451	313		263	240	176	117	195	176	332	223	355	
OGDEN	234	347	278	75	321	451	42	273		418	70	157	78	192	331	34	209	152
PROVO	156	269	200	101	243	373	118	195	78	340	46	79		114	253	43	157	160
ST. GEORGE	199	345	54	353	385	121	371	337	331	156	298	280	253	162		296	409	413
SALT LAKE CITY	199	312	243	78	286	416	74	238	34	383	28	122	43	157	296		170	122
VERNAL	226	297	356	146	141	529	249	223	209	453	147	115	157	233	409	170		293

Total mileage through Utah

Route	Miles
15	401 miles
70	232 miles
80	196 miles
84	119 miles

MORE MILEAGES — PG. 138

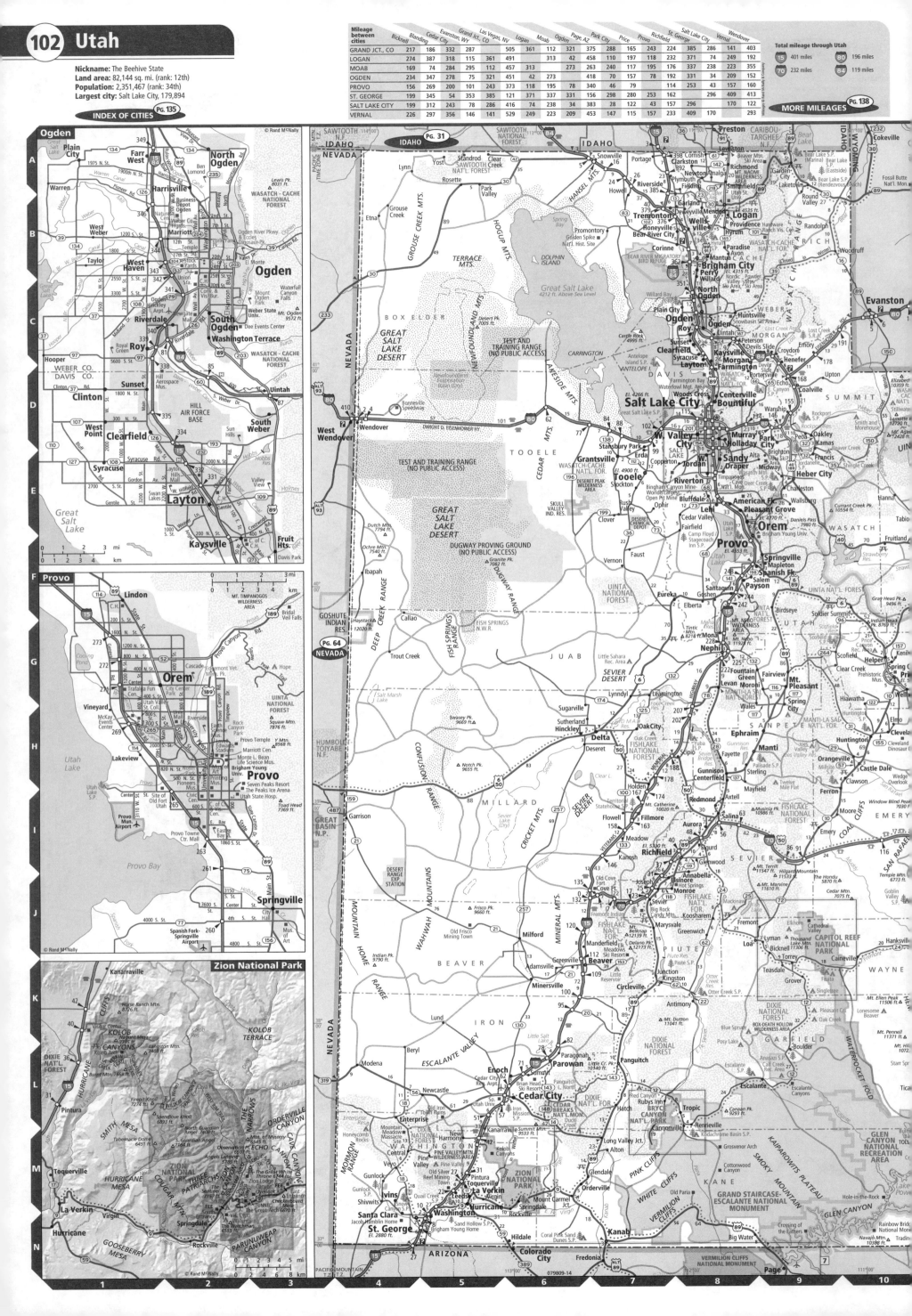

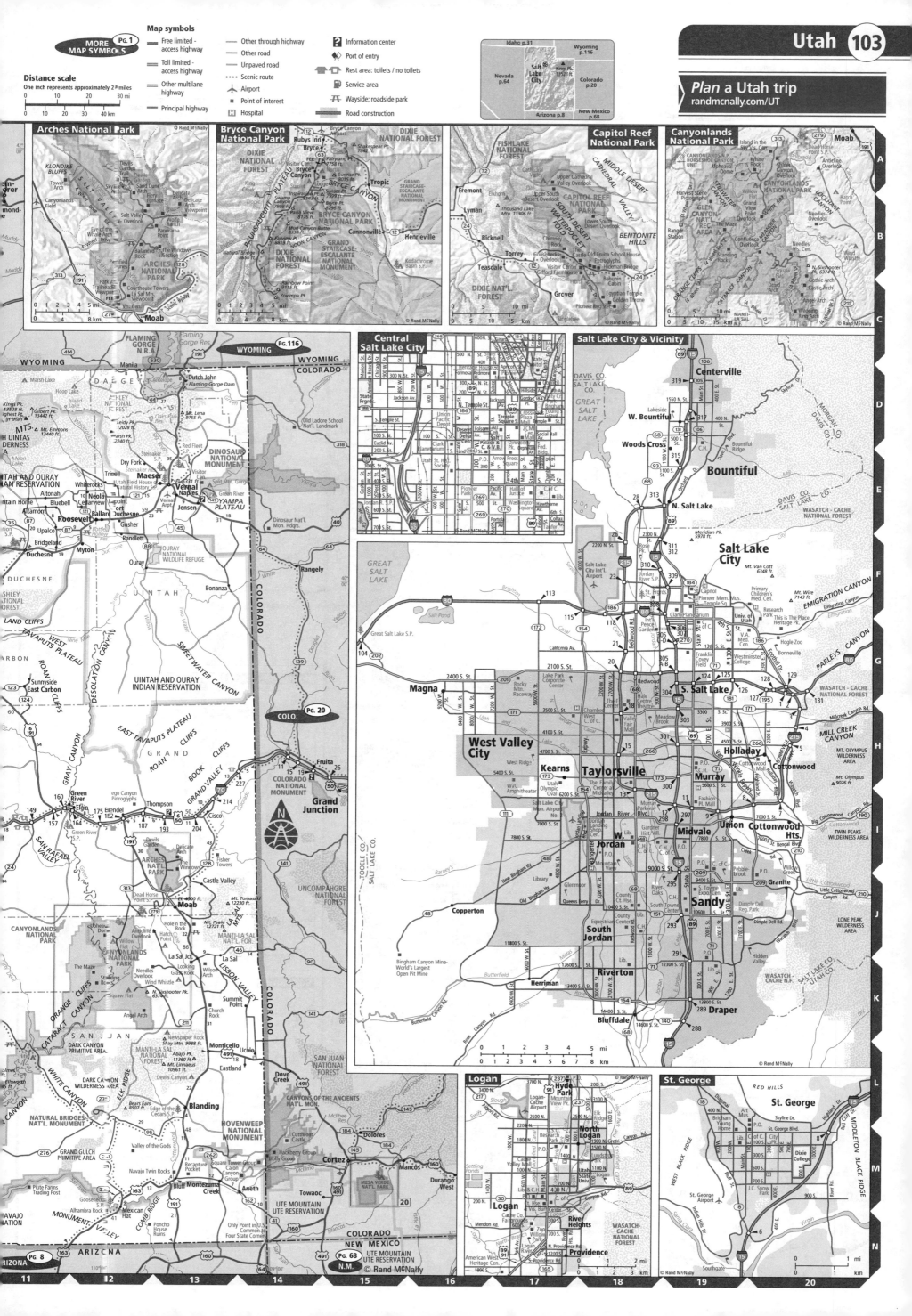

Get travel info
randmcnally.com/VT

Nickname: The Green Mountain State
Land area: 9,250 sq. mi. (rank: 43rd)
Population: 619,107 (rank: 49th)
Largest city: Burlington, 39,148

INDEX OF CITIES PG. 135

Distance scale
One inch represents approximately 14 miles

Mileage between cities	Albany, NY	Brattleboro	Burlington	Montpelier	Newport	Rutland	St. Johnsbury	White River Jct.
ALBANY, NY		81	152	162	246	96	202	145
BRATTLEBORO	81		154	117	166	77	122	65
BURLINGTON	152	154		39	75	67	77	91
MONTPELIER	162	117	39		80	66	38	54
NEWPORT	246	166	75	80		146	44	101
RUTLAND	96	77	67	66	146		102	45
ST. JOHNSBURY	202	122	77	38	44	102		57
WHITE RIVER JCT.	145	65	91	54	101	45	57	

Total mileage through Vermont

89 130 miles		93 11 miles	
91 177 miles		4 64 miles	

MORE MILEAGES PG. 138

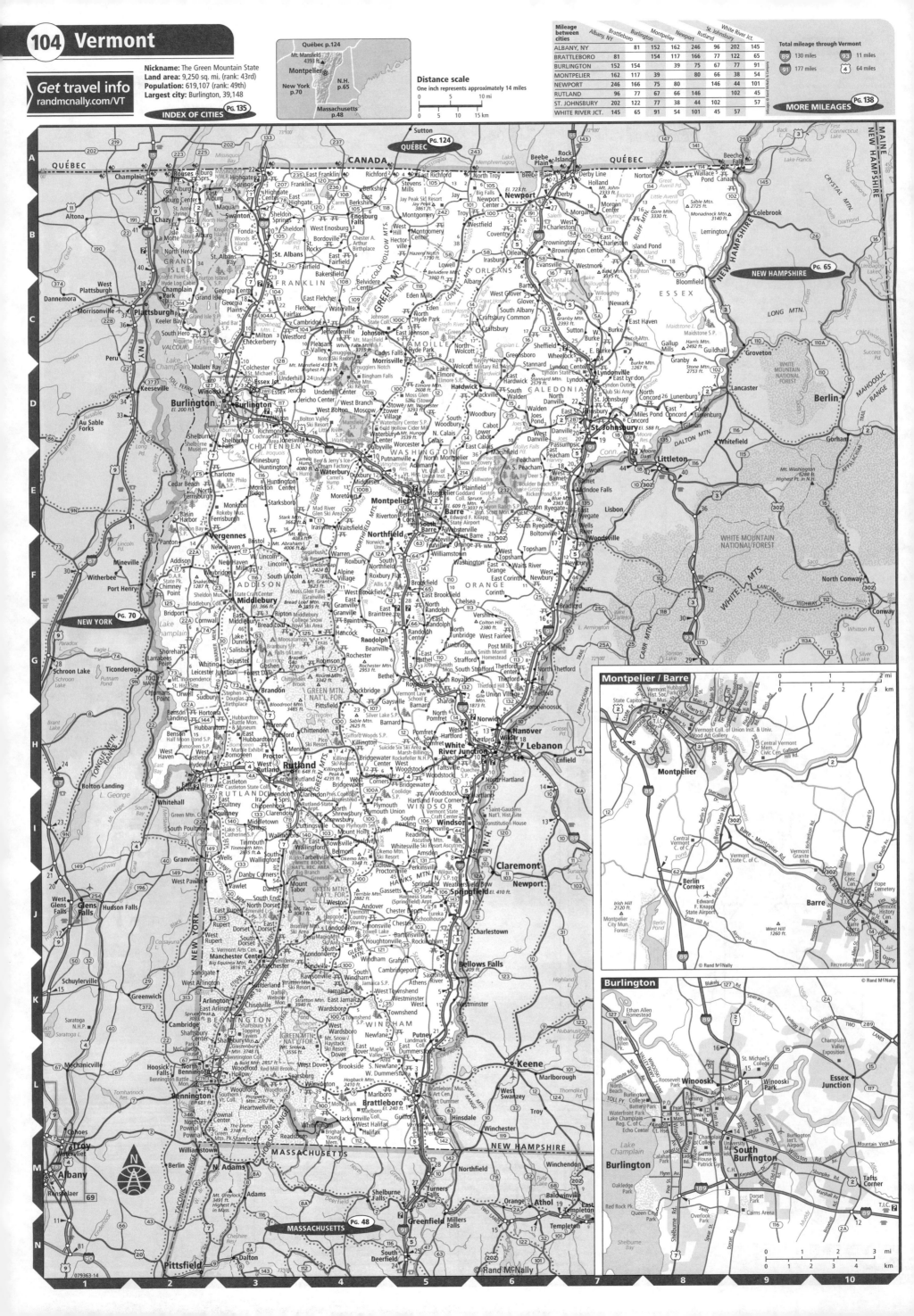

Montpelier / Barre

Burlington

© Rand McNally

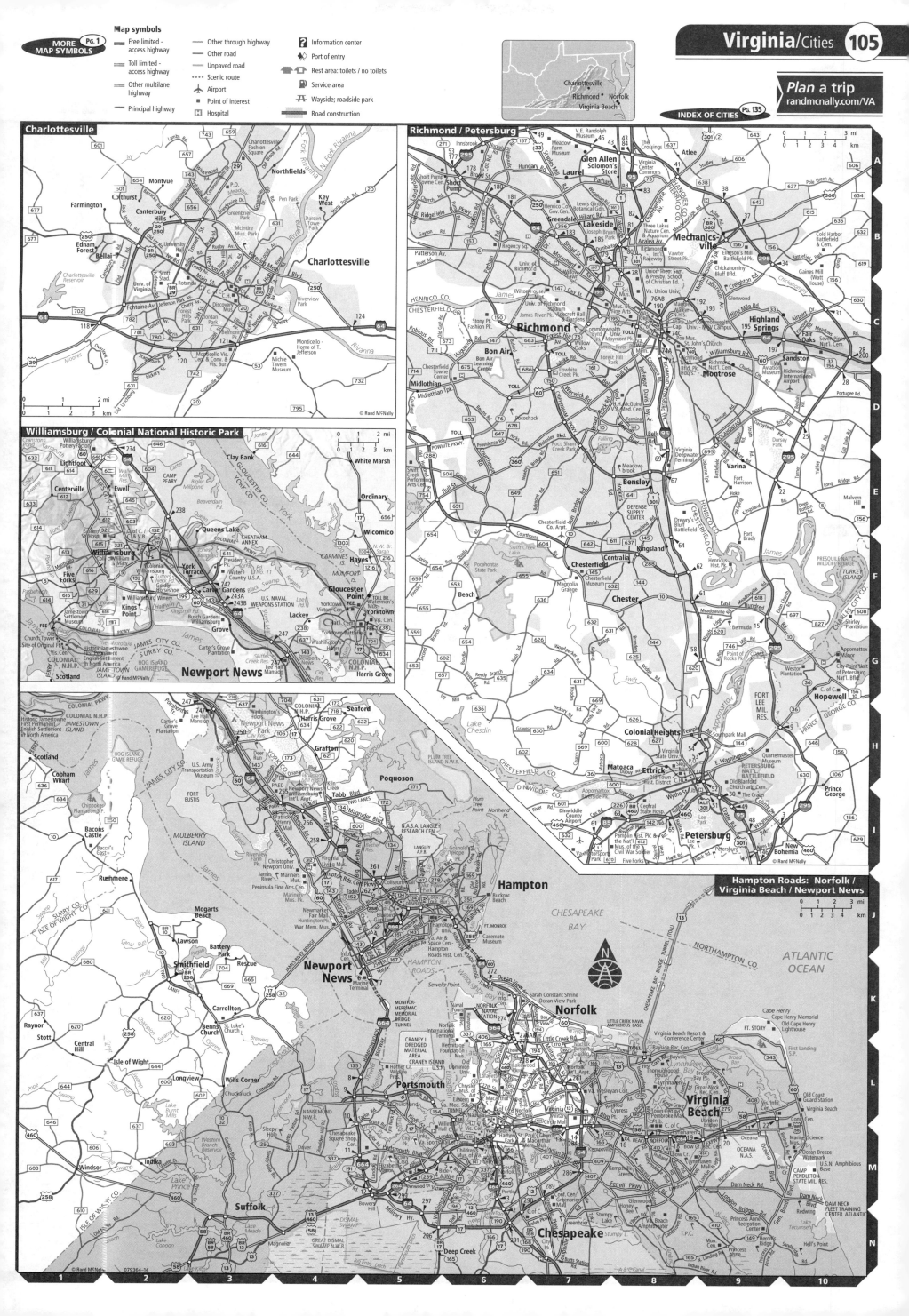

Nickname: Old Dominion
Land area: 39,594 sq. mi. (rank: 37th)
Population: 7,386,330 (rank: 12th)
Largest city: Virginia Beach, 439,467

INDEX OF CITIES PG. 135

MORE MILEAGES PG. 138

Mileage between cities	Bristol	Charlottesville	Chincoteague	Danville	Emporia	Fredericksburg	Hagerstown Md.	Harrisonburg	Lynchburg	Manassas	Norfolk	Richmond	Roanoke	Virginia Beach	Washington, DC	Williamsburg	Winchester	Wytheville
CHARLOTTESVILLE	252		261	126	138	80	167	59	63	95	168	74	114	180	122	126	125	182
EMPORIA	341	138	180	113		119	235	195	127	156	74	64	178	88	170	106	198	271
NORFOLK	418	168	105	186	74	145	261	225	194	182		93	280	17	196	46	224	348
RICHMOND	324	74	186	149	64	55	171	131	118	92	93		105		106	51	134	254
ROANOKE	146	114	373	82	178	194	217	109	54	209	280	186		292	236	238	175	76
WASHINGTON, DC	374	122	161	250	170	54	75	129	185	37	196	106	236	208		154	77	304
WINCHESTER	313	125	242	220	198	82	42	68	157	53	224	134	175	236	77	182		243
WYTHEVILLE	69	182	441	120	271	262	285	177	132	277	348	254	76	360	304	306	243	

Total mileage through Virginia

Route	Miles
64	298 miles
85	69 miles
81	325 miles
95	179 miles

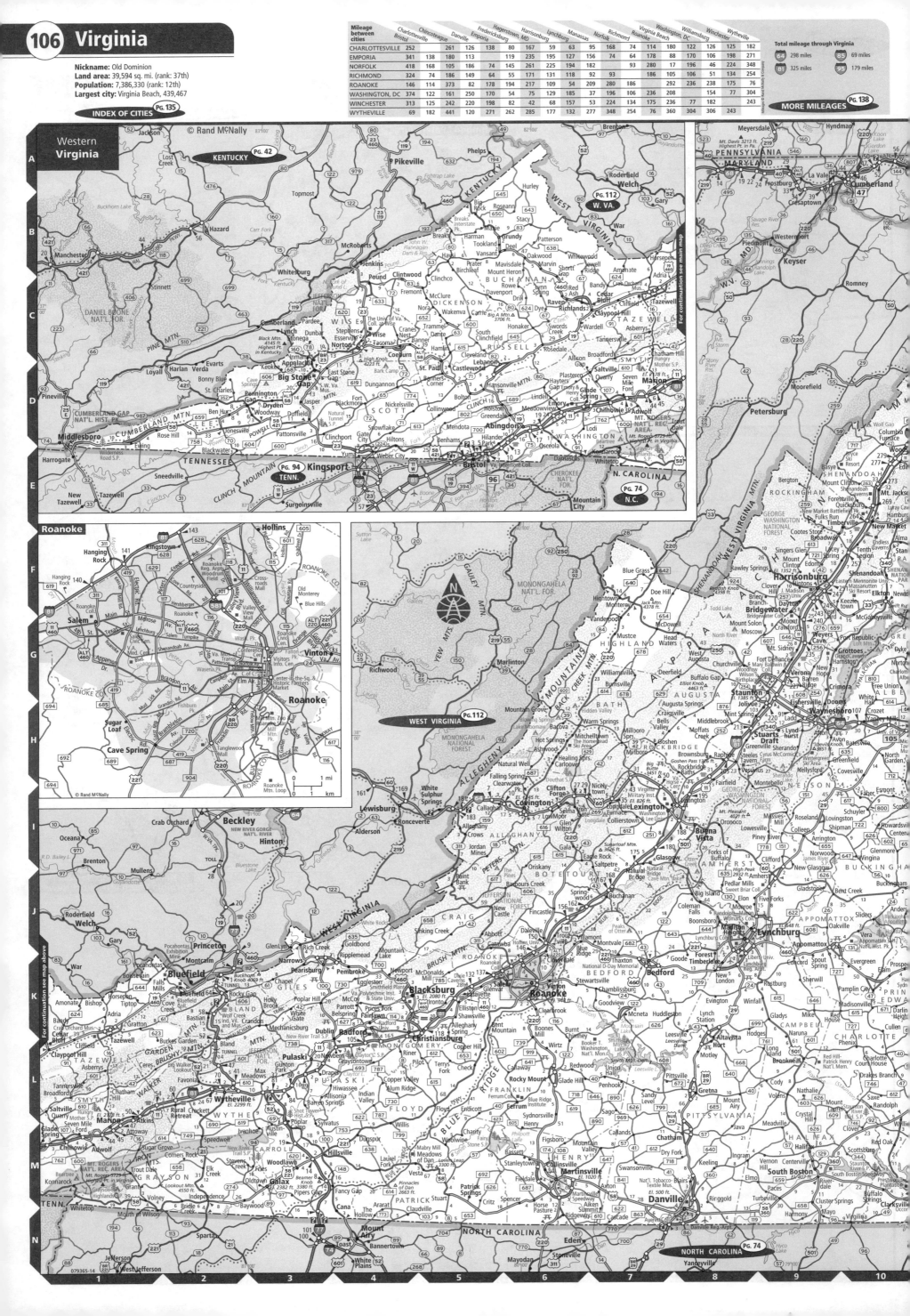

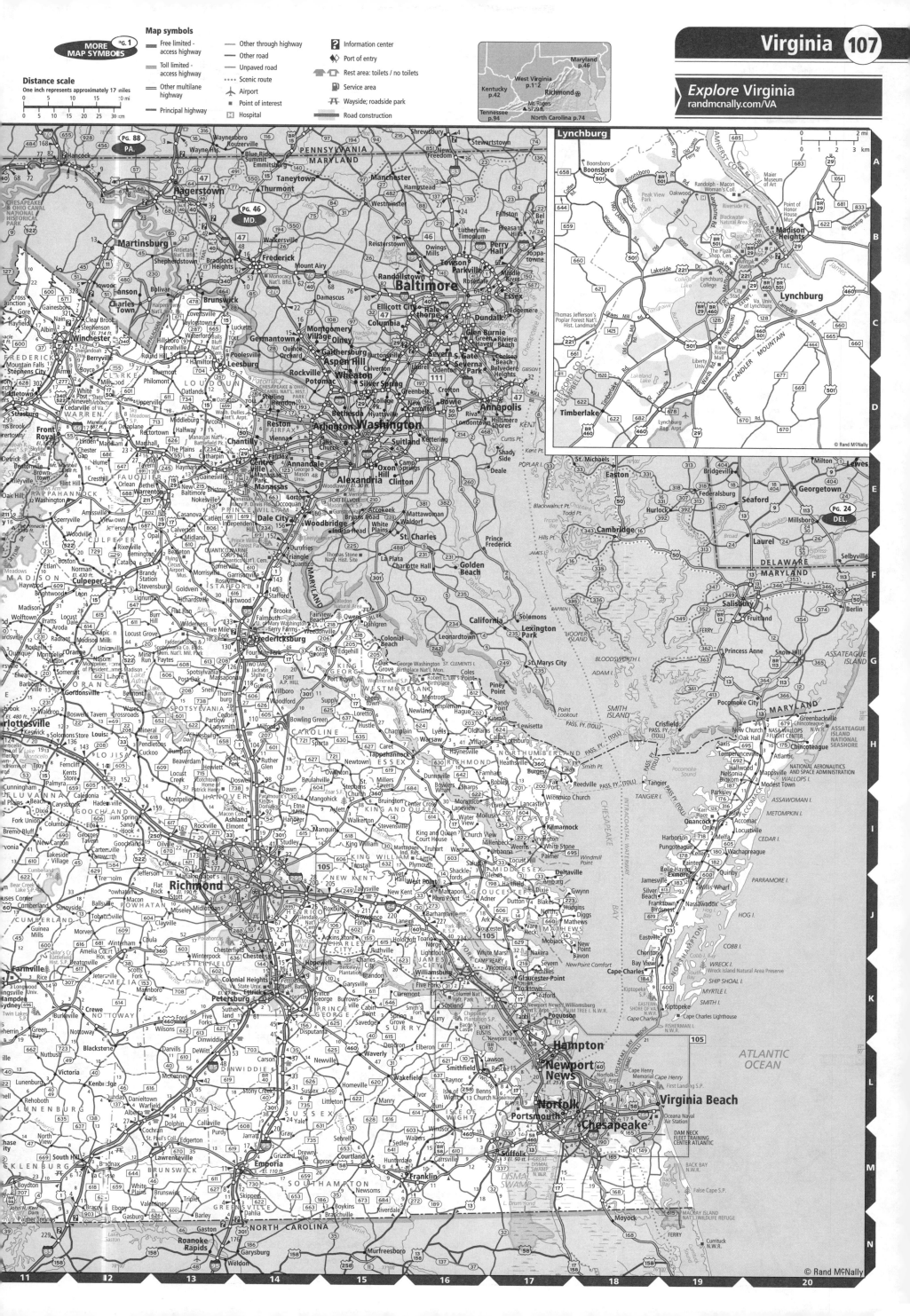

Explore Virginia
randmcnally.com/VA

Lynchburg

Nickname: The Evergreen State
Land area: 66,544 sq. mi. (rank: 20th)
Population: 6,131,445 (rank: 15th)
Largest city: Seattle, 569,101

INDEX OF CITIES — PG. 135

Mileage between cities	Aberdeen	Bellingham	Bremerton	Colville	Kennewick	Lewiston, ID	Longview	Olympia	Omak	Port Angeles	Portland, OR	Seattle	Spokane	Tacoma	The Dalles, OR	Vancouver, BC	Wenatchee	*Via Ferry Yakima
BELLINGHAM	197		152*	326	302	397	217	147	262	208	124*	262	88	365	119	324	55	185	223
KENNEWICK	286	302	265*	210		122	255	260	189	338	213	219	134	232	129	357	140	79
PORTLAND, OR	145	262	174	423	234	334	49	115	377	232		174	352	143	84	317	291	185
SEATTLE	109	88	64*	353	219	314	129	59	241	82*	174		282	31	241	143	153	140
SPOKANE	373	365	328*	71	139	109	371	323	138	401*	352	282		295	268	420	172	202
TACOMA	78	119	33	366	232	327	98	28	254	106*	143	31	295		220	174	186	153
THE DALLES, OR	222	324	251	339	129	250	126	192	293	309	84	241	268	220		379	207	101
YAKIMA	207	223	186*	273	79	200	169	181	192	259*	185	140	202	153	101	278	106	

Total mileage through Washington
5 — 277 miles
90 — 297 miles
82 — 133 miles
101 — 373 miles

MORE MILEAGES — PG. 138

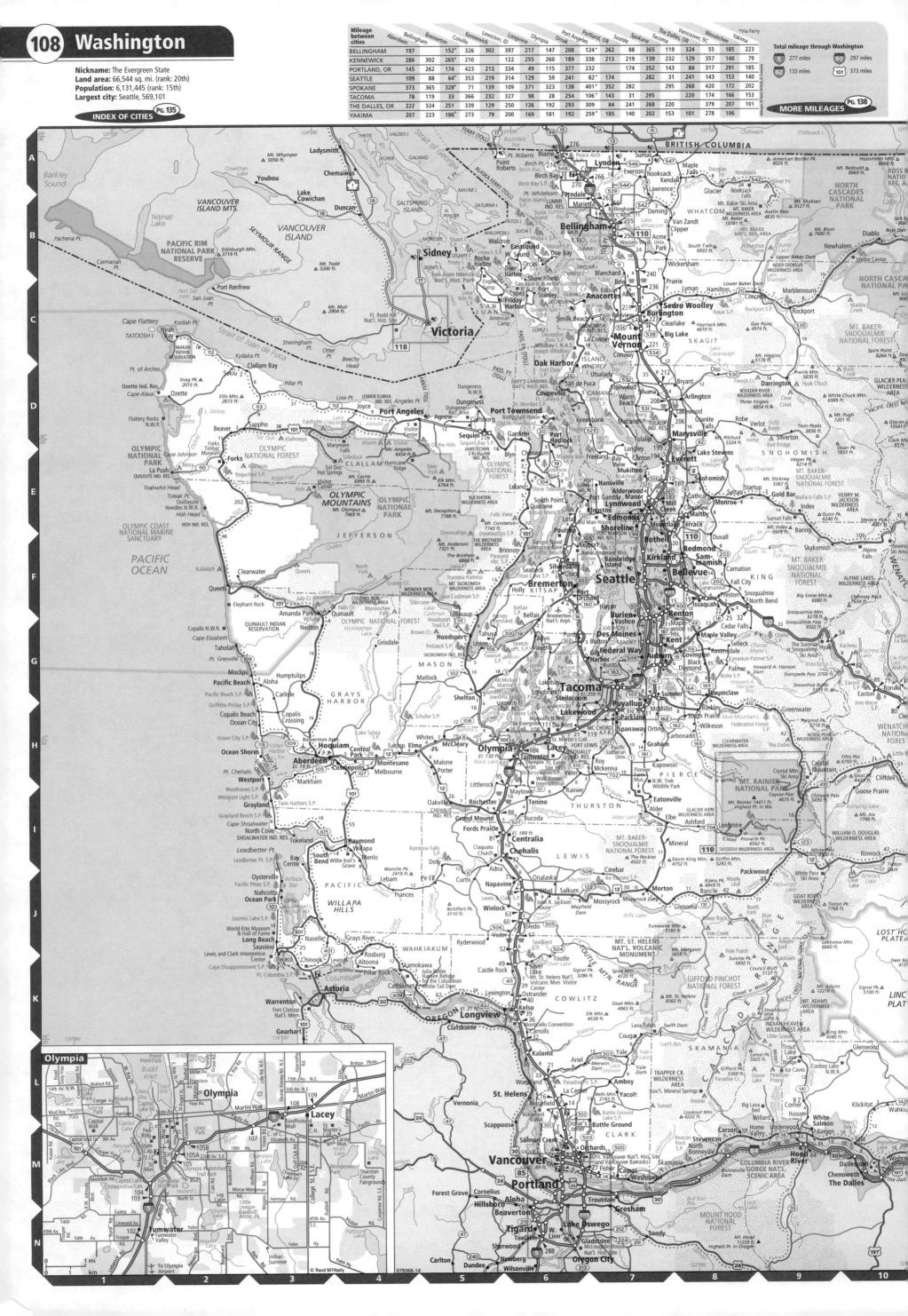

© Rand McNally

079366-14

Map symbols

MORE MAP SYMBOLS PG. 1

- Free limited-access highway
- Toll limited-access highway
- Other multilane highway
- Principal highway
- Other through highway
- Other road
- Unpaved road
- •••• Scenic route
- ✈ Airport
- ■ Point of interest
- H Hospital
- ? Information center
- Port of entry
- Rest area: toilets / no toilets
- Service area
- Wayside; roadside park
- Road construction

Distance scale
One inch represents approximately 23 miles

One inch represents approximately 23 miles

0 5 10 15 20 mi
0 10 20 30 km

British Columbia p.118

Olympia • Mt. Rainier 14411 ft.

Idaho p.31

Oregon p.84

Get more Washington info
randmcnally.com/WA

BRITISH COLUMBIA PG. 118

CANADA

BRITISH COLUMBIA

Grid columns: A B C D E F G H I J K L M N

Grid rows: 11 12 13 14 15 16 17 18 19 20

Selected place names:
Osoyoos, Oroville, Molson, Chesaw, Danville, Laurier, Northport, Grand Forks, Nighthawk, Loomis, Ellisford, Curlew, Republic, Kettle Falls, Metaline Falls, Tonasket, Wauconda, Malo, Colville, Ione, Conconully, Riverside, Okanogan, Omak, Malott, Carlton, Twisp, Winthrop, Mazama, Brewster, Pateros, Bridgeport, Elmer City, Coulee Dam, Grand Coulee, Electric City, Nespelem, Keller, Inchelium, Gifford, Chewelah, Valley, Cedonia, Springdale, Loon Lake, Clayton, Deer Park, Newport, Milan, Spokane, Spokane Valley, Opportunity, Dishman, Greenacres, Post Falls, Coeur d'Alene, Hayden, Dalton Gardens, Rathdrum, Spirit Lake, Chelan, Manson, Mansfield, Withrow, Waterville, Douglas, Coulee City, Hartline, Almira, Wilbur, Creston, Davenport, Reardan, Medical Lake, Cheney, Spangle, Rockford, Fairfield, Waverly, Latah, Plummer, Wenatchee, East Wenatchee, Rock Island, Palisades, Ephrata, Soap Lake, Quincy, George, Moses Lake, Wheeler, Warden, Lind, Ritzville, Sprague, Lamont, St. John, Colfax, Pullman, Moscow, Leavenworth, Cashmere, Peshastin, Monitor, Ellensburg, Kittitas, Vantage, Royal City, Othello, Connell, Mesa, Basin City, Eltopia, Pasco, Kennewick, Richland, West Richland, Benton City, Kiona, Prosser, Grandview, Sunnyside, Outlook, Granger, Zillah, Wapato, Toppenish, White Swan, Yakima, Selah, Naches, Tieton, Cowiche, Mabton, Bickleton, Goldendale, Paterson, Plymouth, Umatilla, Hermiston, Boardman, Stanfield, Pendleton, La Grande, Elgin, Milton-Freewater, Walla Walla, College Place, Lowden, Touchet, Prescott, Waitsburg, Dayton, Starbuck, Dodge, Pomeroy, Pataha City, Clarkston, Lewiston, Asotin, Anatone, Colton, Uniontown, Genesee, Lapwai

U.S. DEPARTMENT OF ENERGY HANFORD SITE

YAKIMA TRAINING CENTER

COLVILLE NATIONAL FOREST

OKANOGAN NATIONAL FOREST

WENATCHEE NATIONAL FOREST

UMATILLA NATIONAL FOREST

WALLOWA-WHITMAN NATIONAL FOREST

KANIKSU NATIONAL FOREST

COLVILLE INDIAN RESERVATION

SPOKANE INDIAN RESERVATION

YAKAMA INDIAN RESERVATION

LAKE ROOSEVELT NAT'L. REC. AREA

PASAYTEN WILDERNESS AREA

LAKE CHELAN NAT'L. REC. AREA

OREGON

PG. 84

PG. 31 IDAHO

Yakima (inset)

0 1 2 mi
0 1 2 3 km

© Rand McNally

Plan a trip
randmcnally.com/WA

INDEX OF CITIES   PG.135

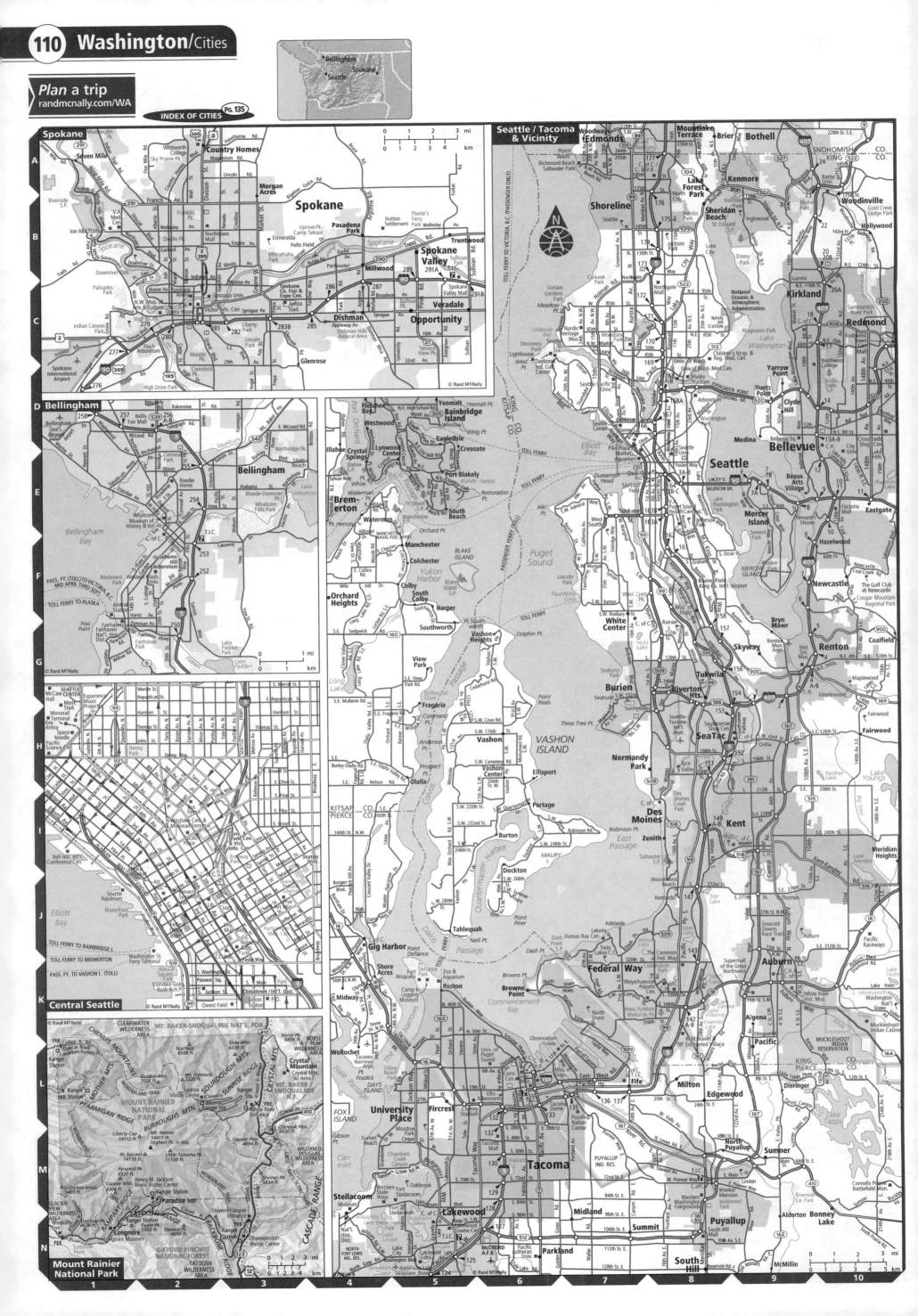

Spokane

Bellingham

Central Seattle

Seattle / Tacoma & Vicinity

Mount Rainier National Park

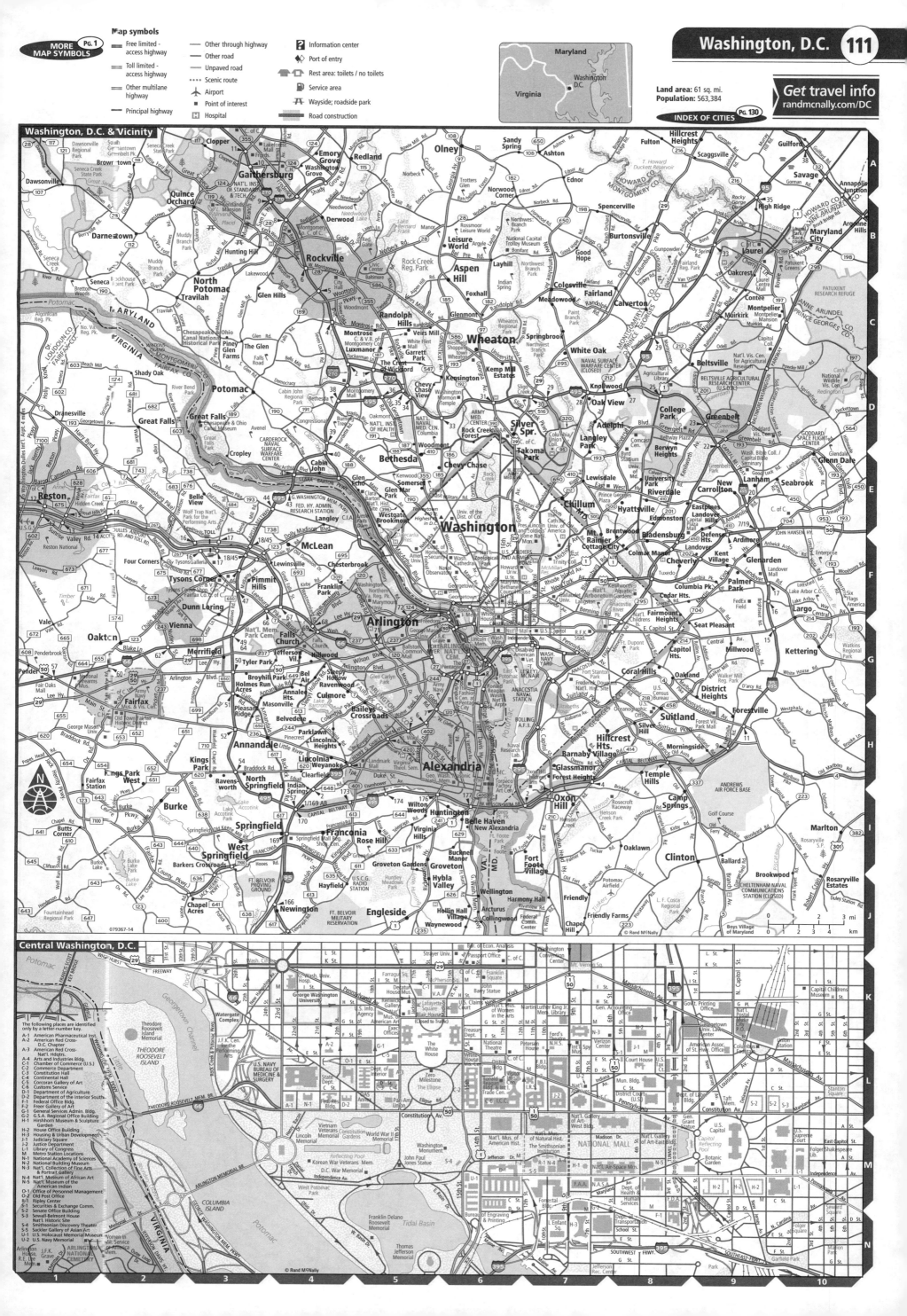

Map symbols

MORE MAP SYMBOLS PG. 1

Free limited-access highway
Toll limited-access highway
Other multilane highway
Principal highway

Other through highway
Other road
Unpaved road
Scenic route
Airport
Point of interest
Hospital

Information center
Port of entry
Rest area: toilets / no toilets
Service area
Wayside; roadside park
Road construction

Land area: 61 sq. mi.
Population: 563,384

INDEX OF CITIES PG. 130

Get travel info
randmcnally.com/DC

Washington, D.C. & Vicinity

Central Washington, D.C.

The following places are identified only by a letter-number key:

A-1 American Pharmaceutical Inst.
A-2 American Red Cross-D.C. Chapter
A-3 American Red Cross-Nat'l. Hdqrs.
A-4 Arts and Industries Bldg.
C-1 Chamber of Commerce (U.S.)
C-2 Commerce Department
C-3 Constitution Hall
C-4 Continental Hall
C-5 Corcoran Gallery of Art
C-6 Customs Service
D-1 Department of Agriculture
D-2 Department of the Interior South
F-1 Federal Office Bldg.
F-2 Freer Gallery of Art
G-1 General Services Admin. Bldg.
G-2 G.S.A. Regional Office Bldg.
H-1 Hirshhorn Museum & Sculpture Garden
H-2 House Office Building
H-3 Housing & Urban Development
J-1 Judiciary Square
J-2 Justice Department
L-1 Library of Congress
M Metro Station Locations
N-1 National Academy of Sciences
N-2 National Building Museum
N-3 Nat'l. Collection of Fine Arts & Portrait Gallery
N-4 Nat'l. Museum of African Art
N-5 Nat'l. Museum of the American Indian
O-1 Office of Personnel Management
O-2 Old Post Office
R-1 Ripley Center
S-1 Securities & Exchange Comm.
S-2 Senate Office Building
S-3 Sewall-Belmont House
S-4 Nat'l. Historic Site
S-5 Smithsonian Discovery Theater
S-6 Sackler Gallery of Asian Art
U-1 U.S. Holocaust Memorial Museum
U-2 U.S. Navy Memorial

© Rand McNally

Plan a trip
randmcnally.com/WV

Nickname: The Mountain State
Land area: 24,078 sq. mi. (rank: 41st)
Population: 1,810,354 (rank: 37th)
Largest city: Charleston, 51,394

INDEX OF CITIES   Pg. 135

Distance scale
One inch represents approximately 20 miles

Mileage between cities	Beckley	Charleston	Cumberland, MD	Huntington	Morgantown	Parkersburg	Wheeling	Wh. Sulphur Springs
BECKLEY		60	241	111	169	135	236	60
CHARLESTON	60		227	51	155	75	176	125
CUMBERLAND, MD	241	227		278	72	181	146	193
HUNTINGTON	111	51	278		206	126	227	176
MORGANTOWN	169	155	72	206		109	74	201
PARKERSBURG	135	75	181	126	109		105	200
WHEELING	236	176	146	227	74	105		301
WH. SULPHUR SPRS.	60	125	193	176	201	200	301	

Total mileage through West Virginia

64	189 miles	77	187 miles
70	14 miles	79	161 miles

MORE MILEAGES   PG. 138

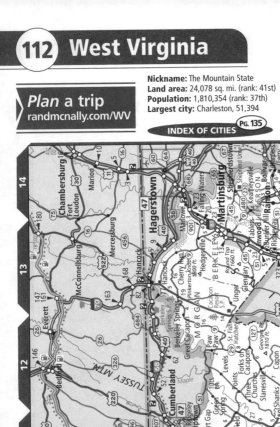

INDEX OF CITIES PG. 136

Nickname: The Badger State
Land area: 54,310 sq. mi. (rank: 25th)
Population: 5,472,299 (rank: 20th)
Largest city: Milwaukee, 586,941

INDEX OF CITIES PG. 136

Mileage between cities	Ashland	Beloit	Chicago, IL	Dubuque, IA	Eau Claire	Green Bay	Hayward	Kenosha	La Crosse	Madison	Manitowoc	Marinette	Milwaukee	Oshkosh	Rhinelander	Sheboygan	Stevens Point	Sturgeon Bay	Superior	Wisconsin Dells
CHICAGO, IL	446	96		175	312	209	419	64	278	146	176	264	92	177	342	148	246	247	460	282	192
EAU CLAIRE	165	220	312	198		198	107	279	87	175	239	225	241	178	161	229	107	294	148	101	122
GREEN BAY	246	191	209	232	198		286	156	206	138	39	55	117	53	129	64	96	42	327	97	133
LA CROSSE	252	186	278	126	87	206	194	245		141	209	257	207	155	204	195	117	250	235	144	88
MADISON	309	54	146	94	175	138	282	115	141		128	189	77	85	205	133	109	182	323	145	55
MILWAUKEE	375	74	92	175	241	117	348	39	207	77	84	172		86	271	56	175	155	389	211	121
SUPERIOR	66	368	460	346	148	327	70	427	235	323	368	300	389	326	185	377	263	371		230	270
WAUSAU	167	190	282	239	101	97	189	249	144	145	124	211	103	63	163	37	141	230		114

Total mileage through Wisconsin

39	182 miles	90	189 miles
43	192 miles	94	341 miles

MORE MILEAGES PG. 138

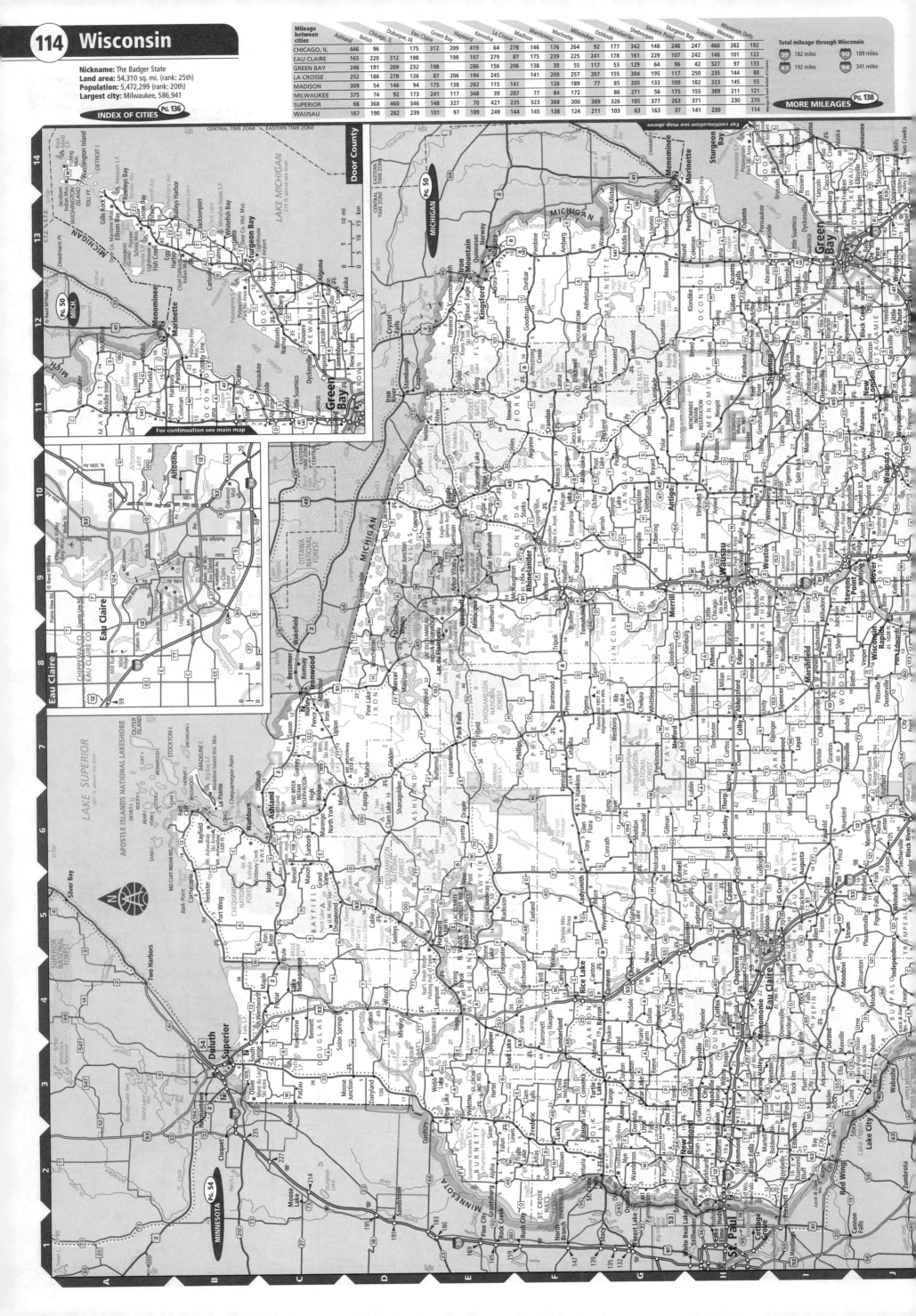

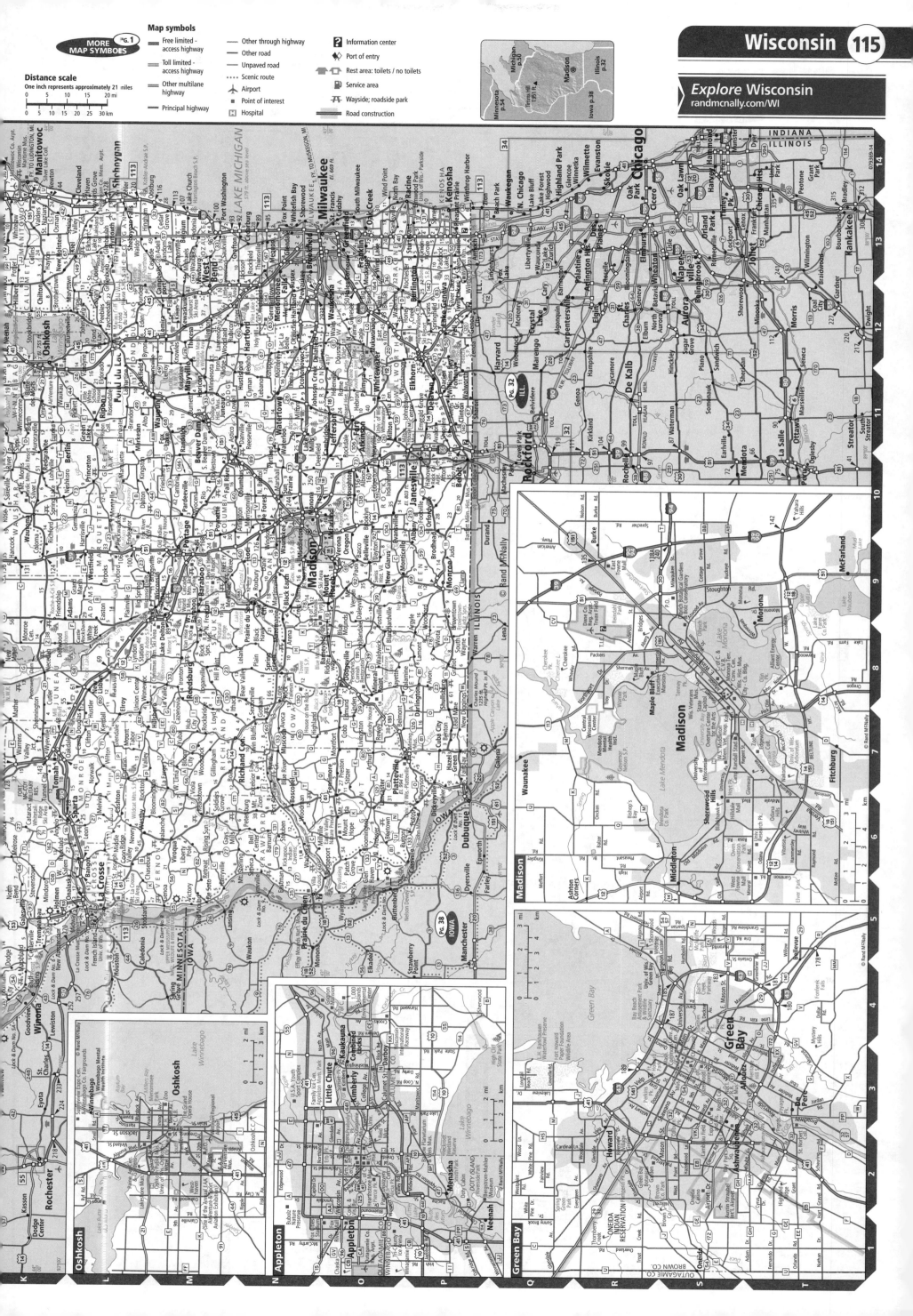

Plan a trip
randmcnally.com/WY

Nicknames: The Equality State
Land area: 97,100 sq. mi. (rank: 9th)
Population: 501,242 (rank: 50th)
Largest city: Cheyenne, 54,374

INDEX OF CITIES   PG. 136

Distance scale
One inch represents approximately 38 miles

Mileage between cities	Casper	Cheyenne	Cody	Jackson	Riverton	Rock Springs	Sheridan	Spearfish, SD
CASPER		180	214	282	119	226	152	223
CHEYENNE	180		395	436	275	258	329	295
CODY	214	395		178	139	282	148	346
JACKSON	282	436	178		166	178	326	509
RIVERTON	119	275	139	166		143	217	346
ROCK SPRINGS	226	258	282	178	143		378	449
SHERIDAN	152	329	148	326	217	378		199
SPEARFISH, SD	223	295	346	509	346	449	199	

Total mileage through Wyoming
301 miles   209 miles
403 miles   505 miles

MORE MILEAGES   PG. 138

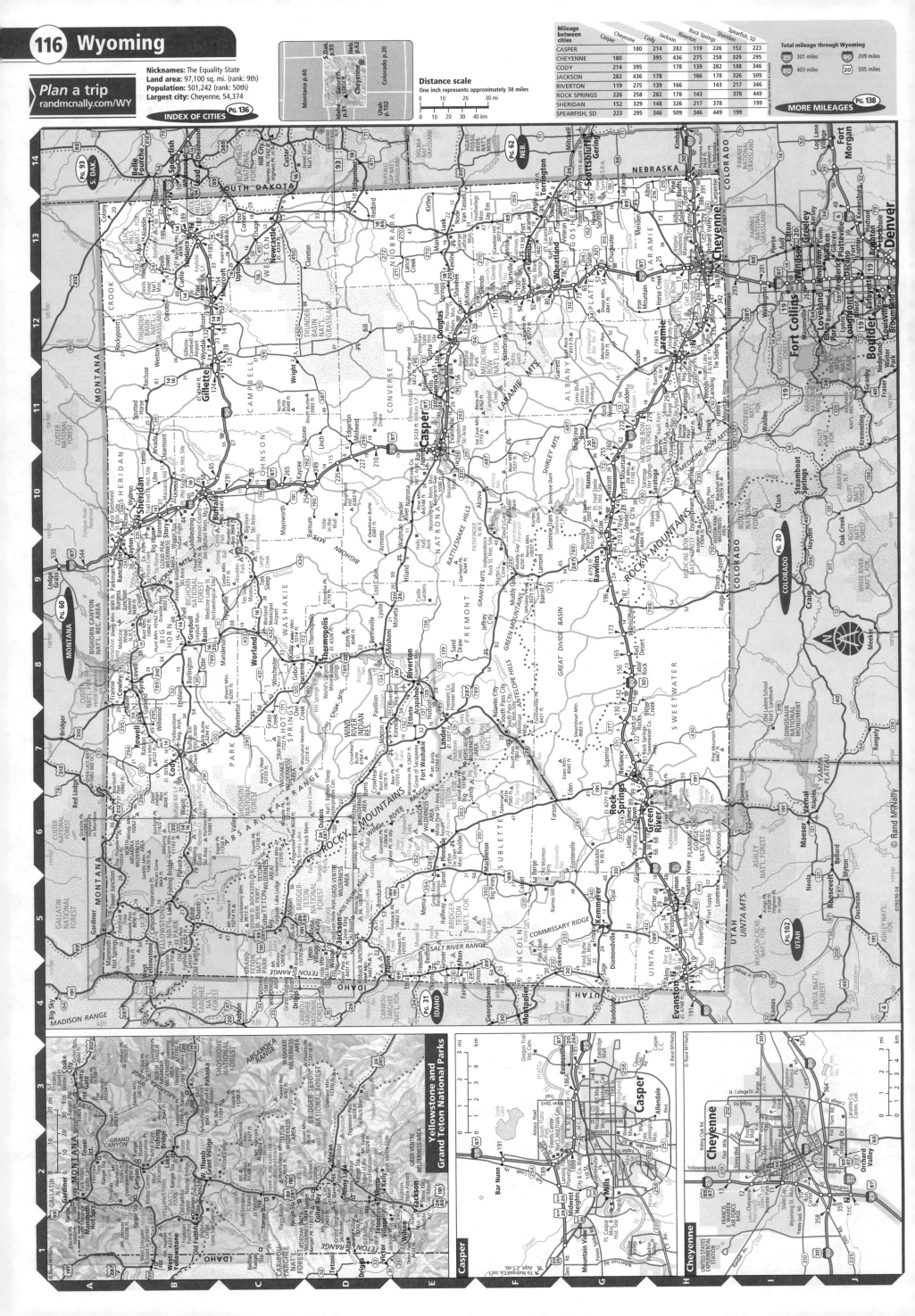

Selected places of interest

Banff National Park	F-3
Cape Breton Highlands National Park	G-13
Elk Island National Park	F-4
Fundy National Park	H-12
Glacier National Park	F-3
Gros Morne National Park	F-13
Jasper National Park	F-3
Kejimkujik National Park	H-12
Kluane National Park	B-2
Kootenay National Park	G-3
Mount Revelstoke National Park	F-3
Parc Nat. de la Mauricie	H-11
Prince Albert National Park	F-5
Prince Edward Island National Park	G-12
Pukaskwa National Park	H-8
Quetico Provincial Park	H-7
St. Lawrence Islands National Park	I-10

MORE MAP SYMBOLS PG. 1

Map symbols

- Free limited - access highway
- Toll limited - access highway
- Principal highway

Distance scale
One inch represents approximately 281 miles

0 100 200 300 mi
0 100 200 300 400 km

INDEX OF CITIES PG. 136

Land area: 3,511,023 sq. mi.
Population: 31,361,611
Largest city: Toronto, 2,481,494

Explore
randmcnally.com

© Rand McNally

Glossary of French Terms

Aeroport	Airport
Arrondissement	District
Baie	Bay
Basilique	Basilica
Barrage	Dam
Bibliothèque	Library
Bois	Woods
Cap	Cape
Centre de recherches	Research centre (or center)
Centre des congrès	Convention centre (or center)
Chemin	Road
Chenal	Channel
Chutes	Falls
Débarquement	Landing
Détroit	Strait
Fleuve	river (that flows to the sea)
Hippodrome	Race track
Hôtel de Ville	City or town hall
Hôtel du Parlement	Parliament building
Île	Island
Jardin botanique	Botanical garden
Jardin	Gardens
Jardin zoologique	Zoological garden (or Zoo)
Lac	Lake
Lieu historique	Historic Site
Lieu historique national	National historic site
Lieu natal	Birthplace
Mont	Mountain
Musée	Museum
Oratoire	Oratory
Parc	Park
Parc marin	Marine park
Parc national	National (and/or Provincial in Québec) park
Pont	Bridge
Promenade	Boulevard
Réserve faunique	Wildlife reserve
Réserve indienne	Indian reserve (or Reservation)
Rivière	River
Rue	Street
Stade	Stadium
Ston ski	Ski area
Tribunal	Court house
Universite	University

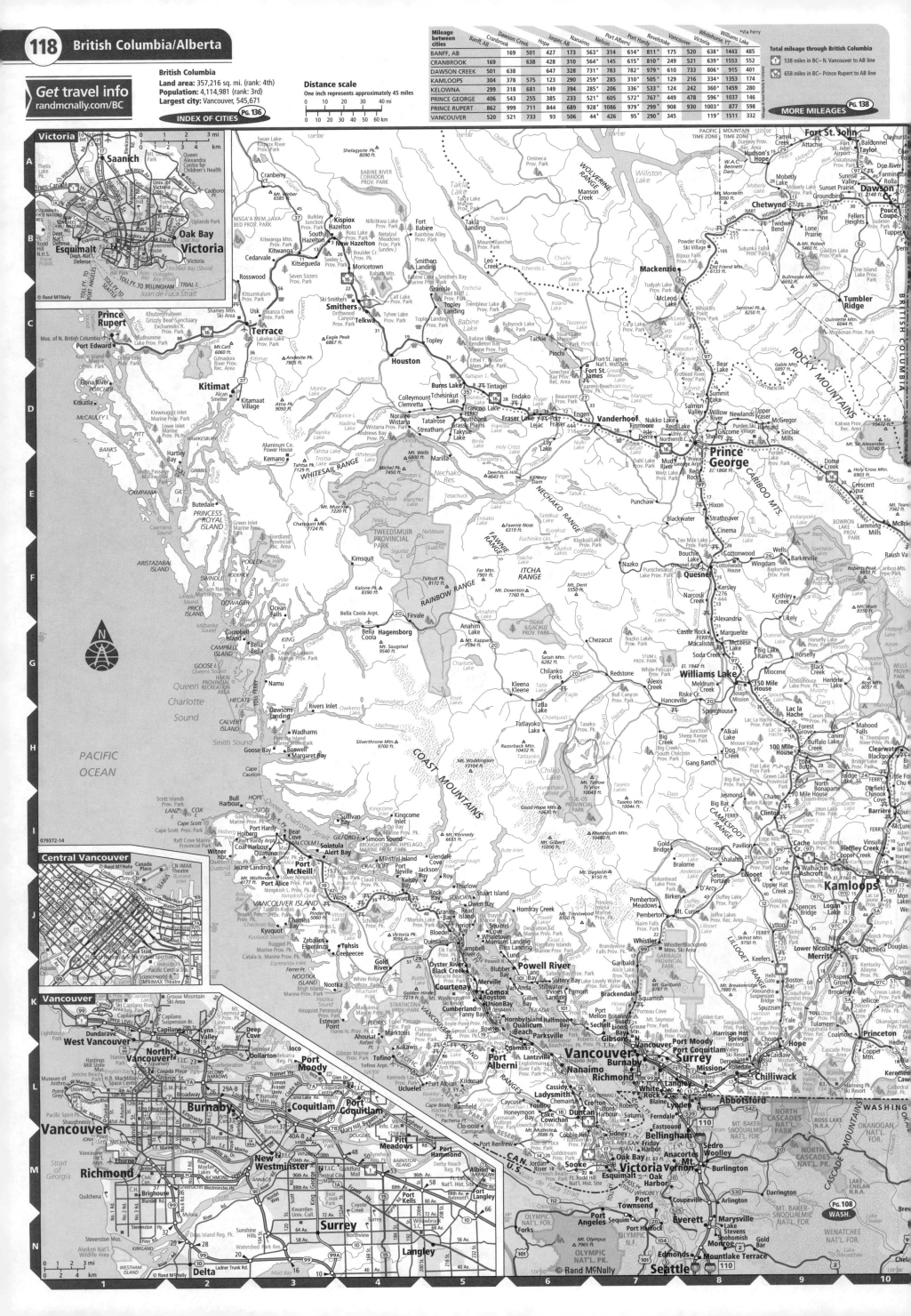

Get travel info
randmcnally.com/BC

British Columbia
Land area: 357,216 sq. mi. (rank: 4th)
Population: 4,114,981 (rank: 3rd)
Largest city: Vancouver, 545,671

INDEX OF CITIES Pg. 136

Distance scale
One inch represents approximately 45 miles
0   10   20   30   40 mi
0   10 20 30 40 50 60 km

MORE MILEAGES Pg. 138

Mileage between cities	Banff, AB	Cranbrook	Dawson Creek	Hope	Jasper, AB	Nanaimo	Nelson	Port Alberni	Port Hardy	Revelstoke	Vancouver	Victoria	Whitehorse, YT	Williams Lake	*Via Ferry
BANFF, AB		169	501	427	173	563*	314	614*	811*	175	520	638*	1443	485	
CRANBROOK	169		638	428	310	564*	145	615*	810*	249	521	639*	1553	552	
DAWSON CREEK	501	638		647	328	731*	783	782*	979*	610	733	806*	915	401	
KAMLOOPS	304	378	575	123	290	259*	285	310*	505*	129	216	334*	1353	174	
KELOWNA	299	318	681	149	394	285*	206	336*	533*	124	242	360*	1459	280	
PRINCE GEORGE	406	543	255	385	233	521*	605	572*	449	478	596*	1037	146	
PRINCE RUPERT	862	999	711	844	810	928*	1086	979*	299*	908	930	1003*	877	598	
VANCOUVER	520	521	733	93	506	44*	426	95*	290*	345		119*	1511	332	

Total mileage through British Columbia
538 miles in BC– N. Vancouver to AB line
658 miles in BC– Prince Rupert to AB line

Alberta
Land area: 248,000 sq. mi. (rank: 6th)
Population: 3,114,390 (rank: 4th)
Largest city: Calgary, 878,866

Plan a trip
randmcnally.com/AB

MORE MILEAGES PG. 138

INDEX OF CITIES PG. 136

Total mileage through Alberta
1 — 332 miles in AB
16 — 397 miles in AB

Mileage between cities	Calgary	Cardston	Crowsnest Pk.	Dawson Creek, BC	Drayton Valley	Drumheller	Edmonton	Fort McMurray	High Level	Jasper	Lethbridge	Red Deer	Slave Lake	Whitecourt
BANFF	81	226	193	501	227	161	254	519	711	173	223	165	413	311
CALGARY		145	141	533	189	80	173	447	630	254	142	84	332	282
DAWSON CREEK, BC	533	678	574		335	539	360	503	303	328	675	444	159	109
EDMONTON	183	318	324	360	86	172		274	453	227	315	84	159	109
LETHBRIDGE	142	46	102	675	331	171	315	589	772	392		226	474	424
MEDICINE HAT	178	149	193	711	367	171	351	556	808	432	103	262	510	460
PEACE RIVER	468	613	601	144	270	474	295	414	182	356	610	382	150	186
VERMILION	294	384	418	480	200	225	121	319	341	338	202	267	223	

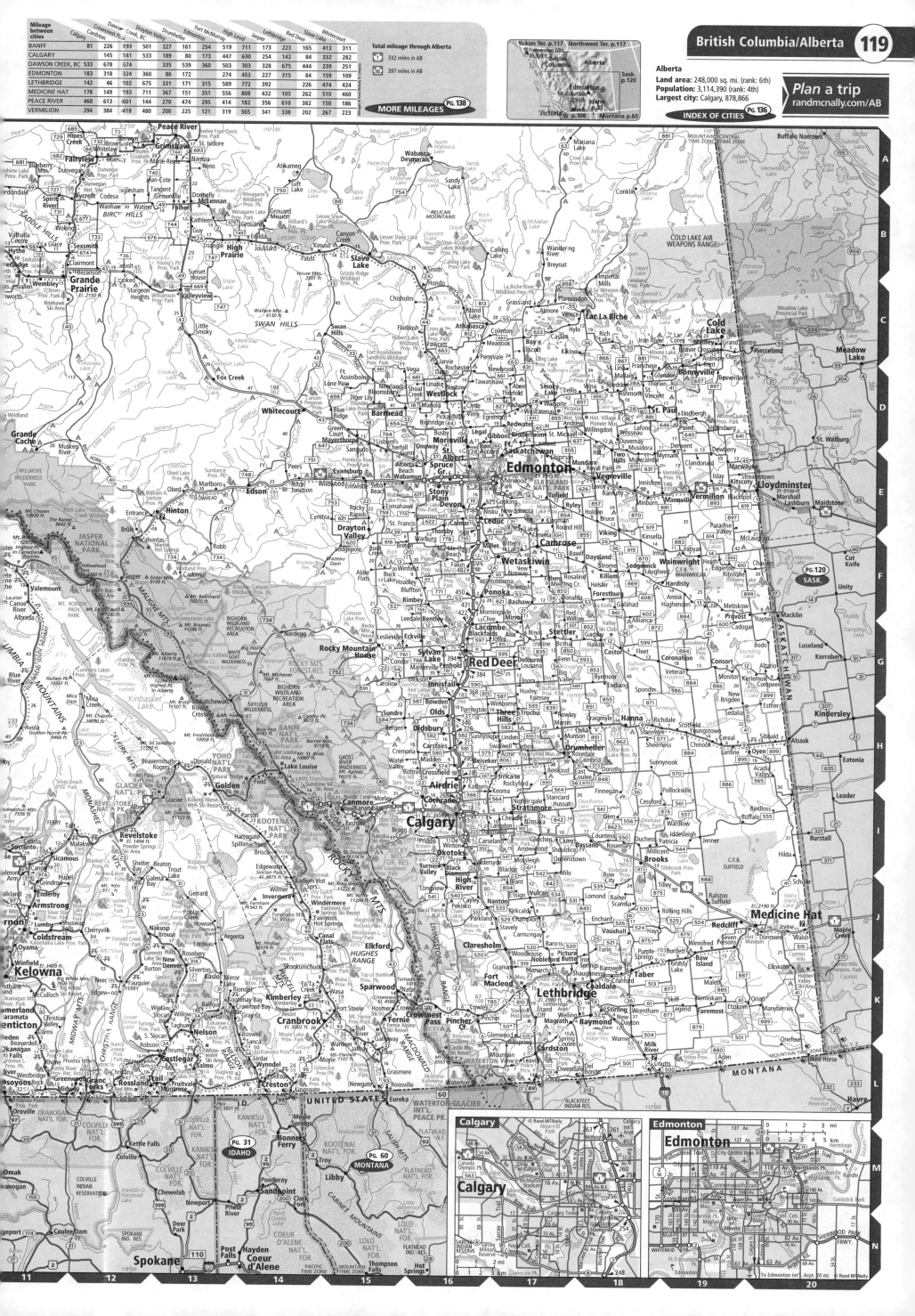

Get travel info
randmcnally.com/SK

Saskatchewan
Land area: 228,445 sq. mi. (rank: 7th)
Population: 995,490 (rank: 6th)
Largest city: Saskatoon, 196,811

Distance scale
One inch represents approximately 35 miles

INDEX OF CITIES — PG. 136

MORE MILEAGES — PG. 138

Mileage between cities	Flin Flon, MB	Hudson Bay	Kindersley	La Loche	La Ronge	Medicine Hat, AB	Melfort	Melville	Moose Jaw	North Battleford	Prince Albert	Regina	Saskatoon	Yorkton
ESTEVAN	471	283	354	662	508	395	299	135	149	368	355	127	283	161
LLOYDMINSTER	458	371	147	335	350	286	275	383	311	88	208	333	173	376
MEADOW LAKE	393	317	214	220	235	365	221	394	322	99	161	384	184	387
PRINCE ALBERT	243	156	212	319	148	396	60	246	223	127		231	87	235
REGINA	438	239	244	539	379	293	173	91	47	245	231		160	117
SASKATOON	330	204	125	379	235	309	108	210	138	85	87	160		203
SWIFT CURRENT	498	389	135	510	404	141	276	241	109	191	255	152	168	267
YORKTON	317	129	307	554	383	408	175	26	162	288	235	117	203	

Total mileage through Saskatchewan
1 — 413 miles in SK
16 — 437 miles in SK

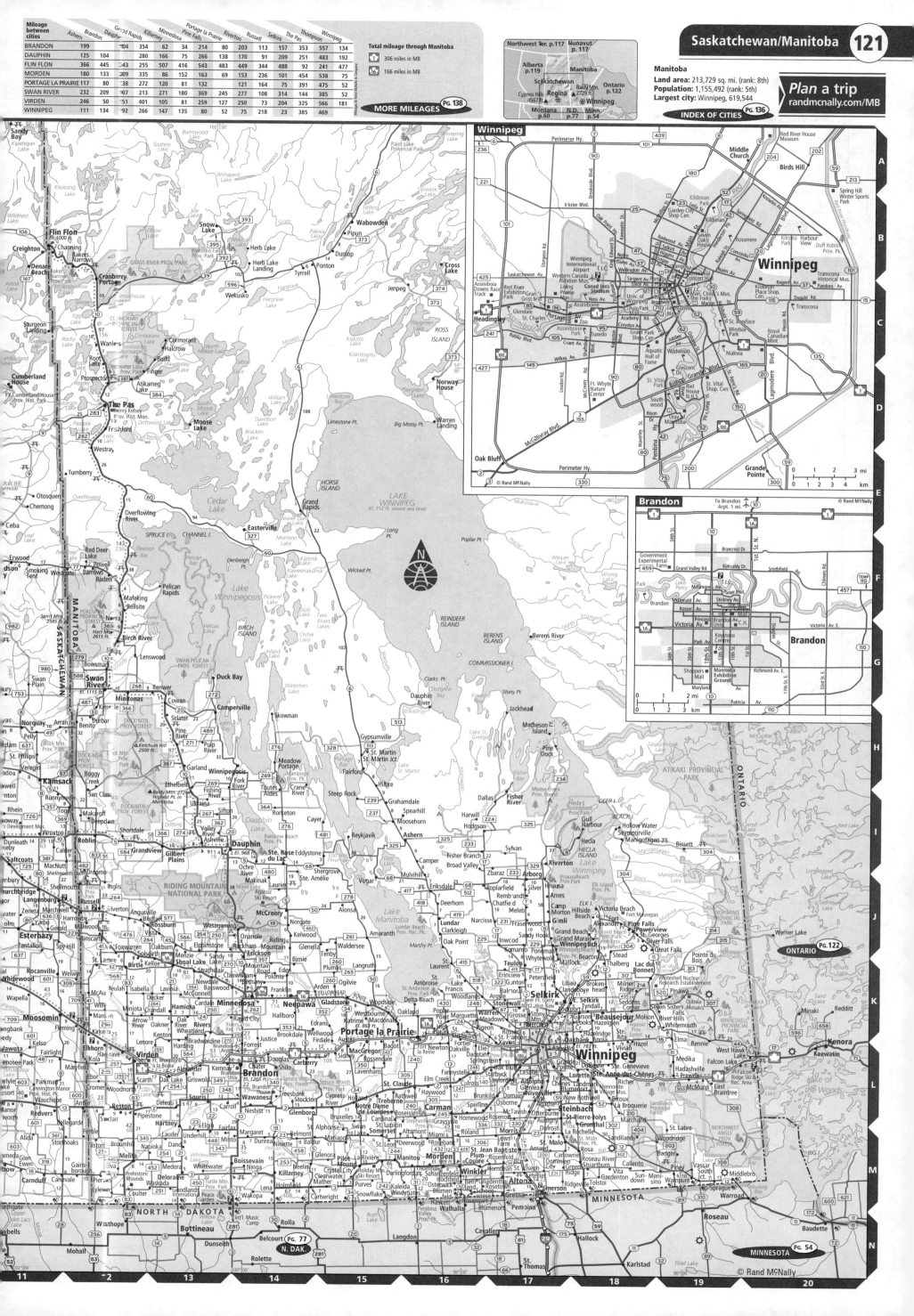

Mileage between cities	Ashern	Brandon	Dauphin	Grand Rapids	Killarney	Minnedosa	Portage La Prairie	Riverton	Russell	Selkirk	The Pas	Thompson	Winnipeg
BRANDON	199		104	354	62	34	214	80	203	113	157	353	557	134
DAUPHIN	125	104		280	166	75	266	138	170	91	209	251	483	192
FLIN FLON	366	445	343	255	507	416	543	483	449	344	488	92	241	477
MORDEN	180	133	209	335	86	152	163	69	153	236	101	454	538	75
PORTAGE LA PRAIRIE	117	80	38	272	120	81	132		121	164	75	391	475	52
SWAN RIVER	232	209	107	213	271	180	369	245	277	108	314	144	385	52
VIRDEN	246	50	151	401	105	81	259	127	250	73	204	325	566	181
WINNIPEG	111	134	192	266	147	135	80	52	75	218	23	385	469	

Total mileage through Manitoba

① 306 miles in MB
⑯ 166 miles in MB

© Rand McNally & Company

MORE MILEAGES PG. 138

Manitoba
Land area: 213,729 sq. mi. (rank: 8th)
Population: 1,155,492 (rank: 5th)
Largest city: Winnipeg, 619,544

INDEX OF CITIES PG. 136

Plan a trip
randmcnally.com/MB

PG. 122
PG. 136

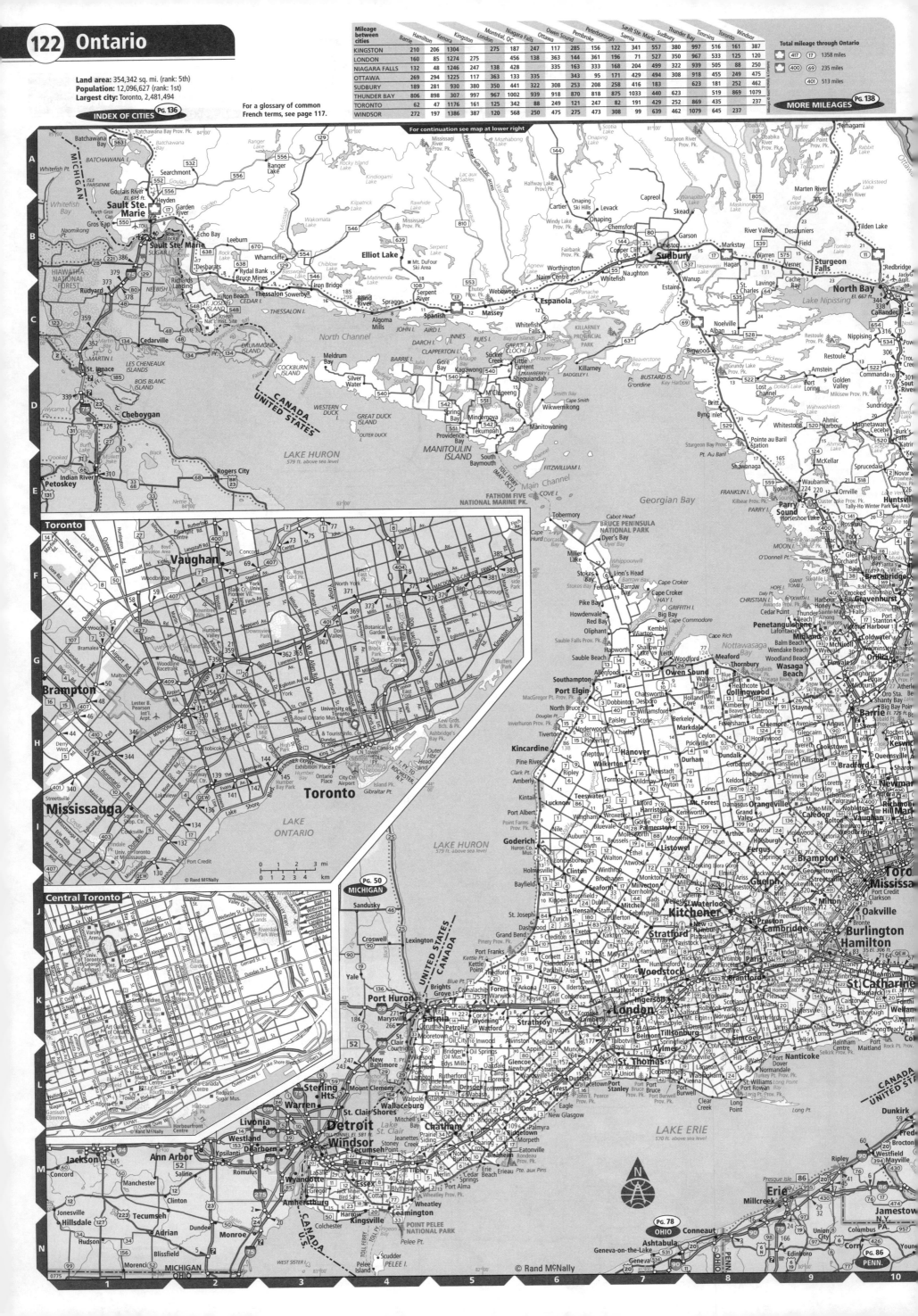

Map symbols

MORE MAP SYMBOLS PG. 1

Distance scale
One inch represents approximately 27 miles
0 10 20 30 40 mi
0 10 20 30 40 km

- Free limited-access highway
- Toll limited-access highway
- Other multilane highway
- Principal highway
- Other through highway
- Other road
- Unpaved road
- Scenic route
- Airport
- Point of interest
- Hospital
- ? Information center
- Port of entry
- Rest area: toilets / no toilets
- Service area
- Wayside; roadside park
- Road construction

Man. p.121
Minn. p.54
Wis. p.114
Mich. p.50
Québec p.124
N.Y. p.70
Toronto
Ishpatina Ridge 2275 ft.

Insets

Kitchener / Cambridge — Waterloo, Kitchener, Cambridge

Ottawa — Ottawa, Gatineau

London

Hamilton — Burlington, Hamilton, Aldershot

Sudbury

St. Catharines — Thorold

Kingston

Thunder Bay

Northern Ontario

Selected place names

Montréal, Laval, Longueuil, Gatineau, Ottawa, Cornwall, Brockville, Kingston, Belleville, Peterborough, Oshawa, Whitby, Ajax, Pickering, Bowmanville, Cobourg, Port Hope, Lindsay, Bancroft, Pembroke, Petawawa, Renfrew, Arnprior, Carleton Place, Smiths Falls, Perth, Deep River, Chalk River, Algonquin Provincial Park, Buffalo, Niagara Falls, Lockport, Medina, Batavia, Thunder Bay, Sudbury, Sault Ste. Marie, Timmins, Kapuskasing, Hearst, Kenora, Dryden, Sioux Lookout, Geraldton, Marathon, Wawa, Duluth, Superior, North Bay, Sturgeon Falls, Espanola, Elliot Lake, New Liskeard, Kirkland Lake, Rouyn-Noranda, Iroquois Falls, Cochrane

© Rand McNally

For continuation see main map

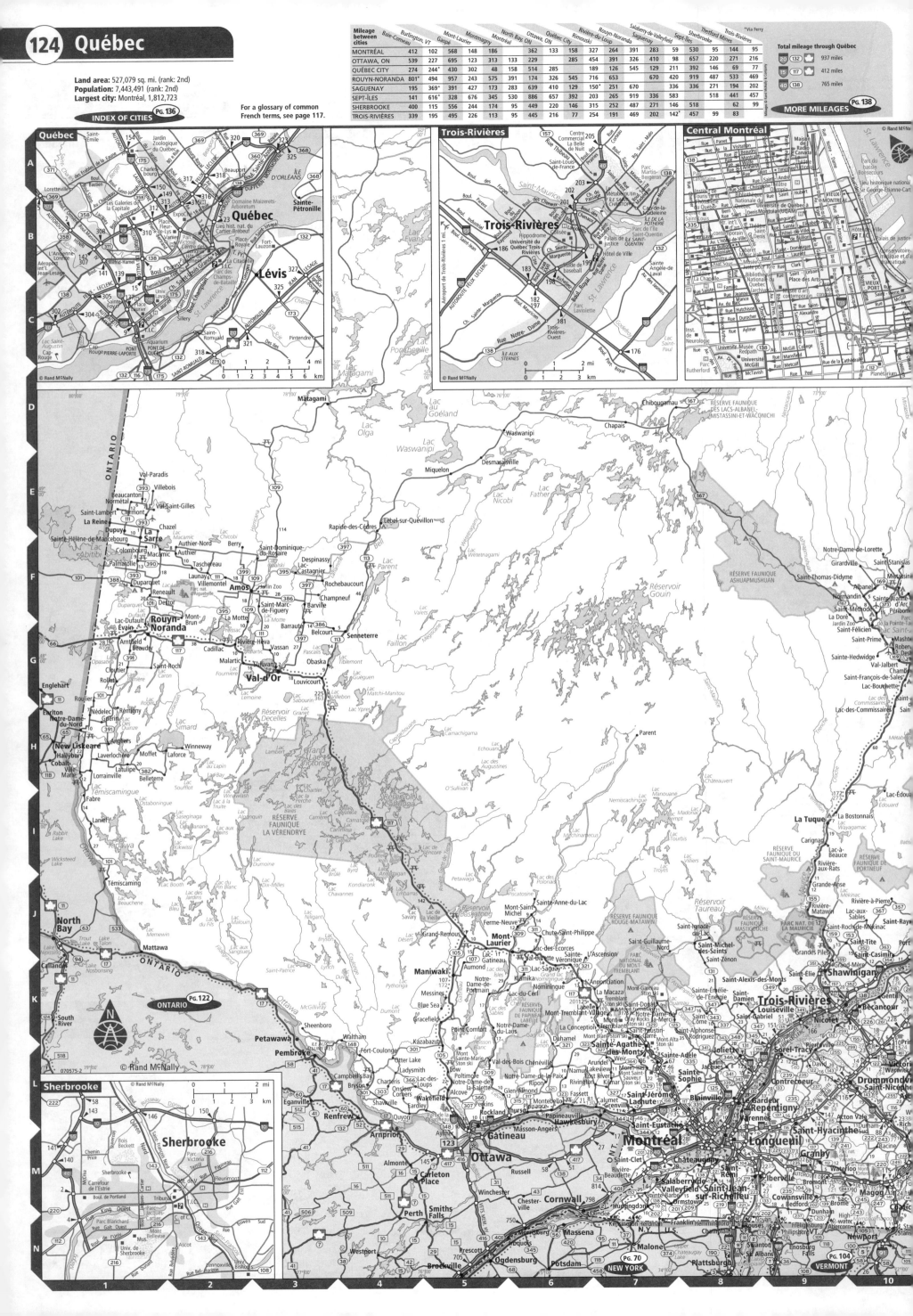

Map symbols

MORE MAP SYMBOLS FIG.1

- Free limited - access highway
- Toll limited - access highway
- Other multilane highway
- Principal highway
- Other through highway
- Other road
- Unpaved road
- •••• Scenic route
- ✈ Airport
- Point of interest
- H Hospital
- ? Information center
- Port of entry
- Rest area: toilets / no toilets
- Service area
- Wayside; roadside park
- Road construction

Distance scale
One inch represents approximately 36 miles

0 10 20 30 mi
0 10 20 30 40 km

Ontario p.122
Newfoundland and Labrador p.127
N.Y. p.70
N.B. p.126
Maine p.45

Get more Québec info
randmcnally.com/QC

© Rand McNally

Montréal

Saguenay

Saguenay

EASTERN TIME ZONE
ATLANTIC TIME ZONE

Sept-Îles
Port-Cartier
Baie-Comeau
Matane
Rimouski
Saguenay
Québec
Lévis
Trois-Rivières
Montréal
Longueuil
Laval
Sherbrooke
Drummondville
Gaspé
Percé
ÎLE D'ANTICOSTI

NEW BRUNSWICK PG.126

PG.122 ONT.
PG.70 N.Y.
PG.104 U.S. VERMONT
PG.65 N.H.
PG.45 MAINE

Southern Québec

INDEX OF CITIES PG. 136

For a glossary of common French terms, see page 117.

MORE MILEAGES PG. 138

Mileage between cities	Amherst, NS	Campbellton, NB	Charlottetown, PE	Corner Brook, NL	Edmundston, NB	Fredericton, NB	Gander, NL	Grand Falls, NL	Halifax, NS	Moncton, NB	New Glasgow, NS	Saint John, NB	St. John's, NL	St. Stephen, NB	Sydney, NS	Truro, NS	Yarmouth, NS *Via Ferry
CHARLOTTETOWN, PE	93	249	319	482	422	241	688	384	164	67	218	597	321	247	104	326	
EDMUNDSTON, NB	336	193	129	417*	860*	177	1080*	37	471	294	446	246	1281*	220	599	409	356
FREDERICTON, NB	158	158	238	239*	682	177	902	139	293	116	268	70	1103*	79	421	231	180
HALIFAX, NS	135	306	386	157*	519*	471	293	739*	433	173	105	271	940*	341	258	64	186
MONCTON, NB	38	131	211	119	562*	294	116	782*	256	173	148	94	983*	164	301	111	365
SAINT JOHN, NB	136	229	309	218	660*	246	70	880*	208	271	94	246	1081*	70	209	110	
ST. JOHN'S, NL	945*	1116*	1196*	597	427	1281*	1103*	201	1243	940*	983*	837*	1081	1151*	688*	878	1132
SYDNEY, NS	263	434	514	247	267*	599	421	487*	561	258	301	155	399	688*		196	450

Total mileage through Atlantic Provinces

2 308 miles (NB)   2 565 miles (NL)
1 101 miles (PE)   104 105 287 miles (NS)

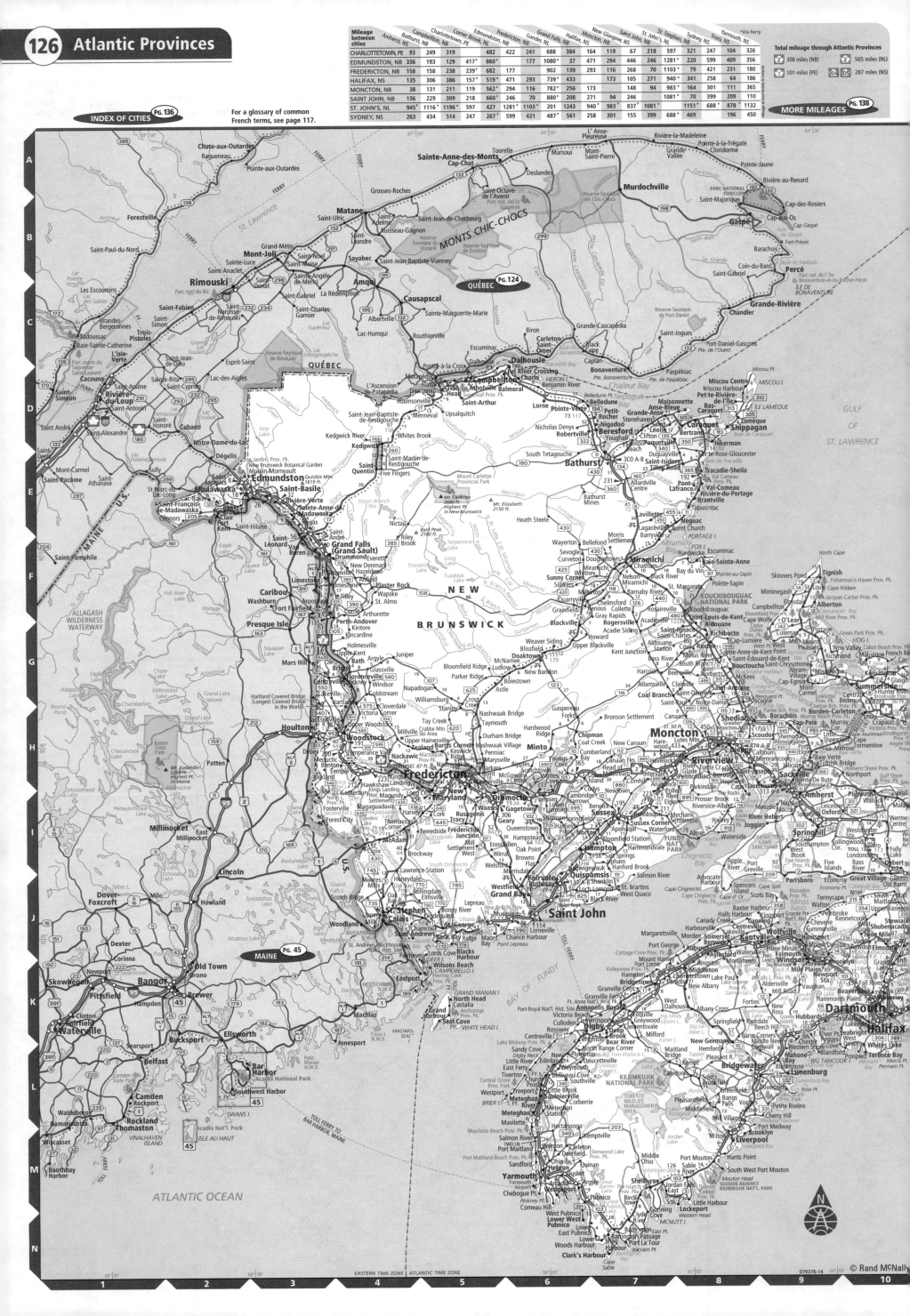

© Rand McNally

079376-14

Explore the Atlantic Provinces
randmcnally.com/AP

New Brunswick
Land area: 27,587 sq. mi. (11)
Population: 750,183 (8)
Largest city: Saint John, 69,661

Newfoundland and Labrador
Land area: 144,353 sq. mi. (10)
Population: 519,270 (9)
Largest city: St. John's, 99,182

Nova Scotia
Land area: 20,594 sq. mi. (12)
Population: 934,392 (7)
Largest city: Halifax, 359,111

Prince Edward Island
Land area: 2,185 sq. mi. (13)
Population: 136,998 (10)
Largest city: Charlottetown, 32,245

Distance scale
One inch represents approximately 31 miles
0 10 20 30 mi
0 10 20 30 40 km

Québec p.124

Newfoundland and Labrador

Fredericton Maine p.45 N.B. P.E.I. Charlottetown Halifax N.S.

St. John's

Newfoundland and Labrador

QUÉBEC

ATLANTIC OCEAN

LABRADOR

Charlottetown

PRINCE EDWARD ISLAND

NOVA SCOTIA

CAPE BRETON ISLAND (N.S.)

NEWFOUNDLAND ISLAND

ATLANTIC OCEAN

Fredericton

Saint John

Halifax

© Rand McNally

Go to randmcnally.com to plan your road trip and get road construction updates.

Mexico
Land area: 758,450 sq. mi.
Population: 97,483,412
Largest city: Mexico City, 8,605,239

Puerto Rico (U.S.)
Land area: 3,425 sq. mi.
Population: 3,808,610
Largest city: San Juan, 421,958

INDEX OF CITIES PG. 136

Distance scale
One inch represents approximately 145 miles

Selected places of interest

Bahía Fosforescente (P.R.) . . F-10	Palenque Ruinas I-11
Barranca del Cobre D-4	Parque Internacional
Catarata de la Mina (P.R.) . . E-14	del Río Bravo C-7
Castillo del Morró (P.R.) . . . D-13	Plaza de la Constitución . . H-2
Chichen Itza Ruinas G-13	Submarine Gardens (P.R.) . . D-13
Grutas de Cacahuamilpa . . . H-8	Teotihuacán Ruinas H-8
Monte Albán Ruinas I-9	Tulum Ruinas G-14
Museo de Arte	Uxmal Ruinas G-12
de Ponce (P.R.) F-11	Xochimilco I-3

United States Citizens Visiting Mexico

To visit Mexico, tourists need proof of U.S. citizenship. Native-born citizens will need either a U.S. passport or a certified birth certificate and a photo ID. Naturalized citizens should carry their naturalization certificate to ensure entry into Mexico and re-entry into the United States.

Tourist cards are valid for any period up to six months, require a fee, and are required for all persons, regardless of age, to visit the interior of Mexico. Cards may be obtained from Mexican border authorities, from Consuls of Mexico, or from Federal Delegates in major cities.

Obtain $27 automobile permit (pay with Master Card or Visa credit card only) good for six months, from the Mexican Customs Office at the border, hold and surrender when leaving Mexico. Carry proof of car ownership (the vehicle's registration card or a letter of authorization from the finance or leasing company). Permits must also be obtained for trailers and boats. Auto insurance policies, other than Mexican, are not valid in Mexico. A short-term liability policy is obtainable at the border.

Each returning U.S. resident may bring back articles for personal use, valued at up to $800.00 free of duty; plant and animal products are carefully regulated whether entering or leaving Mexico. For further information obtain a copy of the booklet, *Know Before You Go* from any U.S. Customs and Border Protection office.

Mileage between principal cities

Miles in red; kilometers in blue

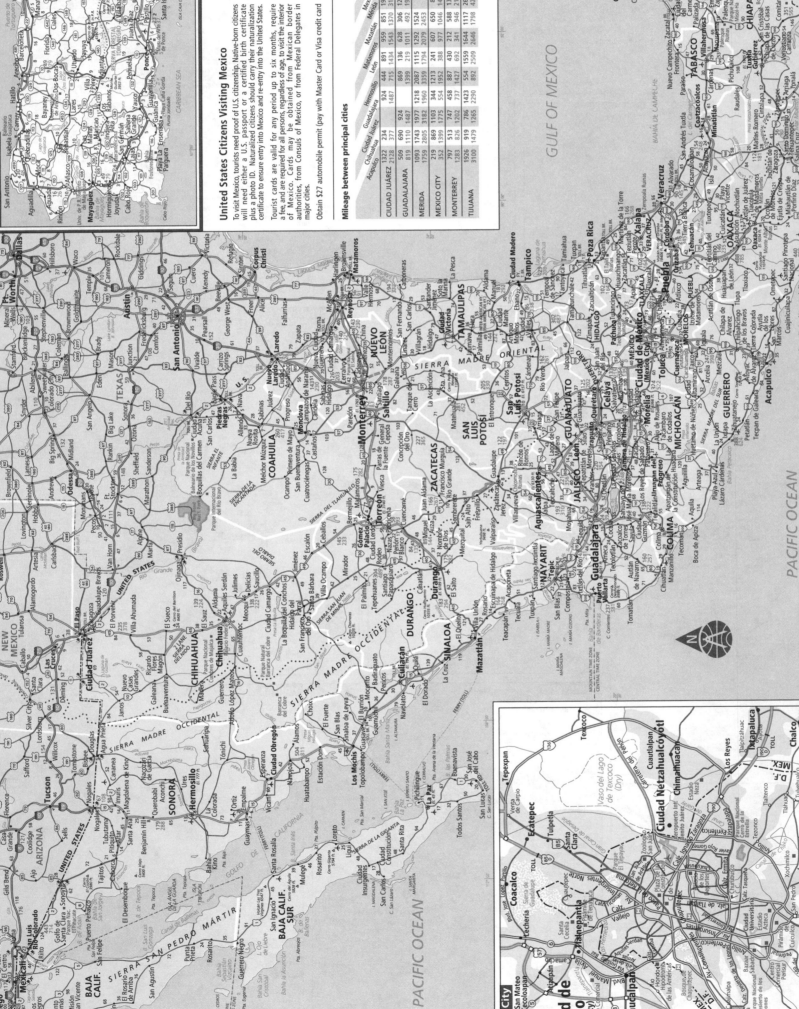

Glossary of Spanish Terms

Avenida (Av.) . . . . . Avenue	Paseo . . . . Drive
Bahía (B.) . . . . Bay	Playa . . . . Beach
Barranca . . . . Canyon	Presa . . . . Reservoir
Cabo (C.) . . . . Cape	Lago (L.) . . . . . . Lake
Calzada (Calz.) . . . Highway	Parque Nacional	(Nac.) . . . . National park
Canal . . . . Canal, strait	Parque Natural . . Wildlife park
Carretera . . . . Highway	Golfo . . . . Gulf
Castillo . . . . Fort	Grutas . . . . Caves
Centro Comercial . . Shopping center	Hipódromo . . . . Race track
Cerro . . . . Mountain	Isla (I.) . . . . Island
Ciudad . . . . City	Punta (Pta.) . . . Point, headland
Deportes . . . . Sports	Sierra . . . . Mountain
Estadio . . . . Stadium	Vía . . . . Road

© Rand McNally

Alabama
Map pp. 4-5

Arizona
Map pp. 8-9
* City keyed to p. 7

Arkansas
Map p. 10

California
Map pp. 12-15

Index keys NA to NN refer
to Northern CA, pp. 12-13,
SA to SN refer to Southern
CA, pp. 14-15.
* City keyed to p. 11
* City keyed to p. 18
* City keyed to p. 16-17

Alaska
Map p. 6

Colorado
Map pp. 20-21
* City keyed to p. 19

Connecticut
Map pp. 22-23

Delaware
Map p. 24

Massachusetts — PLYMOUTH CO., ...

Michigan
Map pp. 50-51
• City keyed to p. 52

Minnesota
Map pp. 54-55
• City keyed to p. 53

Mississippi
Map p. 56

Missouri
Map pp. 58-59
• City keyed to p. 57
‡ Independent city; Not included in any county

Montana
Map pp. 60-61

Nebraska
Map pp. 62-63

Nevada
Map p. 64
• City keyed to p. 11
† City keyed to p. 65
‡ Independent city; Not included in any county

New Hampshire
Map p. 65

New Jersey
Map pp. 66-67
• City keyed to p. 11
† City keyed to p. 65

New Mexico
Map p. 68

New York
Map pp. 69-71

Index keys SA to SJ refer to Southern NY, p. 69. NA to NN refer to Northern NY, pp. 70-71
* City keyed to p. 72-73

North Carolina
Map pp. 74-75

* City keyed to p. 76

North Dakota
Map p. 77

Ohio
Map pp. 78-81

Index keys NA to NN refer to Northern OH, pp. 78-79. SA to SN refer to Southern OH, pp. 80-81

This page is a multi-column gazetteer index listing place names, populations, and grid coordinates for Ohio, Oklahoma, Oregon, Pennsylvania, Rhode Island, South Carolina, South Dakota, and Tennessee.

Oklahoma
Map pp. 82-83

Oregon
Map pp. 84-85

Pennsylvania
Map pp. 86-89

Index keys WA to WT refer to Western PA, pp. 86-87.
EA to ET refer to Eastern PA, pp. 88-89.
* City keyed to p. 90

Rhode Island
Map p. 91

South Carolina
Map p. 92

South Dakota
Map p. 93

Tennessee
Map pp. 94-...
* City keyed to p. 96

Wisconsin
Map pp. 114-115

* City keyed to p. 113

Wyoming
Map p. 116

Canada Cities and Towns
Population figures from latest available census

Alberta
Map pp. 118-119

* City keyed to p. 117

British Columbia
Map pp. 118-119

* City keyed to p. 117

Manitoba
Map pp. 120-121

* City keyed to p. 117

New Brunswick
Map pp. 126-127

Newfoundland and Labrador
Map p. 127

Northwest Territories
Map p. 117

Nova Scotia
Map pp. 126-127

Nunavut
Map p. 117

Ontario
Map pp. 122-123

Prince Edward Island
Map pp. 126-127

Québec
Map pp. 124-125

Saskatchewan
Map pp. 120-121

* City keyed to p. 117

Yukon Territory
Map p. 117

Mexico Cities and Towns
Population figures from latest available census

Mexico
Map p. 128

*, †, ‡, See explanation under state/province title in this index.   County names are listed in capital letters and in boldface type.

ROAD WORK

Road construction and road conditions resources

Road closed. Single lane traffic ahead. Detour. When you are on the road, knowledge is power. Let Rand McNally help you avoid situations that can result in delays, or worse.

There are ways to prepare for construction traffic and avoid the dangers of poor road conditions. Read on:

1. Use the state and province websites and hotlines listed on this page for road construction and road conditions information.
2. Look for the green ribbons (see map section below) that indicate major construction sites on state, province, and city maps throughout the atlas.
3. Go to randmcnally.com/roadconstruction for current U.S. and Canadian road construction information.

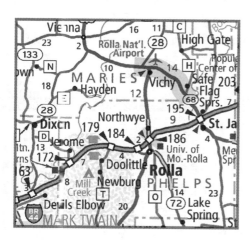

Most of the hotlines and websites listed here offer information on both road construction and road conditions. For those that provide only one or the other, we've used an orange cone ⬘ to indicate road construction information and a blue snowflake ❄ to indicate road conditions information.

Get the info from the 511 hotline

The U.S. Federal Highway Administration has begun implementing a national system of highway and road conditions/construction information for travelers. Under the new plan, travelers can **dial 511 and get up-to-date information on roads and highways.**

Implementation of 511 is the responsibility of state and local agencies.

For more details, visit:
www.fhwa.dot.gov/trafficinfo/511.htm

United States

Alabama
www.dot.state.al.us

Alaska
511
(866) 282-7577
(800) 478-7675 (in AK) ❄
(907) 456-7623 ❄
(907) 269-0450 ⬘
511.alaska.gov

Arizona
511
(888) 411-7623
www.az511.com

Arkansas
(800) 245-1672 ❄
(501) 569-2374 ⬘
www.arkansashighways.com

California
511 (San Francisco Bay and Sacramento areas)
(800) 427-7623 (in CA) ❄
(916) 445-7623 ⬘
www.dot.ca.gov
www.511.org

Colorado
511
(877) 315-7623 (in CO)
(303) 639-1111
www.cotrip.org

Connecticut
(800) 443-6817 (in CT)
(860) 594-2650 ❄
www.ct.gov/dot ⬘

Delaware
www.deldot.net ⬘

Florida
511
www.511tampabay.com
www.fl511.com

Georgia
(404) 635-8000
www.dot.state.ga.us

Hawaii
(808) 536-6566 ⬘
www.hawaii.gov/dot ⬘

Idaho
511
(888) 432-7623
511.idaho.gov

Illinois
(800) 452-4368
(312) 368-4636
www.dot.state.il.us
www.illinoisroads.info

Indiana
(800) 261-7623 ❄
www.in.gov/dot

Iowa
511
(800) 288-1047
www.511ia.org

Kansas
511
(800) 585-7623
511.ksdot.org

Kentucky
511
(866) 737-3767
www.511.ky.gov

Louisiana
www.511la.org

Maine
511
(866) 282-7578
(207) 624-3595
www.511maine.gov

Maryland
(800) 327-3125 ❄
(800) 541-9595 ❄
(410) 582-5650
www.chart.state.md.us

Massachusetts
(617) 374-1234 (SmarTraveler, Greater Boston only) ⬘
www.state.ma.us/eotc/ ⬘

Michigan
(800) 381-8477 ❄
(888) 305-7283 (for West and Southwest Michigan) ⬘
(800) 641-6368 (Metro Detroit) ⬘
www.michigan.gov/mdot/

Minnesota
511
(800) 542-0220
www.511mn.org

Mississippi
(601) 987-1211 ❄
(601) 359-7301 ⬘
www.mdot.state.ms.us

Missouri
(800) 222-6400 (in MO) ❄
www.modot.mo.gov

Montana
511
(800) 226-7623
www.mdt.mt.gov/travinfo/511

Nebraska
511
(800) 906-9069
(402) 471-4533
www.511nebraska.org

Nevada
511
(877) 687-6237 ❄
www.nevadadot.com

New Hampshire
511
(866) 282-7579
www.nh.gov/dot/511

New Jersey
(732) 247-0900, then 2 (turnpike) ❄
(800) 336-5875 (turnpike) ❄
(732) 727-5929 (Garden State Parkway)
www.state.nj.us/njcommuter/ ⬘
www.state.nj.us/turnpike/ ⬘

New Mexico
(800) 432-4269
www.nmshtd.state.nm.us

New York
(800) 847-8929 (thruway) ❄
www.thruway.state.ny.us (thruway)
www.dot.state.ny.us (all other roads) ⬘

North Carolina
511
(877) 511-4662
www.ncsmartlink.org/aboutITS /511.html

North Dakota
511
(866) 696-3511
www.state.nd.us/dot/ divisions/maintenance/ 511-nd.html

Ohio
511 (Cincinnati/northern Kentucky area)
(888) 264-7623 (in OH)
(614) 644-7031 ❄
(440) 234-2030 (turnpike) ❄
(888) 876-7453 (turnpike) ⬘
www.buckeyetraffic.org
www.ohioturnpike.org
www.artimis.org (Cincinnati/ Northern KY area)

Oklahoma
(888) 425-2385 ❄
(405) 425-2385 ⬘
www.okladot.state.ok.us

Oregon
511
(800) 977-6368
(503) 588-2941
www.tripcheck.com

Pennsylvania
(888) 783-6783 (in PA)
(215) 567-5678 (SmarTraveler, Camden/Philadelphia area)
www.dot.state.pa.us

Rhode Island
511
www.tmc.state.ri.us

South Carolina
www.dot.state.sc.us

South Dakota
511
(866) 697-3511
www.sddot.com/511

Tennessee
(800) 342-3258 ❄
(800) 858-6349 ⬘
www.tdot.state.tn.us/ travel.htm

Texas
(800) 452-9292
www.dot.state.tx.us

Utah
511
(800) 492-2400
(866) 511-8824
www.utahcommuterlink.com

Vermont
511
(800) 429-7623
www.aot.state.vt.us/ travelinfo.htm
www.511vt.com

Virginia
511
(800) 367-7623 ❄
(800) 578-4111
www.511virginia.org

Washington
511
(800) 695-7623
www.wsdot.wa.gov/ traffic/

Washington, D.C.
www.ddot.dc.gov ⬘

West Virginia
(877) 982-7623 ❄
www.wvdot.com

Wisconsin
(800) 762-3947
www.dot.state.wi.us

Wyoming
(888) 996-7623 (in WY) ❄
(307) 772-0824 ❄
www.dot.state.wy.us

Canada

Alberta
(403) 246-5853 ❄
www.trans.gov.ab.ca

British Columbia
(604) 660-9770
www.gov.bc.ca/tran/

Manitoba
(877) 627-6237 (in MB) ❄
(204) 945-3704 ❄
www.gov.mb.ca/roadinfo/

New Brunswick
(800) 561-4063 (in NB) ❄
www.gnb.ca/0113

Newfoundland & Labrador
www.roads.gov.nf.ca
www.roads.gov.nl.ca

Nova Scotia
(902) 424-3933 ❄
(800) 307-7669 (in NS) ❄
www.gov.ns.ca/tran

Ontario
(800) 268-4686 (in ON)
(416) 235-4686 (in Toronto)
www.mto.gov.on.ca

Prince Edward Island
(902) 368-4770 ❄
www.gov.pe.ca/ roadconditions ❄

Québec
(877) 393-2363 (in Québec) ❄
(888) 355-0511
www.mtq.gouv.qc.ca/en /index.asp

Saskatchewan
(306) 787-7623 (Regina and surrounding areas, areas outside of province)
(306) 933-8333 (Saskatoon and surrounding areas)
(888) 335-7623 (All other areas)
www.highways.gov.sk.ca

Mexico

www.sct.gob.mx
(in Spanish only)

MILE MARKERS
Mileage chart

This handy chart offers more than 5,300 mileages covering 90 North American cities and U.S. national parks. Want more mileages? Just go to randmcnally.com/MC and type in any two cities or addresses.

Get more info
randmcnally.com/MC